These Apes Appreci

Planet of the Apes a.,.. ~~Philosophy~~

"Who knew that one movie could inspire such fascinating discourse? A thought-provoking collection from some of the brightest minds of our time."

— VANESSA WOODS, bestselling author of *Bonobo Handshake* and *The Genius of Dogs*

"In this entertaining and provocative book, philosophers tackle the implications of the 1968 movie Planet of the Apes *and its many sequels which keep on coming. The book's subtitle,* Great Apes Think Alike, *says it all, regarding not only 'hairy' apes but also the apes most in need of reflection—humans."*

— JEFFREY H. SCHWARTZ, author of *The Red Ape.*

"An engaging and accessible discussion of the myriad scientific, ethical, political, psychological, and artistic questions raised by the Planet of the Apes *franchise, told with a knowledgeableness and dry humor sure to delight fans."*

— EMILIE RAYMOND, author of *From My Cold Dead Hands: Charlton Heston and American Politics*

"Even though apes aren't monkeys, it's still true that this book is more fun than a barrel of monkeys."

— ELLIOTT SOBER, author of *Did Darwin Write the Origin Backwards?*

"A fascinating and multifaceted tour of the radiant hopes and worst fears about humanity and its origins that Planet of the Apes evokes in everyone."

— IAN TATTERSALL, author of *Masters of the Planet: The Search for Our Human Origins*

"If a few intelligent dinosaurs had survived their big extinction event, they might well be surprised and alarmed by the strange development whereby *mammals* took center stage—they seemed so small, weak, and insignificant. From being the planet of the dinosaurs Earth has become the planet of the apes. The *Planet of the Apes* movies draw out the arbitrariness of the current arrangements of world power among species. The naked ape has become the nuclear ape, but she's still an ape—a creature of some absurdity to other proud and ancient species. A stellar cast of ape philosophers has given us *Planet of the Apes and Philosophy*, proving that there may after all be something to be said for the human ape. A philosophical dinosaur might now revise his opinion of those simian upstarts: these parvenus can think!"

— COLIN MCGINN, author of *The Power of Movies: How Screen and Mind Interact*

"Whether you came for the apes and stayed for the philosophy, or came for the philosophy and stayed for the apes, either way this book is an absorbing read."

— SUSAN SCHNEIDER, editor, *Science Fiction and Philosophy*

"This may be the best book on this topic ever written. If you're like me, once you pick it up you may never put it down. What a read!"

— MATT TOLMACH, producer, *The Amazing Spider Man*

"We can't know what Aristotle, Descartes, Spinoza, or Hume would have made of the rising of the apes, but we do have Planet of the Apes and Philosophy— not only a terrific read but highly relevant to urgent issues of our time."

— DALE JAMIESON, author of *Ethics and the Environment*

"John Huss has corralled a tantalizing collection of highly original essays. Planet of the Apes makes an ideal springboard for these philosophers to dive into the morass of research, chimp consciousness, morality, and ethics. Anyone who takes movies—and the plight of animals—seriously will thoroughly enjoy Planet of the Apes and Philosophy."

— ELIZABETH HESS, author, *Nim Chimpsky: The Chimp Who Would Be Human*

"This book is a must, not only for Planet of the Apes *fans, but for anyone interested in what it means to be a primate. Fascinating and thought provoking. A great read!"*

— RICK JAFFA AND AMANDA SILVER, screenwriters of *Rise of the Planet of the Apes* and *Dawn of the Planet of the Apes*

Planet of the Apes and Philosophy

Popular Culture and Philosophy® Series Editor: George A. Reisch

VOLUME 1 *Seinfeld and Philosophy: A Book about Everything and Nothing* (2000)

VOLUME 2 *The Simpsons and Philosophy: The D'oh! of Homer* (2001)

VOLUME 3 *The Matrix and Philosophy: Welcome to the Desert of the Real* (2002)

VOLUME 4 *Buffy the Vampire Slayer and Philosophy: Fear and Trembling in Sunnydale* (2003)

VOLUME 5 *The Lord of the Rings and Philosophy: One Book to Rule Them All* (2003)

VOLUME 9 *Harry Potter and Philosophy: If Aristotle Ran Hogwarts* (2004)

VOLUME 12 *Star Wars and Philosophy: More Powerful than You Can Possibly Imagine* (2005)

VOLUME 13 *Superheroes and Philosophy: Truth, Justice, and the Socratic Way* (2005)

VOLUME 19 *Monty Python and Philosophy: Nudge Nudge, Think Think!* (2006)

VOLUME 24 *Bullshit and Philosophy: Guaranteed to Get Perfect Results Every Time* (2006)

VOLUME 25 *The Beatles and Philosophy: Nothing You Can Think that Can't Be Thunk* (2006)

VOLUME 26 *South Park and Philosophy: Bigger, Longer, and More Penetrating* (2007)

VOLUME 30 *Pink Floyd and Philosophy: Careful with that Axiom, Eugene!* (2007)

VOLUME 31 *Johnny Cash and Philosophy: The Burning Ring of Truth* (2008)

VOLUME 33 *Battlestar Galactica and Philosophy: Mission Accomplished or Mission Frakked Up?* (2008)

VOLUME 34 *iPod and Philosophy: iCon of an ePoch* (2008)

VOLUME 35 *Star Trek and Philosophy: The Wrath of Kant* (2008)

VOLUME 36 *The Legend of Zelda and Philosophy: I Link Therefore I Am* (2008)

VOLUME 37 *The Wizard of Oz and Philosophy: Wicked Wisdom of the West* (2008)

VOLUME 38 *Radiohead and Philosophy: Fitter Happier More Deductive* (2009)

VOLUME 39 *Jimmy Buffett and Philosophy: The Porpoise Driven Life* (2009) Edited by Erin McKenna and Scott L. Pratt

VOLUME 41 *Stephen Colbert and Philosophy: I Am Philosophy (And So Can You!)* (2009) Edited by Aaron Allen Schiller

VOLUME 42 *Supervillains and Philosophy: Sometimes, Evil Is Its Own Reward* (2009) Edited by Ben Dyer

VOLUME 43 *The Golden Compass and Philosophy: God Bites the Dust* (2009) Edited by Richard Greene and Rachel Robison

VOLUME 44 *Led Zeppelin and Philosophy: All Will Be Revealed* (2009) Edited by Scott Calef

VOLUME 45 *World of Warcraft and Philosophy: Wrath of the Philosopher King* (2009) Edited by Luke Cuddy and John Nordlinger

Volume 46 *Mr. Monk and Philosophy: The Curious Case of the Defective Detective* (2010) Edited by D.E. Wittkower

Volume 47 *Anime and Philosophy: Wide Eyed Wonder* (2010) Edited by Josef Steiff and Tristan D. Tamplin

VOLUME 48 *The Red Sox and Philosophy: Green Monster Meditations* (2010) Edited by Michael Macomber

VOLUME 49 *Zombies, Vampires, and Philosophy: New Life for the Undead* (2010) Edited by Richard Greene and K. Silem Mohammad

VOLUME 50 *Facebook and Philosophy: What's on Your Mind?* (2010) Edited by D.E. Wittkower

VOLUME 51 *Soccer and Philosophy: Beautiful Thoughts on the Beautiful Game* (2010) Edited by Ted Richards

VOLUME 52 *Manga and Philosophy: Fullmetal Metaphysician* (2010) Edited by Josef Steiff and Adam Barkman

VOLUME 53 *Martial Arts and Philosophy: Beating and Nothingness* (2010) Edited by Graham Priest and Damon Young

VOLUME 54 *The Onion and Philosophy: Fake News Story True, Alleges Indignant Area Professor* (2010) Edited by Sharon M. Kaye

VOLUME 55 *Doctor Who and Philosophy: Bigger on the Inside* (2010) Edited by Courtland Lewis and Paula Smithka

VOLUME 56 *Dune and Philosophy: Weirding Way of the Mentat* (2011) Edited by Jeffery Nicholas

VOLUME 57 *Rush and Philosophy: Heart and Mind United* (2011) Edited by Jim Berti and Durrell Bowman

VOLUME 58 *Dexter and Philosophy: Mind over Spatter* (2011) Edited by Richard Greene, George A. Reisch, and Rachel Robison-Greene

VOLUME 59 *Halo and Philosophy: Intellect Evolved* (2011) Edited by Luke Cuddy

VOLUME 60 *SpongeBob SquarePants and Philosophy: Soaking Up Secrets Under the Sea!* (2011) Edited by Joseph J. Foy

VOLUME 61 *Sherlock Holmes and Philosophy: The Footprints of a Gigantic Mind* (2011) Edited by Josef Steiff

VOLUME 62 *Inception and Philosophy: Ideas to Die For* (2011) Edited by Thorsten Botz-Bornstein

VOLUME 63 *Philip K. Dick and Philosophy: Do Androids Have Kindred Spirits?* (2011) Edited by D.E. Wittkower

VOLUME 64 *The Rolling Stones and Philosophy: It's Just a Thought Away* (2012) Edited by Luke Dick and George A. Reisch

VOLUME 65 *Chuck Klosterman and Philosophy: The Real and the Cereal* (2012) Edited by Seth Vannatta

VOLUME 66 *Neil Gaiman and Philosophy: Gods Gone Wild!* (2012) Edited by Tracy L. Bealer, Rachel Luria, and Wayne Yuen

VOLUME 67 *Breaking Bad and Philosophy: Badder Living through Chemistry* (2012) Edited by David R. Koepsell and Robert Arp

VOLUME 68 *The Walking Dead and Philosophy: Zombie Apocalypse Now* (2012) Edited by Wayne Yuen

VOLUME 69 *Curb Your Enthusiasm and Philosophy: Awaken the Social Assassin Within* (2012) Edited by Mark Ralkowski

VOLUME 70 *Dungeons and Dragons and Philosophy: Raiding the Temple of Wisdom* (2012) Edited by Jon Cogburn and Mark Silcox

VOLUME 71 *The Catcher in the Rye and Philosophy: A Book for Bastards, Morons, and Madmen* (2012) Edited by Keith Dromm and Heather Salter

VOLUME 72 *Jeopardy! and Philosophy: What Is Knowledge in the Form of a Question?* (2012) Edited by Shaun P. Young

VOLUME 73 *The Wire and Philosophy: This America, Man* (2013) Edited by David Bzdak, Joanna Crosby, and Seth Vannatta

VOLUME 74 *Planet of the Apes and Philosophy: Great Apes Think Alike* (2013) Edited by John Huss

IN PREPARATION:

The Good Wife and Philosophy (2013) Edited by Kimberly Baltzer-Jaray and Robert Arp

Psych and Philosophy (2013) Edited by Robert Arp

Boardwalk Empire and Philosophy (2013) Edited by Richard Greene and Rachel Robison-Greene

Futurama and Philosophy (2013) Edited by Courtland Lewis and Shaun P. Young

Ender's Game and Philosophy (2013) Edited by D.E. Wittkower and Lucinda Rush

Frankenstein and Philosophy (2013) Edited by Nicolas Michaud

How I Met Your Mother and Philosophy (2014) Edited by Lorenzo von Matterhorn

Jurassic Park and Philosophy (2014) Edited by Nicolas Michaud

For full details of all Popular Culture and Philosophy® books, visit www.opencourtbooks.com.

Popular Culture and Philosophy®

Planet of the Apes and Philosophy

Great Apes Think Alike

Edited by
JOHN HUSS

OPEN COURT
Chicago

Volume 74 in the series, Popular Culture and Philosophy ®, edited by George A. Reisch

To order books from Open Court, call toll-free 1-800-815-2280, or visit our website at www.opencourtbooks.com.

Open Court Publishing Company is a division of Carus Publishing Company.

Copyright © 2013 by Carus Publishing Company

First printing 2013

All rights reserved. No part of this publication may be reproduced, stored in a retrieval system, or transmitted, in any form or by any means, electronic, mechanical, photocopying, recording, or otherwise, without the prior written permission of the publisher, Open Court Publishing Company, a division of Carus Publishing Company, 70 East Lake Street, Suite 300, Chicago, Illinois 60601.

Printed and bound in the United States of America.

Library of Congress Cataloging-in-Publication Data

Planet of the apes and philosophy : great apes think alike / edited by John Huss
    pages cm. — (Popular culture and philosophy ; v. 74)
    ISBN 978-0-8126-9822-0 (trade paper : alk. paper) 1. Planet of the apes films—History and criticism. 2. Human-animal relationships. I. Huss, John, 1963- editor of compilation.
      PN1995.9.P495P49 2013
      791.43'72—dc23

                              2013007597

Contents

Great Ape Revolution   ix

Acknowledgments   xii

Part I. Ape Minds   1

1. It's Like He's Thinking or Something
    KRISTIN ANDREWS   3

2. Just Say No to Speech
    SARA WALLER   15

3. Are Apes Sneaky Enough to Be People?
    DON FALLIS   00

Part II. Ape Science   39

4. Science's Crazy Dogma
    BERNARD ROLLIN WITH JOHN HUSS   41

5. Getting a Rise Out of Genetic Engineering
    MASSIMO PIGLIUCCI   53

Part III. Ape Equality   65

6. Who Comes First, Humans or Apes?
    TRAVIS MICHAEL TIMMERMAN   67

7. Of Apes and Men
    JONAS-SÉBASTIEN BEAUDRY   83

Part IV. Ape Spacetime   97

8. We Came from Your Future
    DAVID L. MORGAN   99

9. Escape from the Paradox of the Apes
    RALPH SHAIN   111

Part V. Ape Politics 123

10. Banana Republic
    GREG LITTMANN 125

11. From *Twilight Zone* to Forbidden Zone
    LESLIE DALE FELDMAN 143

12. The Primate Who Knew Too Much
    MICHAEL RUSE 153

Part VI. Ape Ethics 165

13. Captive Kin
    LORI GRUEN 167

14. Rise of the Planet of the Altruists
    JOHN S. WILKINS 177

Part VII. Ape Cinema 191

15. Serkis Act
    JOHN HUSS 193

16. It's a Madhouse! A Madhouse!
    TOM MCBRIDE 203

17. Inside the Underscore for *Planet of the Apes*
    WILLIAM L. MCGINNEY 213

Part VIII. Ape Identity 229

18. Caesar's Identity Crisis
    CHAD TIMM 231

19. Aping Race, Racing Apes
    JASON DAVIS 245

20. Rise of Being-in-the-World
    SHAUN MAY 255

Part IX. Planet 263

21. The Last Man
    NORVA Y.S. LO AND ANDREW BRENNAN 265

22. Planet of the Degenerate Monkeys
    EUGENE HALTON 279

References   293

About the Authors   299

Index   303

Great Ape Revolution

JOHN HUSS

Pick a revolution and there's a *Planet of the Apes* movie with something to say about it.

The Scientific Revolution? Standing before an Ape Tribunal discussing space travel, Charlton Heston's George Taylor calls to mind Galileo, who once made the ridiculous claim that the Earth is just another planet, whizzing through space and spinning at an incredible speed. All at once, an affront to science, religion, and common sense. Heresy!

And if Copernicus, Galileo, and ultimately Newton dispatched us from our place at the center of the universe, surely the Darwinian Revolution finished the job, toppling us humans from our place at the pinnacle of evolution. This is exactly what *Planet of the Apes*, beginning with Pierre Boulle's 1963 novel, took to its logical extreme—in a way only science fiction and philosophical imagination can.

The reboot, *Rise of the Planet of the Apes*, reminds us that we are in the midst of a Molecular Revolution—with new tools for the diagnosis and treatment of disease, modification of the genomes of humans, apes, and crop plants. It also warns us that with great power comes great responsibility. The consequences of our tinkerings extend well beyond the borders of the human body. To those human chauvinists who fail to recognize that we share this planet with other species, this is your wake-up call.

The original film, *Planet of the Apes*, came out in 1968, in the wake of the Summer of Love. If you have any doubt that the filmmakers were in the grips of the Sexual Revolution, just take a look at this book's cover. When I see such interspecies erotica, I remember what philosopher Elizabeth Anscombe once said: "You might as well accept any sexual goings-on, if you accept contraceptive intercourse." Whether that argument can get us over the species line is another matter.

Political revolutions? When *Conquest of the Planet of the Apes* was released, it was easy to see in it a refracted image of the Watts Riots, and race riots erupting in Los Angeles, Newark, and other cities. Eric Greene has called the *Planet of the Apes* series "an American Myth" and an allegory for race relations, but the movies are not only an *American* myth: they have resonated outside of America as well. They seem to hold a mirror up to us, without fully dictating what gets reflected back, freeing us up to describe what we see without the cultural and political baggage of our world. To take one example, once the revolution in Tahrir Square had settled into making a transition to a new elected government, Egyptian President Mohamed Morsi used *Planet of the Apes* as an allegory for, well, it's hard to say exactly what, but here he is quoted in *Time* magazine:

> I remember a movie. Which one? *Planet of the Apes.* . . .When the big monkey, he was head of the supreme court I think . . . and there was a big scientist working for him, cleaning things, has been chained there. It was the Planet of the Apes after the destructive act of a big war, and atomic bombs. . . . The scientist was asking him to do something. . . . "Don't forget you are a monkey," he tells him, "Don't ask me about this dirty work." What did the big ape, the monkey say? He said, "You're human, you did it to yourself." That's the conclusion. Can *we* do something better for ourselves? I saw it thirty years ago. That is the role of the art.

I don't fully understand what President Morsi said, but I agree with him. I too saw *Planet of the Apes* some thirty years ago. And whatever else he may have been talking about, President Morsi could just as easily have been discussing philosophy. We who have written this book can all attest to the proposition that philosophy is dirty work.

Chained to our desks, we try our utmost to clean up a messy reality and make it comprehensible and rational, first to ourselves, and then to others. We start from premises no *Planet of the Apes* fan would deny. Then we ascend, through reason, to conclusions that no one but a *Planet of the Apes* fan will accept. But that's only one job of the philosopher. The other job is to listen, to be open to the responses of others, to learn.

As you'll see, we who wrote this book are open to your response. In fact, we invite it. On Facebook. Now. Well, you might want to read a few chapters first.

President Morsi is right. *Planet of the Apes* is art. It stays with us and reminds us: We *are* human. We *did* do this to ourselves. And yes, we *can* do something better, for ourselves and for the other inhabitants of the planet we share.

Acknowledgments

The authors would like to thank all those who helped make this book possible. Sharon Cebula provided editorial suggestions and assistance on a number of chapters. George Reisch offered constructive criticism and editorial guidance. Joanna Trzeciak helped out from the initial stages of the project through the submission of the final manuscript.

In 2011, philosopher Peter Singer published "A Planet for All Apes," a review essay of two movies that had come out a week apart: the documentary *Project Nim* and Amanda Silver and Rick Jaffa's *Rise of the Planet of the Apes*. Singer's essay was a catalyst for this book, and we thank him for his encouragement and help in the early stages of outreach to authors.

I

Ape Minds

1
It's Like He's Thinking or Something

KRISTIN ANDREWS

One day, your dog starts to speak in what sounds like some kind of Scandinavian language. She looks at you, cocks her head, and says, "Getum við farið í göngutúr?"

All of a sudden, the familiar has become monstrous. You knew your dog well enough up till now; you looked into her eyes every day and saw her loyalty and affection. But now you look at her in horror. Animals aren't supposed to talk! Worse yet, what is she thinking? What is her *plan*?

We usually feel as though we understand our friends, parents, co-workers, and partners. But when our friends act out of character, we tend to be temporarily baffled. We wonder why they're behaving that way. At least with such people we have recourse to a shared language, which serves as a tool to try to come back to a point of understanding. Without the luxury of a common tongue, gaining understanding of people's unexpected acts is all the more difficult.

This problem is especially salient in the *Planet of the Apes* movies. In the original film, for example, Charlton Heston's Taylor tries to make friends with the mute humans, but in response to Taylor's friendly greeting, they shrink back in terror. Humans aren't supposed to talk! Or in *Rise of the Planet of the Apes*, after Caesar exposes the apes in the San Bruno Primate Shelter to ALZ 113, remember how they gather together in a kind of conference, systematically grunting to one another, planning their uprising? John Landon, the boss of the facility, looks on bewildered. In our world, other apes aren't supposed to plot against us!

When individuals act as they're supposed to act, we feel as if we can understand them even without language. You understand your dog's desire to go for a walk when she ambles up to the door, cocks her head at you, and barks. But when she asks for a walk in Icelandic, that's when you start to worry. New parents carefully study subtle distinctions in the tonality of cries to figure out whether their babies want food, a diaper change, or sleep. Or they download the Baby Cry Translator app. Even with an iPhone, dealing with crying babies can be frustrating, but it is rarely scary. Talking babies, like babies with revolving heads, are another matter all together.

Just as we can understand babies and dogs who can't talk, little children can come to understand us. In this sense, human children can mindread—they can predict what others are going to do, and think about what others want and how others feel. Mindreading is especially handy when someone acts in a way we wouldn't expect, because a developed mindreading ability allows us to figure out people's reasons for acting. Why does Nova touch Taylor's neck, the bruise on her own arm, and then the bruise on Taylor's arm? Zira explains Nova's pantomime by reading Nova's mind: she remarks that Nova remembers the blood transfusion.

A lack of shared language is not the only impediment to our cross-species mindreading success. We also often suffer from a lack of familiarity with the normal behavior of the mindreadee in question. Cornelius first scoffs at Zira's interpretation of Nova's pantomime, and many of our attempts to mindread other species are likewise controversial. For example, when visiting Samboja Lestari Orangutan Rehabilitation Center in Borneo, I got to know a young orphan male orangutan named Cecep, who spent his days in a forest school so he could learn the skills he needed to live in the wild.

Cecep liked to play in the dirt, and the babysitters who took care of the orangutans would often use leaves to wipe the dirt off his fur. One day I watched Cecep sit in front of Anne Russon, a psychologist who studies orangutan cognition. Cecep had dirt on top of his head, and he picked up a leaf and handed it to Anne. She cleaned the dirt off his head with the leaf, just like the babysitters often did. Then Anne dropped the leaf so Cecep gave her another. But this time Anne played dumb, and didn't clean Cecep's head. After a few seconds, Cecep took the leaf back from Anne, rubbed it on his own head, and then gave it back to her. Anne got the message, so she cleaned Cecep's head again. Anne and I interpreted Cecep's act of handing Anne the leaf as a request to clean his head; he was assuming that there was a shared expectation about what to do with the leaf. When he didn't get what he wanted, Cecep had to elaborate, and pantomime what he wanted Anne to do with the leaf. Anne and I later wrote about this and other instances of orangutan pantomime in the journal *Biology Letters*.

Some scientists think we are unjustified in our interpretation of Cecep's behavior. They do not think that Cecep truly understands the interaction; his behavior is mere mimicry, or coincidence. Without controlled experimental studies, some scientists object, we can't be sure what Cecep is thinking. (We can't even be sure *that* he is thinking.) While some scientists think the problem of interpretation is an empirical problem that could be investigated by different kinds of studies, it is perhaps more accurately described as a philosophical problem. This philosophical problem is that science alone cannot answer the question of what Cecep is thinking, because animal cognition research — like human psychology research — is grounded in folk psychology.

When philosophers speak of *folk psychology*, they mean our understanding of others as people who act for reasons, who have feelings and plans and moods and personalities. Folk psychology is the commonsense understanding of other minds that emerges (in part) from mindreading. But how accurate is folk psychology in the interpretation of other species? Are we right to think that our dog is happy to see us, or that our cat thinks it is time for lunch? What exactly are we doing to other animals when we try to read their minds? And what makes us want to mindread another species in the first place?

It's Like He's Thinking or Something

One answer to the last question is that we want to mindread other animals because we think they have minds. Philosophers like René Descartes (1596–1650) and Donald Davidson (1917–2003) were never interested in asking what an animal thinks, because they believed that animals can't think. Both philosophers argued that language is necessary for having thoughts. After all, if someone doesn't have words, how can we characterize what they are thinking using words? What are they thinking in, if not in language?

There are a number of reasons to be unconvinced by this line of thought. For one, some philosophers, such as Jerry Fodor, argue that animals might think in a language of thought, while lacking an external language. We shouldn't assume that because they don't have the kind of language that results in blabber, animals don't have language at all. Alternatively, it may be that animals—and humans—might sometimes think in images, or diagrams, or some other medium altogether; the assumption that humans think only in language might actually be false, too. Indeed, if we accept that babies can think before they're very good at using language, we have to accept that thought without language is possible. At the end of the day, the arguments that language is required for mind often come off as arguments from ignorance—I can't imagine how someone can think without language, so it must be impossible, the critic seems to say.

Sometimes we feel sure that someone has a mind even though they don't talk. Consider how Taylor tries to show Zira that he has a mind. Because he can't talk at first, he has to mouth words in response to her questions. Zira is amazed by his actions, and says to Dr. Zaius "Can you believe it? It looks like he's talking. . . . I could have sworn he was answering you." Dr. Zaius, ever the good scientist, dismisses Taylor's movements as nothing more than clever mimicry. Then when Zira wonders aloud how Taylor would do on the Hopkins manual dexterity test, and Taylor wiggles his fingers, she is astonished. . . . "Perhaps he understood."

In this scene, Zira is trying to discern Taylor's mind through his behavior; she's mired in the problem of other minds. Philosophers have long grappled with the other minds problem, which is a question about how we know that other humans have minds. I know that I have a mind, because I directly experience it—I feel my own pain and taste the food that goes into my own mouth. I think my own thoughts. But I can't taste the food you eat, or feel your pain, or think your thoughts. At least not directly. Sure, you can tell me what you're thinking, but maybe you're just a cleverly designed robot. Your speech isn't direct evidence that you have a mind.

There are a couple ways philosophers have addressed the other minds problem. John Stuart Mill (1806–1873) claimed that he knows others have minds because he knows that he has a mind, and that other people are like him in relevant ways. But for each similarity we find between two people, we can find a difference. I'm similar to you because I speak English. But I might be different from you because I have a bad memory, or enjoy eating fried tempeh, or am female. My physical body is probably very similar to yours in a lot of ways, but there are subtle differences between our bodies, including our brains. Because we might be different in important ways, we can't use the argument from analogy to defend our belief in other human minds, much less other animal minds.

Another strategy for defending the existence of other minds is to infer mind in order to explain behavior. If you don't have a mind, I really don't have a good explanation for why you're reading this chapter right now. Just as Zira doesn't have a good alternative explanation for why Taylor is engaged in a conversational sort of give and take, or why he wiggles his fingers when she wonders aloud about his manual dexterity. Why does he do these things? He must understand! Nothing else makes sense of his actions! The apes who want to figure out Taylor finally conclude that he has a mind, because it's the best way to explain the sorts of things he does. Of course, once Taylor starts talking, Caesar starts signing, and Koba writes Jacobs's name on her tablet, others immediately accept that they have minds, totally convinced by their use of language.

He Shows a Definite Gift for Mimicry

But before Taylor uses language, not everyone is convinced by Zira's reasoning. What one person explains by appeal to mind, others explain in other terms. Dr. Zaius, for example, explains that Taylor, "shows a definite gift for mimicry" and he at least pretends to conclude that his explanation of Taylor's tricks is better than Zira's.

To decide whether Zira is justified in her interpretation of Taylor's behavior, or whether Anne and I were justified in our interpretation of Cecep's, we have to do a little philosophy of science. When we explain something a human does (in the enterprise of either folk psychology or contemporary scientific psychology), we often talk about what she thinks, or what she wants, or her emotions, moods, or personality traits. For most of the twentieth century, the dominant way of thinking in psychology was behaviorism. Behaviorism avoided all talk about unobservable thinking processes or states of mind. For the behaviorists, the idea that scientists could explain behavior in terms of mental states such as *wanting*, *hoping*, or *wondering* was heresy.

Though behaviorism started losing traction for human psychology in the 1960s, it was still going strong in animal psychology. In the 1970s, the biologist Donald Griffin (1915–2003) challenged the behaviorist way of thinking in animal cognition, arguing that we need to talk about animals' mental states to explain some animal behavior. Today, while some use of folk psychology is the norm in animal cognition research, there remain questions about how far we can go.

Scientists are generally happy to say that many animal species do things because of what they perceive and what they remember. Some animal species are thought to learn new things by building associations, and can classify objects in ways that make some scientists think that they have concepts, even if they don't have words. Psychologist Sara Shettleworth, in her 2013 book *Fundamentals of Comparative Cognition*, reviews evidence for learning, concepts, mental maps, tool construction and use, problem solving, numerical understanding, and other interesting capacities in different species. But many scientists deny that non-human animals, despite all of these capacities, are folk psychologists at all.

If these scientists are right, this would make all non-human animals radically unlike humans. From birth, human infants respond to social stimuli such as faces, and engage in the give and take of social imitation. And by four years old, they're already thinking about what other people are thinking! But it's unclear whether other animals understand that there are other minds, or minds at all! Knowing that there are other minds may be important for being able to communicate—after all, why communicate if there isn't a mind to communicate to? So perhaps when Zira thinks Taylor is trying to speak, and when Anne and I think that Cecep was requesting to be cleaned, we're thinking that our respective communicators are also able to mindread. And maybe that assumption is really the problem.

Why do we think young children can mindread? Developmental psychologists usually point to their ability to attribute a false belief to a character in a story. The original false belief task, invented by developmental psychologists Heinz Wimmer and Josef Perner, involves giving the child a puppet show: Maxi the puppet is holding a piece of chocolate, but he wants to save it for later, so he hides it in a box and then leaves the room. While Maxi is out, his mother finds the chocolate in the box and moves it to a cupboard. Maxi returns to the scene, the show is stopped, and children are asked to predict where Maxi will go to look for his chocolate. Children who are able to say that Maxi will look for the chocolate in the box, where he left it, are said to be mindreaders. But most children younger than four predict that Maxi will look for the chocolate in the cupboard, where it is now. The idea is that the children who predict that Maxi will look for the chocolate in the box know that Maxi has a false belief, and in order to be a folk psychologist, you need to know that others have beliefs that can be true or false.

To try to find the same sort of evidence for mindreading abilities in other species, psychologists have invented nonverbal versions of the false belief task, with mixed results. In a review of all the mindreading experiments given to chimpanzees, the psychologists Josep Call and Michael Tomasello claim that there's no evidence that chimps understand that others have false beliefs. Chimps do seem to understand what others can see, what others know, and what others' goals and intentions are, according to Call and Tomasello. But if they don't understand that others can have beliefs that are false, then they cannot be full-blown folk psychologists. It follows that Anne and I aren't justified in interpreting Cecep's behavior as a communicative pantomime. And Zira, without recourse to controlled experimentation on Taylor using a nonverbal version of the false belief test, isn't justified in thinking Taylor is trying to communicate, either.

You Read Me Well Enough

But this seems wrong. Remember how babies and their caregivers can come to understand one another, or how you and your dog understand each other? There is some sort of communication going on when your dog asks, in doggish, to go for a walk. She communicates with a bark and a look. It is far too conservative to dictate that communication requires mind-reading of the false belief sort. Consider the idea that belief is something that is expressed in a full sentence: "I believe that *the San Bruno Primate should be shut down,*" or "I believe that *Charlton Heston is a lousy actor.*" When children start to speak, like when baby Caesar starts to sign, we already know that they're trying to communicate, even though they can't communicate in sentences. The baby who reaches and says "cookie" is making her desires pretty well known, and we can translate her one word utterance into the sentence "I want a cookie." We don't just communicate sentences, but also feelings and goals. A shared smile is communication. While Taylor and Nova can't use language together, they can communicate through touch and eye contact. Nova wants to be with Taylor; she willingly goes with him to live in the Forbidden Zone. They understand each other without exchanging words.

The narrow focus on belief reading ignores all the other ways we read minds. On a daily basis, we rarely think of the other people in our lives in terms of what they believe. When we do wonder about what someone believes, it's usually because we're trying to explain some strange thing they did. This points to a problem with the idea that we understand others by thinking about the contents of their heads. We do not, in fact, think of others as just the set of the sentences they are thinking. Rather than abstractly reading minds, we share minds and read people by doing things together and learning about one another's normal behaviors and personal idiosyncrasies. This understanding is built over time as we get used to doing things together and learn how to interact with one another.

In order to understand a new roommate or a new dog, you first have to get to know them. By cooking together, planning out how to pay the bills, going for walks, or playing fetch, we come to learn how to co-ordinate with the other person we're sharing our space with, and to judge the right time to introduce a kitten to the household, or suggest throwing a party. As I argue in my 2012 book *Do Apes Read Minds? Toward a New Folk Psychology*, we come to know others by interacting with them, and moving together. Like a dance, we share our minds through gestures, movements, facial expressions, gaze, and posture.

Anne and I don't need to withhold judgment about whether Cecep was communicating because we know him, and we consider his pantomiming behavior in the context of the other things we know about him. When we make an inference to the best explanation, we have to take all available evidence into account. So let me tell you another story about Cecep.

He was one of the leaders of the little group of forest school orangutans, and the babysitters nicknamed him The Policeman because he often broke up fights and seemed to want to keep the peace. Aldrin, one of the other orangutans in the group, wasn't doing very well. Aldrin didn't run around the forest with the other orangutans; instead he would sit and hug a babysitter, and whimper if no one would cuddle him. He only once climbed a tree when I was there, and the other orangutans usually ignored him. But one day things were very different: the babysitters found a turtle. Now, as a human reader, this might not sound terribly exciting, but orangutans are terrified of turtles—something even Darwin remarked on. When the orangutans, including Aldrin, saw the turtle they all fled into the trees in terror. Later that day when it was time to head back to camp, the babysitters realized that Aldrin wasn't with them. They never saw him come down from the tree. Then the babysitters noticed that Cecep wasn't around either. When they went back to where the turtle had been, they found Aldrin and Cecep perched in different trees. Cecep was up in a tree in front of Aldrin's, and he looked back at Aldrin, caught his eye, and then moved on to the next tree. Aldrin followed Cecep, who led Aldrin from tree to tree until they reached the path back to camp. Though Cecep had been looking back at Aldrin from time to time, when he got down to the ground he just scampered away, joining the rest of the group. And Aldrin followed. That's just the kind of guy Cecep is.

When we see only one incident of a behavior that looks as if it was done for a reason, a mentalistic explanation may not be very well justified. But as we gather observations of incident after incident that cries out for an explanation in terms of reasons for action, we become more and more justified in our interpretation. While the mentalistic hypothesis is only weakly supported by each individual incident, the *overhypothesis* that explains the large set of data is much stronger. As the philosopher Nelson Goodman defines it, an 'overhypothesis' is a hypothesis used to justify a set of more specific hypotheses, and it is a basic tool in human reasoning that allows us to form generalizations. It is one of the amazing features of human beings that we are able to learn so much starting from so little, and much of this ability is due to our powers of induction.

To justify the interpretation of a behavior via induction, we need more information than just the description of the behavior. We need to know what happened before the behavior, and what happened after. It also helps to know the idiosyncratic history of the behaving individual, as well as the normal behavior of the relevant species. No behavior occurs outside of a larger context. So we shouldn't interpret any behavior without taking its context into account.

They're All Tame Until They Take a Chunk Out of You

Context plays an especially important role in the interpretation of behavior insofar as minds have evolved in—and are naturally designed to work within—particular contexts. If our environment affects our minds, then in order to know the natural ape mind, scientists need to gather inductive data about ape behavior in natural ape environments. Most cognition research is done with caged animals. Think about how unimpressive Taylor is in his cage, or how well the scientists understand Caesar's mother Bright Eyes in hers.

Now think about how much mental work you offload onto your environment, and imagine trying to get by without the information in your phone. Try doing your taxes without a computer or even a pencil and paper. We have good memories because we write things down in our calendars. We are organized because we have to-do lists. We know how to do many things, from getting to work to buying dinner, because we live in the same kind of environment in which we learned these skills. Elderly people with dementia can often live surprising well in their own homes, because they let the house serve as part of their mind. Take this person out of her home, and she often deteriorates quite quickly. We all need our environments to help us think, and we all need familiar tools to show off our skills. A tailor is useless without thread and needle, just as an orangutan may be useless without trees to climb and build nests in.

Experiments on great apes can help us find out what apes can do, but we can't count on them to tell us what apes can't do. We especially can't let them tell us that apes can't do something when we have access to a body of observations that together force us toward an explanation in terms of that very ability. Imagine trying to understand what great apes can do while only studying the apes at the San Bruno Primate Shelter, or the apes at Gen Sys. Or imagine the intelligent simians of *Planet of the Apes* trying to learn about all the things twentieth-century humans can do by studying Taylor alone in a cage without clothes or a voice. When you're in a cage, you act caged, and a tame animal is a compromised one. Since caging and taming changes the individual, we need to study uncaged wild animals if we really want to know what they're thinking.

2
Just Say No to Speech

Sara Waller

In the beginning, there was the word of Taylor. Our hero's loneliness in space is captured in language, a soliloquy spoken to an empty galaxy. He asks, "Does man, that marvel of the universe, that glorious paradox who sent me to the stars, still make war against his brother? Keep his neighbor's children starving?"

Taylor's language in the opening scene of *Planet of the Apes* (1968) conveys not only intelligence, but empathy and hope that future humanity is better than the humanity he left hundreds of years in the past. He wants to speak, and to be heard, which is precisely what he cannot do alone in space, or after being shot in the throat. Language—wielded by humans or by apes—seems to endow its possessors with superiority and moral worth, allows space travel, religion, and science, and lets us confess: "I am lonely."

And with language, we have made ourselves lonely, as we often seem to have empathy only for other creatures that speak. Language becomes a weapon in its ability to indicate thought, and its absence is easily construed as an absence of intelligence. For creatures without language, we have a great variety of measures that can be used to bestow, or reject, their intelligence. Once intelligence has been dismissed, it seems that rights, personhood, and respect are gone as well; our empathy is reserved for our intellectual equals.

Tyranny of Language

The word 'barbarian' is a clear example of how language can be used to prop up prejudice and oppression. To the ancient Greeks, other languages such as Persian sounded so much like 'bar bar bar bar' that 'barbarian' came to mean 'one who is brutish' and 'one who does not speak the language of the civilized' (that being Greek, of course). The word served to diminish anyone who spoke differently, both in intellect and in moral character, and so, in our moral concern for such a person as well. After all, who would go to great lengths to protect or care for a strange foreigner who is crude, hostile, threatening, and babbling? And the barbarians cannot defend themselves from this charge, for all they can do in return is say 'bar bar bar bar' thus proving their inferiority. We see this prejudice play out across the *Planet of the Apes* films. Dodge Landon, the cruel chimp keeper in *Rise of the Planet of the Apes* mocks the intelligent and imprisoned chimps mercilessly, imitating the sounds Caesar makes and calling him "stupid monkey." And in the original film, Dr. Zaius remarks of Taylor how amusing it is that a man would act like an ape, mimicking speech.

We know the *Planet of the Apes* films present us with metaphors for racism as well—and racism is often reinforced through linguistic oppression. America's voting restriction laws of 1894 present us with another good example of the tyranny of language as the measure of minds. These laws prohibited anyone who could not read or write in English from approaching the polls. A wonderful device for those who were wealthy and educated, the law effectively kept the lower classes from casting votes and thereby gaining advantages such as education and literacy. These laws were in many cases abused by whites in power telling potential black voters that they had failed the test—not because they had really failed to answer the questions, but because it was in the interests of racists to implement any effective method of oppression.

Tell a potential minority voter he has failed the test, and not only has his vote been blocked, but he might also believe that he is illiterate and uneducated, and so unworthy of protesting or fighting back against the majority and their elegant language skills. Giggling at animals such as Taylor and saying 'human see, human do' is also effectively demoralizing, not to mention hosing them down and subjecting them to ridicule.

Standard IQ tests in use today may be accused of similar bias. The two most accepted tests are the Stanford-Binet Intelligence Test, and the Wechsler Adult Intelligence Test. If you know your IQ, it is because you took one of these tests (probably while you were in middle school). The basic format of these tests is a conversation between an examiner and the person being 'measured,' and the examiner asks questions focusing on vocabulary, mathematics, and ability to recall information. The results of the test depend on the ability of the examinee to understand instructions and respond clearly. But the structure of the test itself seems to double the importance of language skill in taking the test. The most crucial part of the test—the part that most reliably determines one's overall IQ—is the vocabulary section. Indeed, IQ tests have been criticized for bias precisely because those who speak a dialect of English may receive a lower IQ score simply due to a difference in response to certain words that appear on the test. Speakers of creoles, and people who have learned English as a second language, all risk being assigned a lower IQ because their responses are non-standard. We measure your mind in a test made of the language, by the language, and for the language.

Poor Taylor's mind gets measured, and dismissed, in much the same way. It seems that ape psychologists followed right along with this human linguistic prejudice. Zira, perhaps the most empathetic and charitable of the ape researchers, cajoles the imprisoned humans to do more than peer and grunt. "Well, . . . And what do we want this morning? Do we want something? Come on, . . . speak." She's thrilled with "Bright Eyes" precisely because he seems to be attempting to speak (or perhaps pretending he can speak), even though she is met with skepticism from her colleagues. Once the prejudice against non-speaking humans is in place, there is nothing Taylor can do to prove himself smart—much as there is little or nothing the 'Bright Eyes' in *Rise of the Planet of the Apes* can do to persuade her human keepers that she is merely protecting her child, or that Caesar can do to appease the next door neighbor who is convinced he is vicious. Muteness, human or ape, seems a sure way to become oppressed. Even Taylor is not immune from the tyranny of language as he gazes at the beautiful

Nova, and wonders aloud if she is capable of love, given her lack of speech.

We'll Start with the Wisconsin Multiphasic

Once a language barrier has been established (between Greeks and barbarians, humans and apes, researchers and studied animals), we can try to understand the mind of the other through non-linguistic tests. Dr. Zira immediately muses about how Taylor might do on the "Hopkins Manual Dexterity Test," no doubt a Hollywood version of the real Minnesota Manual Dexterity Test, in which one must nimbly put discs in holes as quickly as possible. While dexterity is a far cry from an indicator of intelligence (Stephen Hawking, for example, would fail such a test), it's easy for us to read into these test results, thinking that those who are smart are also dexterous, and vice versa.

In *Escape from the Planet of the Apes*, Dr. Zira and Cornelius arrive on twentieth-century Earth and are subjected to testing. They have agreed not to divulge their ability to speak without gathering some information on how the humans might react. Since they seem mute to the curious humans, tests seem the right way to investigate these apes-gone-astronaut. The first test is called the "Wisconsin Multiphasic" in homage to two well-known and well-respected psychological tests: the Wisconsin Card Sorting Task, and the Minnesota Multiphasic Personality Inventory. In the real Wisconsin task, subjects are asked to identify and respond to patterns presented in cards, and the more aptly they do it, the more they are said to have good *executive function*. Akin to outright intelligence, executive function is the ability to plan, solve problems, work through steps of a problem, and complete a logical sequence of events or tasks. The Minnesota Multiphasic is a completely different kind of test. It is a several-hundred-question-long psychological survey aimed at discovering the inner workings of your personality. Are you depressive? Neurotic? Your score on the MMPI will tell you.

Amusingly, the fictional Wisconsin Multiphasic test that Zira is subjected to seems to be a simple memory task. But it's given in a way that is standard for much psychological testing. She sits opposite the examiner, and is allowed to see objects presented by the tester. Then, a shade is drawn between them, and the examiner adds more objects. She must select the old objects and ignore the new ones, showing she can remember what was first presented. When she succeeds at this, the human psychologist presents her with the container for all the objects—with holes cut in the right shape for every object. Lightly insulted, Dr. Zira completes the task without effort.

The human psychologists are very pleased with Zira's results, and present her with a classic task first given to chimpanzees by researcher Wolfgang Kohler in 1913. In this task, as in the film, a banana is suspended out of reach, and the hungry chimpanzees have to find a way to obtain it using things in their environment, such as boxes. Kohler's famous studies showed that chimpanzees did not have to use trial and error in order to learn and solve problems: that is, they could solve such a problem on the first try, using *insight*, a clear mark of intelligence. In the movie, the boxes have almost Tetris-like shapes, made for easy stacking. Kohler's original task was a bit harder, with ordinary boxes that were not so easily stacked. Dr. Zira, who probably learned about, if not performed, similar experiments with humans as she pursued her doctoral work in psychology, stacks the boxes in a familiar and deliberate way, and then sits with the banana easily in reach, gazing at her human examiners. Why doesn't she take it after completing the task? "Because I loathe bananas," Dr. Zira shouts. And with that, just as with Taylor's "Take your stinking paws off me, you damn dirty ape" in the original movie, and Caesar's exclamation of "No" in *Rise of the Planet of the Apes*, the notion of the "animal," and its intelligence and moral status, is forever changed.

Delightfully, Dr. Zira's exclamation is accurate to real ape preferences in comparative psychology laboratories—everyone who works with chimpanzees recognizes that they prefer grapes. Indeed, recent studies by Frans de Waal show that chimpanzees who receive cucumbers for completing a task, but can see that their companion in the neighboring cage are receiving grapes for the same work, first become enraged and shake the cage, then throw the cucumber back at the experimenter, and finally refuse to do the task altogether until the grape is given rightfully and equally to both working parties. DeWaal's recent TED talk entitled "Moral Behavior in Animals" reveals some delightful moments of these experiments and can be found on YouTube.

Rise of the Planet of the Apes opens with "Bright Eyes" completing "the Lucas Tower," which is modeled on a well-known and often-employed real psychological task called the Tower of Hanoi. Composed of three small poles and a series of discs of decreasing sizes, the object of the task is to move the disks from the left hand post to the right hand post without ever placing a larger disc on top of a smaller disc. It's considered a task of "executive function" because it demands that the subject plan ahead so as to never misplace the discs. Bright Eyes is doing amazingly well at the task, completing it in twenty moves. Caesar later masters the same task in fifteen moves at a young age, with a plot line that mirrors the research of Sue Savage-Rumbaugh. This researcher worked with bonobos (a chimp-like ape species), and trained the mother of the famous bonobo, Kanzi, on a symbol board, hoping to get her to associate symbols with meanings and thus use the board as a proxy for speech. The mother of Kanzi never did do well on the symbol board, but Kanzi did, suggesting that a young brain is indeed more amicable to training than an adult brain—and that a young monkey can indeed benefit intellectually from experiencing the training aimed at its mother.

Finally, in *Rise of the Planet of the Apes*, young Caesar exhibits intelligence as he swings about the kitchen, steals a cookie, and swings back to replace the lid on the cookie jar in order to cover his tracks. In doing this, he passes a well-respected "deception task" in comparative psychology. Animals that can fake out other animals through deception are thought to be intelligent because they must understand that the animals being tricked have mental states—specifically, beliefs—and that these beliefs can be manipulated in a variety of ways.

Ravens, for example, will steal the fish from the lines of ice fishermen, and then carefully place the line back in the water so that the unsuspecting human does not know he was robbed. Likewise, an octopus in a west-coast aquarium would slither from its tank at night to eat the luscious salmon and crabs in neighboring tanks, slither back into its own tank, and shut the top. The baffled humans lost several shipments of crab and fish before they installed a camera in the aquarium to find out what was happening at night. This story marked the beginning of serious consideration of octopus intelligence by comparative psychologists. No wonder Caesar is shown stealing cookies at an early age—he's portrayed as exceptionally bright every step of the way.

But, as Zira quips in *Escape from the Planet of the Apes,* "Primitive? . . . These tests are prehistoric! They couldn't test the intelligence of a newt." Cognitive ethologists argue that laboratory tests such as these show us little of animal intelligence, and that we must measure the intelligence of all creatures through observation of their behaviors in a natural environment. They argue that the lab is too artificial, and too biased toward human values to really help us understand what animals are thinking, and how smart they might be.

Astronaut Behavior 101

Measures of intelligence from cognitive ethology—the kind of research that observes animals in their natural environment—are based on things the animal does to preserve itself and plan for its future. The original crash landing of Taylor and his colleagues reveals many of the operative principles in cognitive ethological observation. The first thing they do is attempt to establish where they are in space and time: "It's not so much where we are, it's when we are," quips Taylor. They ponder the accuracy of their instruments, contemplating the tools they used to get to the planet, and wonder just how off course they may be. Notions of location and time are important measures of intelligence for ethologists. Birds such as bluejays that can remember not only where their favorite food is, but how old it is (as it gets less tasty as it ages) put bird brains on the map of animal intelligence research because they demonstrate a sense of time as well as an excellent memory.

The crash-landed humans proceed to try to figure out what went wrong. Why did Stewart die? Is the theory of relativity accurate, or was there a miscalculation in trajectory? Problem solving is a well-respected measure of intelligence, and understanding cause and effect relationships is an important part of problem solving. Soon, however, as their ship sinks into the lake and they realize that the problem cannot be solved because they are "here to stay," they turn to more practical matters of locating ammunition, food, and shelter. Determining that they have enough food for three days, much like bluejays, they decide that they need to search for future supplies. From their actions, they exhibit intelligence, for they can remember, plan, and problem-solve. In a habitat that is not so natural, the team passes several cognitive ethological milestones in the measure of intelligence.

Once we see that they can take care of themselves, another, more sophisticated cognitive function enters the arena. The dialogue shifts from survival to emotion. The astronauts discuss their grief for the lost colleague Stewart. Mourning behavior is seen as an indicator of not only memory, but emotional attachment, which in turn is taken by cognitive ethologists to be an important precursor to moral behavior. No wonder we're so fascinated by elephants, who travel for miles to visit the boneyards of their ancestors, and spend hours fondling the skeletons of their relatives. They seem to remember, and feel, in just the way human beings do as we visit gravesides and perform ceremonies. Recently it has been reported by researcher Marc Bekoff that magpies also perform ceremonies for their dead, carefully placing grass and baubles near the deceased before flying away.

And from grief at the loss of Stewart, the conversation turns to the more abstract grief at the loss of their civilization, of everyone they have ever known, and of their once-important ambitions, now so meaningless as they traverse the desert. Emotions run high as the astronauts contemplate the fate of the Earth as well as their own futures. With the range of emotion and abstract thought the astronauts display, we can imagine that the apes are thankful for their scarecrows up on the hills, for by cognitive ethological measures, these astronauts do seem to be intelligent—and intelligence is often dangerous. (But of course, the most frightening thing about them is still that they can speak.)

At the end of *Planet of the Apes* one of the best accepted measures of intelligence in the world of ethological research is found—evidence of play. That talking doll, a toy, is of great significance, for play suggests counterfactual reasoning—imagining the world as it is not, and interacting with things that aren't real.

Social play is even more important as a measure of intelligence, because beings that play together must somehow agree with each other about an imaginary universe in which they will both participate. When children play cowboys and Indians or war, they do not kill each other because they understand that the scenario they co-create is not real. That takes tremendous cognitive ability: to imagine, to remember, to treat one's friends as friends, as well as to create a narrative about something in an imaginative plane that is shared. The doll at the end of the film speaks volumes about cognition well beyond language—cognition that includes co-operation, imagination, and the envisioning of how things could be different.

Is Language the Last Word on Intelligence?

We're reminded of just how important language is as a measure of intelligence when we learn early in *Rise of the Planet of the Apes* that by eighteen months Caesar was signing up to twenty-four words, when in *Planet of the Apes* we see that Landon has been subject to some sort of language-erasing lobotomy, and when in *Escape from the Planet of the Apes,* the apes caution each other with "Our safety is in our silence."

There is no threat from the apes in *Conquest of the Planet of the Apes*—no matter how many intelligent "tricks" they perform—until Caesar mutters "Lousy human bastards." Amidst the chaos at the chimp facility in *Rise of the Planet of the Apes* the stupefied human population asks "What happened?" The answer given in the film is not that the chimps broke free, nor is it that they organized, planned, and co-ordinated an attack on human civilization. Rather, says Rodney, "He spoke."

But should language be such a threat, and such an important measure of intelligence? One philosopher, Quine, just says 'No.'

Quine developed a thought experiment to illustrate a concept called *the inscrutability of reference*, by which he meant that we don't really ever know for sure what anyone else is referring to, even if that person is speaking the same language that we are. Take, for example, the case of an anthropologist who has been assigned to decipher a newly discovered foreign language that is solely spoken by an isolated tribe. There are no natural translators for the language. In his example, Quine suggests that the smart anthropologist will go out and observe the tribe's speech behaviors just as any cognitive ethologist would, taking notes in a notebook every time a certain word is spoken. On day one, a member of the tribe walks out of her hut, points at a rabbit, and utters the sound "Gavagai." The anthropologist makes note of this, guessing that perhaps 'gavagai' means rabbit. On day two, a man walks out of the brush, points in the direction of a rabbit, and also says 'gavagai.' Our anthropologist again makes a note of this, and is pleased with herself for having figured out what some words in this language might mean.

But Quine suggests that our anthropologist is overly confident, because there is ultimately no way to know exactly what these natives are pointing to when they speak. Perhaps, in their minds, they are pointing to *undetached rabbit parts* or *temporal slices of rabbitness* or something that we have not even conceived of yet. Since there is no way to tell the difference between our ordinary conception of *rabbit* and *undetached rabbit parts*, there is no way for us to know exactly what the tribe members mean when they say 'gavagai.' Indeed, Quine concludes, there really is no way for us to be sure that we know what anyone is referring to at any given time, because we cannot see inside the mind of another person. While uttering 'gavagai' might still get us the result of a rabbit, we don't know how the other person conceives of the rabbitty-like-thing she hands to us in our discussion.

Since we can't be sure exactly what anyone means when he or she uses a word, there seems to be a real worry regarding using language as the ultimate measure of intelligence. There is a real-world example that helps to reveal just how prejudiced we are toward language. People with Williams-Beuren syndrome often have strong speaking ability and tend to be very cheerful, friendly, trusting, and talkative. In other words, on first meeting, they can be completely charming. However, the down side of the condition is moderate mental retardation. No matter how verbal they are, they often have difficulty doing many of the other tasks we associate with intelligence, such as problem-solving, planning, learning, and memory. As biased as we are toward language, there are still cases that show that language is not the last word on intelligence.

Be Clever—Be Quiet

Perhaps remaining silent is more intelligent than using language. Is this why Nova continuously tried to stop Taylor from speaking? She put her hand over his mouth, smeared out his word written in the dirt, and persisted in refusing to say her name. Perhaps she knew something about speech that Taylor didn't—that it can be used against the orator, that it can be misinterpreted, that it can create prejudice, bias, injustice, and bombs.

Nova may well be protecting him from the consequences of his speech, which may be seen as a threat in their religious setting—analogous to the pre-Darwinian era—in which the simian brain alone is believed to have the spark of the divine. Zira and Cornelius urge Taylor to "be clever . . . be quiet" at his trial. Indeed, the films of *Planet of the Apes* as a body of work suggest repeatedly that the smart are the silent, perhaps obliquely suggesting that the animals do not speak to us because of their intellectual superiority. Zira and Cornelius themselves attempt to seem speechless as they arrive on earth in *Escape.* As Milo says, in *Escape from the Planet of the Apes*— this is "a time not for lies, but for silence."

In *Beneath the Planet of the Apes,* Brent looks at the eroded subway station and wonders about the nature of the mute: "Are you what we were before we learned to talk and made fools of ourselves?" Language has led to the destruction and devastation he sees around him. Is this why the native humans do not speak in the early movies? None of the brain surgery and psychological testing that take place in simian psychological research of the early films answers the question of the mute humans. All we know from the first film is that the key to human muteness is not to be found in human physiology. Could it lie instead in a decision the humans made?

Beyond annihilating the planet, language has led us to destroying each other, simian or human. In *Escape from the Planet of the Apes,* we're warned "If you are caught by the gorillas you must remember never to speak . . . If they catch you speaking they will dissect you and kill you in that order." Even the Caesar of *Conquest of the Planet of the Apes* must pretend he is silent like the other pet chimpanzees, for his own safety. And the Caesar of *Rise of the Planet of the Apes* finds himself a circus-trained orangutan companion who tells him, "Man no like smart ape." In an oppressive society, it may well be smarter to follow the methods of American slaves, who developed a linguistic vernacular like "black English" that seemed stupid and halting to their captors but was actually sophisticated and as rule-bound as any language is. To be smarter than your oppressors, play stupid. And a great method for appearing stupid is to behave as if you don't comprehend language, or enact it poorly. As MacDonald says in *Battle for the Planet of the Apes*, "Brightness has never been encouraged among slaves."

Cornelius's advice to a morally outraged Zira in *Escape from the Planet of the Apes* was "Have a grape, dear, and look the other way," but this urge to refuse to re-think our judgments of intelligence and what they so often seem to allow in terms of "sub-human" treatment is exactly what these films help us to overcome. By watching the *Planet of the Apes* movies, we look right at our own prejudices, tendencies toward unfairness, and biases about intelligence. The series helps us do better than drink more "grape juice" and lapse into our denial about the treatment of others who do not speak (or who fail to speak our language). Through art such as movies, we have the ability to go beyond our prejudices regarding intelligence and re-think our treatment of non-human animals. We just say no to our bias toward language as the most important measure of intelligence and moral worth.

3
Are Apes Sneaky Enough to Be People?

DON FALLIS

Pierre Boulle's novel *Planet of the Apes* is clearly an allegory about how we should and should not treat other people. In *Planet of the Apes as American Myth*, Eric Greene suggests that, taken as a whole, the *Planet of the Apes* movies present a case against the enslavement and oppression of people who seem to us to be more primitive or less than fully human.

But also, Boulle's novel and the subsequent movie series directly raise the question of what it takes to be a *person*. Are any nonhuman animals, such as apes, smart enough to count as persons? In his recent review of the documentary *Project Nim*, Princeton philosopher Peter Singer suggests that the answer is *Yes*.

One obvious indicator of superior intelligence and cognitive development, and the one that Singer focuses on, is the ability to use *language*. But while several researchers have tried to teach primates (such as Koko and Nim Chimpsky) to use sign language, the results have been inconclusive. For instance, it has been suggested that these researchers were (much like the trainers of Clever Hans, the horse that could allegedly do arithmetic) unconsciously giving the apes cues about what to sign and that the apes were just imitating them.

Maybe the apes were just *aping* the humans. In the original 1968 movie, the apes are at first quite skeptical of Taylor's ability to use language. The keeper thinks that his attempts to speak (which he is unable to do because he has been shot in the throat) are a case of "human-see-human-do." Cornelius is sure that even Taylor's written notes are just a "stunt."

But another possible indicator of intelligence (and, thus, of personhood) is the ability to *deceive*. In fact, many years before Boulle's novel, Robert Heinlein (1907–1988) wrote a science fiction story called "Jerry Is a Man," in which genetically enhanced apes are able to perform menial tasks and have some ability to speak. When the human characters are deciding whether one of these apes is a person (and, thus, should not be euthanized when he is no longer able to work), a critical piece of evidence is that Jerry is able to lie.

Such deception requires fairly sophisticated cognitive capacities that we usually only associate with humans. In order to deceive, you must be what Tufts philosopher Daniel Dennett calls, in his 1981 book *Brainstorms*, a "second-order intentional system." Not only must you be capable of having beliefs, desires, and other intentions, you must be capable of having beliefs and desires *about* beliefs and desires. In particular, it must be possible for you to *want* someone else to have a *false belief*.

General Thade, from Tim Burton's *Planet of the Apes*, is a good example of a mendacious second-order intentional system. In order to get permission to eliminate the humans, he lies to Senator Sandar. Thade tells the senator that his daughter Ari has been kidnapped by the humans. He does this because he *wants* the senator to have the *false belief* that they kidnapped her.

We'll Check This with the Authenticator

In addition to deception requiring sophisticated cognitive capacities, many psychologists argue that deception is how we became humans in the first place. According to Andrew Whiten and Richard Byrne's *Machiavellian Intelligence* hypothesis, the evolutionary advantage of being able to deceive other members of one's social group is what led to the remarkable brain size and intelligence that separates us from the rest of the animal kingdom.

As the philosopher David Livingstone Smith explains in a 2005 article in *Scientific American Mind*, "social complexity propelled our ancestors to become progressively more intelligent and increasingly adept at wheeling, dealing, bluffing and conniving." Those individuals who had a greater ability to deceive (and a greater ability to detect deceivers) were more likely to pass on their genes.

If it's so advantageous to be able to detect deception, it's a little bit strange that humans are so bad at it. Experimental studies suggest that most of us are able to detect liars at only slightly better than chance. We're not at all like the subterranean mutant humans with telepathic capabilities (a.k.a. the Keepers of the Divine Bomb in *Beneath the Planet of the Apes*) who can simply tell that Brent is lying when he says that "the Apes are a primitive, semi-articulate and underdeveloped race whose weapons have not progressed beyond the club and the sling!" In order to be sure that someone is not lying to us, we've had to develop assistive technologies, such as the sodium pentothal that Dr. Otto Hasslein uses on Zira in *Escape from the Planet of the Apes* or the "Authenticator" that Inspector Kolp uses on Armando in *Conquest of the Planet of the Apes*.

In his book *Telling Lies*, Paul Ekman—the inspiration for Cal Lightman, the protagonist of the TV show *Lie To Me*—offers an explanation for why we need such technological assistance. He claims that "our ancestral environment did not prepare us to be astute lie catchers. . . . Serious lies probably did not occur often, because a lack of privacy would have made the chances of being caught high" (pp. 341–42). But Ekman's suggestion here, which conflicts with the *Machiavellian Intelligence* hypothesis, can't be right. Anybody who is part of a family knows that a lot of deception goes on even though privacy can be hard to come by. But does this apply to ape families or just human families?

You Damn Dirty Apes!

Just like humans, the highly intelligent apes in the *Planet of the Apes* series certainly have the ability to deceive. General Thade is a notable example, but he's not the only untrustworthy ape in the series by a long shot. In *Escape from the Planet of the Apes*, after the "ape-nauts" land on present-day Earth and are taken to the Los Angeles Zoo, they pretend that they are unable to talk. And once Cornelius and Zira do start talking, they start lying. They tell the Presidential Commission that they do not know Taylor, and they conceal how apes treat humans in the time that they come from. In *Conquest of the*

Planet of the Apes and in *Rise of the Planet of the Apes*, Caesar also has to pretend to be just a normal, non-talking, ape. But not only that, in *Conquest of the Planet of the Apes*, Caesar feigns being electrocuted so that the humans will think that he's dead. (Fortunately Mr. MacDonald had just turned off the power.)

The apes in the series don't just deceive humans. They frequently attempt to deceive other apes. In Boulle's novel, Cornelius tricks the other apes by substituting Ulysse Mérou, Nova, and their child for the three primitive humans that (much like Ham the Astrochimp) were originally going to man an artificial satellite. In *Beneath the Planet of the Apes*, Zira tells Dr. Zaius that "Cornelius hit me . . . for my bad behavior at the meeting." She tells this lie in order to explain the bloody bandage that she had been using to clean Brent's gunshot wound. In the original film, in order to help Taylor escape, Zira's nephew Lucius lies to the keeper about taking Taylor to the zoo. And let's not forget the unnamed ape that cheats at cards and one that wears a toupée in Burton's movie.

Admittedly, the apes in the series are not always very good at carrying out their deception. In *Conquest of the Planet of the Apes*, Caesar basically just needs to keep his mouth shut in order to look like a normal ape. But he can't stop himself from shouting, "Lousy human bastards!" at some guards that are roughly subduing a gorilla. Also, in *Rise of the Planet of the Apes*, even though the circus orangutan warns him that humans don't like smart apes, Caesar does not do much to hide his intelligence. For instance, when the apes are holding a meeting in the large enclosure at the San Bruno Primate Shelter and the keeper unexpectedly arrives, the rest of the apes start milling about as if nothing is going on. But Caesar just turns and gives the keeper a defiant look. (Fortunately for Caesar, the keeper can't believe what he's seeing and decides to ignore it.)

Some of the apes in the series don't like to engage in deception. In *Escape from the Planet of the Apes*, Dr. Lewis Dixon performs some tests on Zira and Cornelius at the zoo. In one test, Zira builds a staircase out of blocks that will allow her to reach a banana hanging from the ceiling, but then she doesn't grab the banana. Dr. Stephanie Branton wonders out loud, "Why doesn't she take it?" to which Zira unexpectedly replies,

"Because I loathe bananas." When Cornelius and Dr. Milo criticize her for revealing her ability to speak, she says, "I hate deceit."

Nevertheless, like the other talking apes, Caesar and Zira certainly have the ability to deceive. In fact, they even advise others to do it, as when Zira tells Brent how to appear to be a normal, non-talking, human. Also, in *Conquest of the Planet of the Apes*, it's clear that Caesar must have explained to his troops how to outsmart the armed riot police.

Now, these highly intelligent apes may not be quite as intelligent as humans. Although they are clearly the masters of a fairly civilized world, this is only possible because there was a pre-existing *human* civilization to copy. For instance, as Mérou notes, most of what it takes to sustain such a civilization is

> a question of conditioned reflexes. At the still higher level of administration, it seemed even easier to concede the quality of aping. To continue our system, the gorillas would merely have to imitate certain attitudes and deliver a few harangues, all based on the same model. (p. 101)

It's not clear that the apes could have created such a civilization on their own. After all, the technology of the Planet of the Apes has not advanced very much since the apes took over. Even so, these apes are pretty clearly sneaky enough to be people.

It's not at all surprising that creatures who are smart enough to talk would also be smart enough to deceive. The really interesting question is whether or not *real* apes have the ability to deceive and, thus, whether or not they should count as persons.

Is She Not an Animal?

While the question of whether apes *in our own world* can deceive is intrinsically interesting, you might wonder what relevance it has for the *Planet of the Apes*. It's actually quite relevant. Because the roles of humans and apes have been reversed, asking whether real apes have the ability to deceive is equivalent to asking whether the *humans* on the Planet of the Apes have the ability to deceive and, thus, should count as persons.

Apes are the masters of the Planet of the Apes and humans are the primitive animals. Thus, these apes are legitimately shocked when they run into a human that can speak. In fact, given how primitive the humans are, it's a little weird how attached Taylor gets to Nova. It would arguably be more appropriate for him to treat her as a pet than as a scantily-clad love interest. In Boulle's novel, Mérou is at least embarrassed about his relationship with Nova: "Is she not an animal? . . . I blush at the thought of our former intimacy" (p. 92).

Now, in Burton's film, all of the humans—not just Marky Mark—on the Planet of the Apes can speak. But this is inconsistent with the novel and the other movies. Admittedly, Nova finally does manage to utter the single word "Taylor" in *Beneath the Planet of the Apes* ("With great effort, she stammers out the syllables of my name, which I have taught her to articulate," p. 109.) Also, in the novel, the genius chimpanzee Helius is able to get a few primitive humans to speak by directing electrical impulses at certain spots in their brains. This procedure allows the humans to tap into "atavistic memories" of their ancestors who could speak, "reviving a past several thousands of years old" (p. 115). But these are clearly exceptional cases. In general, the primitive humans on the Planet of the Apes do not use language. But are they able to deceive?

Apes that Can Read Your Mind

Determining whether real apes, or the primitive humans on the Planet of the Apes, can deceive is a good way of determining whether they are second-order intentional systems. Or, as most contemporary philosophers would put it, it is a good way of determining whether they are *mindreaders*. And by mindreading, these philosophers do not mean an extra-sensory psychic ability of the sort possessed by the Keepers of the Divine Bomb. They just mean the ability to attribute beliefs and desires to others. It's the sort of mindreading that we all use every day to explain and predict the behavior of other humans. It's the sort of mindreading that Mérou claims that Zira is capable of when he tells us that "My eyes met Zira's and I saw that the clever she-ape had read my thoughts" (p. 86).

You can only intentionally deceive someone if you can conceive of her having false beliefs. So the ability to deceive would suggest that real apes are mindreaders. And it looks as though real apes do have this ability. Like many other species, apes give alarm calls in order to warn other apes about predators in the vicinity. However, apes sometimes give *fake* alarm calls in order to frighten other apes away from food. In other words, they essentially cry "Wolf!" when there is no wolf so that they can grab up the abandoned food for themselves.

In fact, there is some anecdotal evidence that real apes can actually *lie*. For instance, Koko the gorilla, who was trained to use American Sign Language, had a pet kitten. When her keepers asked her about a large steel sink that Koko had ripped from the wall, she signed, "Cat did it."

At least a few of the primitive humans on the Planet of the Apes also exhibit such deceptive abilities. In the novel, the gorillas hunt humans by driving them toward a clearing and then shooting them down with rifles. As in the films, most of these primitive humans rush into the open space and are easily slaughtered. But as Mérou reports:

> others gave evidence of more cunning, like old boars who have been hunted several times and have learned a number of tricks. These crept forward on all fours, paused for a moment on the edge of the clearing, studied the nearest hunter through the leaves, and waited for the moment when his attention was drawn in another direction. Then, in one bound and at full speed, they crossed the deadly alley. Several of them thus succeeded in reaching the opposite side unhurt, and disappeared into the forest. (pp. 32–33)

Allow Me to Expose this Hoax

But not everybody is going to be convinced by this sort of evidence. For instance, in his *Discourse on Method*, René Descartes (1596–1650) claimed that nonhuman animals are not conscious at all. They do not have beliefs or desires, much less the ability to attribute beliefs and desires to others. They are simply unthinking and unfeeling "beast machines" who have essentially been programmed by God (or for the modern Cartesian, by evolution) to behave in these apparently deceptive ways.

However, if we're going to worry that nonhuman animals are essentially robots, we might as well worry that other humans are robots. In fact, we might also worry that every-thing is an illusion created by the Keepers of the Divine Bomb. That's exactly the sort of thing that Descartes was famously concerned about in his *Meditations on First Philosophy*. But most philosophers are not quite that skeptical. Most philosophers think that apes *are* conscious and that they are "intentional systems" as defined by Dennett.

Even so, many philosophers are not sure that apes are *second-order* intentional systems. Although apes sometimes give fake alarm calls in order to steal food, it does not necessarily mean that these "sneaky" apes have any intentions with respect to the beliefs of other apes. They may just have learned to associate a. making a certain noise and b. other apes running away and leaving food behind. In other words, these apes may be engaging in what scientists call *functional* deception rather than *intentional* deception.

There's another reason why it can be difficult to be sure how smart non-human primates are on the basis of laboratory studies. In addition to primatologists being accused of *unconsciously biasing* the results of experiments, Marc Hauser, formerly of Harvard University, has been accused of scientific misconduct, much like Cornelius and Zira in the original film. However, in his case, the issue is not simply that his results contradict the Sacred Scrolls. It is alleged that he *intentionally fabricated* some of his results about rhesus monkeys and cotton-top tamarins. So, even if we can't be sure that apes are sneaky enough to be people, we do have a pretty good idea that some of these scientists are.

If we refuse to conclude that apes are mindreaders despite their apparently deceptive behavior, we're following a fairly plausible scientific rule that Mérou discusses. When he's unable to convince Dr. Zaius and the other orangutans of his intelligence, he tells us that

> they were only prepared to attribute my talents to a sort of instinct and a keen sense of mimicry. They had probably adopted the scientific rule that one of our learned men at home summarized as follows: "In no case may we interpret an action as the outcome of the exercise of a higher psychical faculty if it can be interpreted as the outcome of one that stands lower in the psychological scale." (p. 54)

Although the orangutans were mistaken about Mérou, we would certainly want to follow this rule (a.k.a. Lloyd Morgan's canon) when explaining the apparently deceptive behavior of many other species. For instance, some species of birds will fake having a broken wing in order to draw predators away from their nests. In fact, just like apes, a few species of birds will give fake alarm calls in order to steal food from other birds. But birds are clearly not sneaky enough to be people. They just associate (via learning or instinct) performing a particular action (in a particular circumstance) with achieving a particular effect.

Dogs are admittedly closer to being people than birds. But it is pretty clear that they also lack the cognitive capabilities required to engage in intentional deception. Dennett does tell the story of a dog that "tricks" its master into getting out of the comfy chair by going to the door as if it needs to go out. But as Dennett points out, such behavior does not make the dog a mindreader. He has just learned that his master does *that* (gets up) whenever he does *this* (goes to the door). In his *Philosophical Investigations*, Ludwig Wittgenstein simply takes it for granted that dogs are not capable of intentional deception:

> Why can't a dog simulate pain? Is he too honest? Could one teach a dog to simulate pain? Perhaps it is possible to teach him to howl on particular occasions as if he were in pain, even when he is not. But the surroundings which are necessary for this behaviour to be real simulation are missing. (p. 90)

Functional deception of the sort that birds and dogs engage in is not limited to non-linguistic creatures. Just as real apes systematically benefit from other apes being misled by fake alarm calls, the orangutans on the Planet of the Apes systematically benefit from "propagating grotesque errors among simian youth" (p. 75). Since they have traditionally held a very privileged position in ape society, these orangutans benefit from maintaining the status quo. Although the orangutans on the Planet of the Apes are capable of intentional deception, they may not be guilty of it here. Like many ideologues on our own planet, they may believe everything that they say.

We'll Begin with the Wisconsin Multiphasic

Although they initially looked like pretty good evidence, the fake alarm calls do not prove that real apes can read minds. But apes might, nevertheless, be mindreaders. To find out, we'll need to perform some further tests.

In addition to the Wisconsin Multiphasic test conducted on Cornelius and Zira by Dr. Dixon in *Escape from the Planet of the Apes*, primatologists have devised many other ways to test the cognitive capacities of primates. Most notably, Brian Hare, Josep Call, and Michael Tomasello have performed some experiments that suggest that apes are indeed mindreaders.

In an experiment described in the journal *Animal Behaviour*, a dominant chimpanzee and a subordinate chimpanzee were placed in cages on opposite sides of a room that contained two pieces of food. But one of the two pieces of food was placed next to an opaque barrier so that, while the subordinate chimp could see it, the dominant chimp could not. The chimpanzees were then released from their cages, with the subordinate chimp given a slight head start. Now, dominant chimpanzees tend to punish subordinate chimpanzees who challenge them for food. So, unsurprisingly, the subordinate chimp preferred to go after the piece of food that was hidden from the dominant chimp. But we should only expect this sort of behavior if the subordinate chimp knew that the dominant chimp did not know that there was food behind the barrier. Thus, this behavior suggests that chimpanzees can attribute beliefs to other chimpanzees.

As with the fake alarm calls, the results of this experiment could possibly be explained without assuming that the subordinate chimp is a mindreader. The chimpanzee might have learned that it's safe to go after food whenever there is something solid between the food and any dominant chimpanzees in the area. However, this is just one of several experiments that have yielded essentially the same results. For instance, if apes have a choice between openly reaching for a piece of food and reaching for it though an opaque tunnel that hides their action, they consistently choose the covert option. In addition, many of these experiments presented the apes with situations, such as transparent barriers and experimenters with buckets on their heads, that neither they nor their ancestors would have experienced in the wild.

According to Occam's Razor, we should prefer the *simplest* possible explanation of these results. The hypothesis that these apes have an ability to read minds which they deploy in all sorts of novel circumstances provides a simple, unified explanation of the results of all of these experiments. In order to explain their behavior without this hypothesis, we have to assume that these apes have learned a whole bunch of varied associations that it is unlikely that they had any opportunity to learn. Thus, if someone wants to deny that apes are mindreaders, she quickly starts to look like a conspiracy theorist who keeps having to make her theory more and more convoluted in order to account for the available data. (I said more about the irrationality of believing in conspiracy theories in my chapter in *Philip K. Dick and Philosophy*.) In other words, this is a case where Occam's Razor trumps Lloyd Morgan's canon.

They are Sneaky, but Are They Sneaky Enough?

While it looks as if real apes are mindreaders, it also looks as if their mindreading capabilities are somewhat limited compared with the mindreading capabilities of humans. In particular, the scientific evidence suggests that apes are not able to attribute *false* beliefs to others. And if they cannot attribute false beliefs to others, then they cannot intend others to acquire false beliefs.

Hare, Call, and Tomasello devised a variation on their food competition experiment. In this variation, there were two opaque barriers rather than one, and there was one piece of food rather than two. At the beginning of the experiment, the experimenter placed the food behind one of the two barriers so that it was only visible to the subordinate chimp. Then the chimps were released (with the subordinate given a slight head start).

The primatologists ran three versions of this experiment. In the first (*informed*) version, although the dominant chimp could not see the food once it was behind the barrier, he was allowed to see where the food was placed (and the subordinate chimp saw that he saw this). In the second (*uninformed*) version, the dominant chimp was not allowed to see where the food was placed (and the subordinate chimp saw that he did not see this). In the third (*misinformed*) version, the dominant chimp was allowed to see where the food was placed, but then his view was blocked and the food was moved behind the other barrier (and the subordinate chimp saw what he did and did not see).

When the chimps were released, the subordinate was more likely to go for the food if the dominant chimp did not know where the food was located. However, if the subordinate had been able to attribute *false beliefs* to the dominant chimp, he should have been even more likely to go for the food when the dominant chimp incorrectly thought that food was in one place when it was really in another place. (If the subordinate were able to understand that the dominant chimp was *misinformed* and not just uninformed, he would have been sure that the dominant chimp would head off in the wrong direction.) But the experimenters found that the subordinate chimp performed the same in both the uninformed and misinformed versions of the experiment. Unlike even very young human children, apes consistently fail to pass such *false belief tests*.

There's clearly a difference between deceiving someone and merely withholding information from someone. As Dr. Milo explains to Zira (after she unwisely reveals her ability to speak to Dr. Dixon), "There is a time for truth, and a time, not for lies, but for silence." And it looks like real apes can only intentionally withhold information in order to keep others in the dark about something. Unlike General Thade, they cannot intend others to acquire false beliefs. And so, real apes may not be sneaky enough to be people.[1]

[1] I would like to thank Kristin Andrews, Tony Doyle, John Huss, James Mahon, Kay Mathiesen, Bill Taylor, and Dan Zelinski for helpful suggestions on this chapter.

II

Ape Science

4
Science's Crazy Dogma

BERNARD E. ROLLIN WITH JOHN HUSS

In 1968, the year that *Planet of the Apes* was released, I was insufferable. Halfway through my doctorate in philosophy at Columbia University, with a couple of trivial publications gracing my resume, and a Fulbright Fellowship at the University of Edinburgh behind me, I was so cool and aloof that I appreciated virtually nothing. If movies were not grainy and incomprehensible, I sneered at them. As for *Planet of the Apes*, I regretted spending a dollar to see it, advised anyone who would listen not to see it, and dismissed it as incoherent, pretentious, hokey, pseudo-intellectual Hollywood drivel.

Yet today, after working on the ethics of scientific research—especially animal research—for more than thirty-five years, and then viewing the movie again, I find it to be an astute, telling, and devastating depiction and critique of what I have called "scientific ideology" or the "common sense" of science. Few movies better illustrate the ubiquitous psychological effects of absurd ideology than *Planet of the Apes*.

Nazi Ideology

It's easy to underestimate the power of ideology to be a source of great evil. Consider the Holocaust: The German government estimates that it took at least fifty thousand full-time workers to carry out the Holocaust smoothly. Is it possible to believe, asks historian Daniel Goldhagen, that there were in fact fifty thousand psychopaths roaming around in Germany waiting to be tapped for such killing?

Not likely, says Goldhagen. So how can we explain such plainly immoral acts as panels of physicians judging that thousands of physically and mentally "defective" children had lives "not worth living" and thereby authorizing their death by lethal injection? Similarly, Goldhagen writes about auxiliary policemen from Germany who were brought to the Eastern front to kill women, children, and "undesirables"—Jews, Gypsies, and many others. Not only were those unwilling to do so not punished, they were rewarded and sent home. Nonetheless, most of them served voluntarily and eagerly.

Goldhagen and others have explained this unexpected behavior by appeal to ideological conditioning. For example, Robert Jay Lifton has demonstrated that German doctors were trained not only in the treatment of individual human beings, but also in removing "pathogens" from the body politic—mentally and physically "defective" people who consumed resources but contributed nothing to society. Similarly, Goldhagen recounts long-standing German ideology that characterizes "outsiders" like the Jews as parasites. Ideologies create predictable, unreflective, automatic, and thoughtless responses to difficult questions. They allow us to act without thinking, and eclipse common sense, common decency, and even basic logic (witness Catholic ideology declaring that something can be both three and one at the same time). It is characteristic of ideology that once we've been trained to embrace it, it seems obvious and unquestionable to us.

Dr. Zaius, Minister of Science and Chief Defender of the Faith

In the 1968 movie, the reigning ideology is the superiority of apes to any and all other life forms. There are scenes where Taylor tries to communicate with his captors, at first through gestures, and eventually using words. He protests, "I can speak. . . . I can talk, can't you see?" Still, the apes reject these self-verifying utterances with formulaic responses: "He keeps pretending he can talk." "He has a gift for mimicry." "Human see, human do."

These responses violate both facts and logic. In frustration, Taylor declares "You are a scientist—don't you believe your own eyes?" Indeed, the very fact the apes are able to converse with Taylor shows conclusively that he is communicating. Were he simply engaging in "mimicry" or "pretending" there could be no flow and give and take of argument—Taylor's responses would not be appropriate, nor could the apes answer him in kind. In short, despite the fact that their dialogue with Taylor belies the content of their own argument, the apes hold fast to their claims, a classic ideological strategy.

Indeed, this is precisely the strategy employed by scientific ideology to dismiss both empirical and conceptual evidence of animal thought and animal communication. Some propositions are so deeply embedded in the background beliefs of scientists that they become almost irrefutable. They are held, dogmatically, in the face of all evidence and argument to the contrary. When science hardens into ideology in this way the result is a near-religion known as "scientism." When you're in the grip of a scientistic worldview, "facts" that are evident to both sense experience and common sense are ruled out as irrelevant.

Perhaps surprisingly, in the character of Zaius, science and religion are conflated. Zaius is both Minister of Science *and* Chief Defender of the Faith, and his reaction to Taylor's behavior is consonant with that dual role. As Taylor rightly remarks, "Are they afraid of me? I can't hurt them . . . but I threaten them somehow. Threaten their faith in simian superiority. They have to kill me." Faith and science converge in contemporary science's unwillingness to consider the morality of harming and killing animals for the sake of advancing scientific knowledge. The failure of science to acknowledge the obvious fact that non-human animals can be hurt and harmed and the correlative failure to apply ethical categories to patently hurtful animal use is very much a matter of scientific *faith*, not reason, and thus looks very much like religiously based *dogma*, rather than rational ethics.

Scientific Ideology

Ideologies operate in many different areas—religious, political, sociological, economic, ethnic. So it's not surprising that a scientific ideology has emerged. After all, science has been the dominant way of knowing about the world in Western societies since the Renaissance. In order to fully explain how *Planet of the Apes* is relevant to contemporary ideologically-based moral abuses, I have to summarize what I have studied and taught for nearly forty years. I call it *scientific ideology* or *the common sense of science*. It is to scientific life what common sense is to daily life.

Ask a typical working scientist what separates science from religion, speculative metaphysics, or shamanistic worldviews. Most would immediately say that science tests all claims through observation and experiment. This aspect of scientific ideology dates to Sir Isaac Newton, who proclaimed that he did not "feign hypotheses" (*"hypotheses non fingo"*) but operated directly from experience. The fact that Newton in fact *did* use such non-observable (and therefore *hypothetical*) notions as gravity, action at a distance, and absolute space and time did not stop him from explicitly ruling out hypotheses. Members of the Royal Society, arguably the first association of scientists, apparently took him literally, gathered data for their 'common-place books', and fully expected major scientific breakthroughs to emerge. For the most part, those breakthroughs never came.

Defending Science against Nonsense

The insistence on experience as the bedrock for science continues from Newton to the twentieth century, where it led to *logical positivism,* a movement that was designed to eliminate from science anything that could not be verified by the senses. At its most extreme, it aimed to reduce all of science to a set of general truths logically derivable from observations. Anything not based on sensory experience or logic was to be cast aside as meaningless. A classic example can be found in Einstein's rejection of Newton's concepts of absolute space and time, on the grounds that such talk was untestable.

But the logical positivist program was only partly eliminative, of course. Logical positivism's "positive" program was to encourage the formulation of views in such a way that their predictions could be tested by experience. In a sense, this requirement may very well have bequeathed us the *Planet of the Apes* franchise. On January 14th, 1972, when astronauts Taylor, Landon, Dodge, and Stewart took flight aboard the Icarus, their mission was to test the Hasslein Curve theory of Dr. Otto Hasslein, which predicted that over the course of eighteen months (ship time) that the crew would spend in flight, most of it in suspended animation, they would be propelled over two thousand years forward in Earth time, a prediction that was confirmed as the ship's clock reads November 25th, 3978 at the time it crashes.

Although logical positivism took many forms, the message to scientists and their students (like me), was that proper science shouldn't allow unverifiable statements. This left scientists free to dismiss religious claims, metaphysical claims, or other speculative assertions not merely as false, and irrelevant to science, but also as meaningless. Only what could be verified (or falsified) empirically was meaningful. A looser requirement was that a claim should be verifiable in principle. "In principle" meant "someday," given technological progress.

So although the statement "In the distant future, Earth will be ruled by an advanced simian society" could not in fact be verified or falsified in 1972, it was still meaningful, since we could see how it could be verified, for example by building rocket ships and sending astronauts deep into outer space and back at near light speed. Such a statement is totally unlike the statement "There are intelligent beings in Heaven," because, however our technology is perfected, we don't even know what it would be like to visit Heaven, since it is not a physical place. Thus, according to the logical positivist, it's a meaningless statement.

Is Science Value-Free?

What does all this have to do with ethics? Quite a bit, it turns out. The philosopher Ludwig Wittgenstein, who greatly influenced the logical positivists, remarked in a public lecture around 1930, that if you take an inventory of all the *facts* in the universe, you will not find it a *fact* that killing is wrong. In other words, ethics is not part of the furniture of the scientific universe. You can't, in principle, test the proposition that "Killing is wrong." It can neither be verified nor falsified. So, according to Wittgenstein, ethical judgments are empirically and scientifically meaningless. It's a short leap of logic to the conclusion that ethics lies outside the scope of science, along with all judgments regarding values. The slogan that I learned in my science courses in the 1960s, and which is still being taught in too many places, is that "Science is value-free."

The denial of the relevance of ethics to science was taught both explicitly and implicitly. One could find it stated in science textbooks. For example, in the late 1980s when I was researching a book on animal pain, I looked at basic biology texts, two of which a colleague and I had used, ironically enough, in an honors biology course we team-taught for twenty-five years attempting to combine biology and its philosophical and ethical aspects. The widely used Keeton and Gould textbook, in what one of my colleagues calls the "throat-clearing introduction," loudly declares that "Science cannot make value judgments . . . cannot make moral judgments." In the same vein, Mader, in her popular biology text, asserted that "Science does not make ethical or moral decisions." The standard line affirms that science at most provides society with *facts* relevant to making moral decisions, but never makes such decisions itself.

So according to the logical positivists, moral discussion is empirically meaningless. But that is not the whole story. Positivists felt compelled to explain why intelligent people continued to make moral judgments and continued to argue about them. Their explanation goes like this. When people say things like "killing is wrong," which seem to be statements about reality, they are in fact describing nothing. Rather, they are "emoting," expressing their own revulsion at killing. "Killing is wrong" really *expresses* "Killing, yuk!" And when we seem to debate killing, we are not really arguing about ethics (which we can't do any more than you and I can debate whether we like or don't like the Tim Burton remake), but rather disputing each other's facts. For example, a so-called debate over the morality of capital punishment is my expressing revulsion at capital punishment while you express approval. What we can debate are factual questions such as whether or not capital punishment serves as a deterrent against murder.

It's therefore not surprising that when scientists were drawn into social discussions of ethical issues they were every bit as emotional as their untutored opponents. According to positivist ideology these issues *are nothing but emotional*; therefore, the notion of rational ethics is an oxymoron, and he who generates the most effective emotional response "wins."

So in the 1970s and 1980s debate over the morality of animal research, most scientists either totally ignored the issue, or countered criticisms with emotional appeals to the health of children. For example, in one film entitled "Will I Be All Right, Doctor?" (the question asked by a frightened child), made by defenders of unrestricted research, the response was "Yes, if *they* leave us alone to do what we want with animals." So unabashedly mawkish was the film, that when it was aired at a national meeting of laboratory animal veterinarians, whom you'd expect to be about the most sympathetic audience you could find, one veterinarian exclaimed that he was "ashamed to be associated with a film that is pitched lower than the worst anti-vivisectionist clap-trap!"

Other ads placed by the research community affirmed that ninety percent of the animals used in research were mice and rats, animals "people kill in their kitchens anyway." Sometimes questions raised about animal use, as once occurred in a science editorial, elicited the reply that "Animal use is not an ethical question—it is a scientific necessity," as if it cannot be, and is not, both.

Stop Thinking You Can Think!

Denying the relevance of values in general and ethics in particular to science has blinded scientists to issues of major concern to society. But that's not all. There is another major component of scientific ideology that harmonizes perfectly with the value-free dictum. That was the claim that science can't legitimately talk about consciousness or subjective experiences—since they are unobservable—which led to a question about their existence—even pain! (John Watson, the founder of Behaviorism came close to saying that we don't have thoughts, we only think we do!)

As you can imagine, agnosticism about animal pain quickly devolved into atheism. During the 1970s and 1980s, two veterinarians, an attorney, and I conceptualized, drafted, and ultimately persuaded Congress to pass two pieces of 1985 federal legislation assuring some minimal concern on the part of researchers for the welfare of laboratory animals. In the course of my discussions with Congress, I was asked why a law regulating animal research was needed. I replied that the scientific community did not use analgesics (painkillers) for animals used in the most painful experiments. Congress replied that the research community claimed it did use painkillers very liberally, and it was my job to prove they did not.

After much thought, I approached a friend who was a librarian at the Library of Congress, and asked him to do a literature search on analgesics for laboratory animals. That search revealed no articles. I then asked him to expand the search to analgesics for animals. The search found two papers, one of which affirmed that there should be papers! Fortunately, this strategy plainly indicated the need for legislation.

The Psychologist's Dilemma

Here's a personal anecdote strangely reminiscent of the sort of "logic" employed by Dr. Zaius when he denies to Taylor's face that Taylor is capable of thought. In 1982, I was invited to give the prestigious C.W. Hume lecture on animal welfare at the University of London. I was also asked by the organizers to comment on a paper dealing with pain in dogs. The speaker was a prominent British pain physiologist who dwelt at length on how different the electrochemical activity in the cerebral cortex of dogs during the administration of painful stimuli was from that of people. He concluded that dogs did not feel pain in any sense humans could relate to. My response was uncharacteristically brief. I pointed out that he was a prominent pain researcher who did pain research on dogs and extrapolated the results to people. He agreed. I then pointed out that either his speech or his life's work was false, since, of course, if dogs don't feel pain, they can't model human pain!

In further illustration of this twisted logic, consider what's known as the "psychologist's dilemma." If animals do not, as scientific ideology suggests, experience fear, loneliness, boredom, anxiety, or similar emotions, what's the point of studying these states in "animal models?" And if they do experience them in a way that is analogous to the way we do, how can it possibly be moral to create those states in them? This is an excellent example, as it shows plainly the way in which denying the existence of the animal mind works hand-in-hand with denying the relevance of ethics to science.

Recall Taylor's plaintive lament to Zaius—"Don't you believe your own eyes?" The ability of ideology to blind us even to patent sense experience has a long history. For example, when Galileo was accused of heresy, in part because he denied the Moon was perfect, and he implored the bishops to see for themselves by looking through his telescope, they refused to look. The reason is that they already "knew" the Moon was perfect. And if someone had made them look, we can imagine the answer—"Galileo has built an instrument that distorts the perfect moon and makes it look flawed."

You're a Scientist—Don't You Believe Your Own Eyes?

Neither logic nor sense experience can overcome ideological bias, as *Planet of the Apes* clearly illustrates. Early on in my work on ethics and animal research, I could not fathom how veterinarians could be blind to obvious animal pain. On one occasion, I was walking through the surgery wards of our veterinary hospital with the hospital director. I could hear the animals whining and crying. "Why don't you give them any analgesics?" I challenged him. "Oh," he said. "That is not pain, it is after-effects of anesthesia!" Such is the power of ideology.

On another occasion, I telephoned a veterinarian who had written one of the very rare (at the time) papers dealing with pain control and animals. I asked him if he ever encounters colleagues who deny that animals feel pain. "Sure," he said. "How do you deal with that?" I asked. "Well," he responded, "I ask them to take a hundred pound Rottweiler and put him on their examination table. Then I tell them to take a vice grip, fit it around the dog's nuts, then squeeze. He'll tell you he feels pain by ripping your God damn face off!" His answer was based in common sense and experience, yet would of course never convince the ideologue. This is the exact point made in the movie.

Blinded by Science

One of the most extraordinary consequences of scientific ideology was the denial of pain not only in animals, but in newborn humans. For a long time, indeed, until the 1990s, open-heart surgery was performed on newborn human babies without anesthesia. Curariform drugs were instead utilized to hold the babies still. Such drugs have no analgesic or anesthetic properties; they are drugs that *paralyze* by depolarizing the neuromuscular junction. If anything, they increase pain by virtue of paralyzing the diaphragm muscles, causing black terror.

In defense of this practice, as well as the practice of withholding pain control from animals, the International Association for the Study of Pain (IASP) affirmed that to feel pain requires the possession of language. This idea comes down to us from René Descartes (1596–1650), who claimed that non-human animals, not having language, are not conscious. They are machines that have no souls and therefore no feelings. This teaching exonerates Descartes's followers when they perform literal *vivisection*—cutting up live animals for scientific purposes, and it also provides blanket permission to ignore pain control in nonlinguistic beings, including human babies. Likewise in Ape City, whose Dr. Zira we take to be the very model of the progressive, humane scientist, experimental neurosurgery is performed on humans, precisely because they—with the notable exception of Taylor—are mute!

Unfortunately, no one at IASP ever explained the connection between possession of language and the ability to feel pain. Did these people genuinely believe that at some unspecified point in development, when babies acquire linguistic ability, along with this, like the prize in a box of Cracker Jacks, they also magically begin to feel pain? Did they genuinely believe that animals, despite patent pain behavior of innumerable kinds, are not capable of experiencing pain? If so, what happens to Charles Darwin's view that there is continuity between humans and other animals because of our common ancestry? If our common ancestry has given us physiological and anatomical traits continuous with those of other animals, why aren't our psychological traits—such as the ability to feel pain—equally continuous, as Darwin himself believed?

If It's True, They'll Have to Accept It

At Taylor's trial, he makes one claim after another that, according to the members of the ape tribunal, could not possibly be true. So outraged are they at the heresies he utters that they cover their eyes, ears, and mouths: see no evil, hear no evil, speak no evil.

Visibly irritated, they refused to listen to a word Taylor says. When I recently viewed this scene once more, I was reminded of the time when liberal members of IASP invited me to speak at their annual meeting. There I gave a detailed talk attacking their view of pain in relation to language. In my thirty-plus years of giving invited lectures all over the world to groups ranging from cowboys to animal researchers, I never experienced as much hostility and hatred as I did from the IASP audience. People were white with rage, and stalked out of my talk without anyone asking a question of me or responding to my arguments.

Afterwards, a physician who had been involved in writing the pain policy approached me to explain. He pointed out that one of the most common illnesses that incapacitate workers is lower back pain. However, lower back pain is often present in the absence of a visible injury. Wanting to address this problem on compassionate grounds, IASP decided that reporting lower back pain was enough to justify its presence. I was astounded! I pointed out that apparently what they were trying to say was that a verbal report of lower back pain was a *sufficient condition* for assuming its presence. But what they ended up affirming was that verbal reports, and therefore linguistic capacity, were *necessary conditions* for attribution of pain, a fundamental error in freshman logic!

Stop Telling Me You Can Talk!

Such egregious errors in reasoning are tellingly satirized in *Planet of the Apes,* when Zaius affirms that Taylor's use of language does not prove that a human has linguistic ability! What leaps to mind is the ancient account of the pre-Socratic philosopher Heraclitus's dictum that "You can't step into the same river twice." His student, Cratylus, eager to go his master one better, resoundingly declared that "You can't step into the same river *once,*" which is of course utter nonsense! Proudly resting your position on the presence of pain on a confusion between necessary and sufficient conditions is as absurd as saying that a being who uses language is incapable of speech.

For most of human history, human superiority to the rest of the animal kingdom was assured by the alleged presence of an immortal soul in humans but not in animals. In the hands of Descartes, and through the present day, the uniqueness of humans has been vested in the presence of language, now that belief in the soul is scientifically unacceptable. To this day, for much of the scientific community, attribution of thought or feeling to animals commits the career-killing fallacy of 'anthropomorphism', though of late, the psychiatric community has begun inexplicably to seek animal models of psychiatric illness such as schizophrenia and depression, both of which are majorly defined in terms of subjective experiences.

The ability of too many scientists to deny that animals have thoughts and feelings, while quietly assuming in their research that animals do have thoughts and feelings, helps us understand how Zaius can be Minister of Science and Chief Defender of the Faith, for there is much in scientific ideology that is reminiscent of religious ideology. Consider the claim that only experientially verified judgments are scientifically admissible. Yet such judgments are built upon the observations of individual scientists, which are instances of their subjective experiences. If science is to describe an objective world independent of our subjective experiences, science cannot be based in reports of experiences by scientists, these experiences being inherently *subjective*. In other words, if extreme positivism is true, a science of the objective world is impossible. And this in turn begins to sound a good deal like religious ideology.

David Hume once remarked that, while the mistakes of religion are dangerous, the mistakes of philosophy are merely ridiculous. The mistakes of ideology—both scientific and religious—are both ridiculous and dangerous. The two mutually reinforcing components of scientific ideology, namely the notion that science is value-free and ethics-free, and that science must be agnostic about consciousness, taken together have caused incalculable damage to science, society, and human and non-human animals. Yet the powerful hold of scientific ideology upon its adherents remains largely invisible to scientific practitioners, and also to the general public except in cases where science fails to grapple with the ethical issues raised by its activities. In this regard, *Planet of the Apes* can serve as a valuable lens focusing light on the hitherto ignored.[1]

---

[1] Thanks to Sharon Cebula, Pete Weiss, George Reisch, and Joanna Trzeciak for helpful feedback.

5
Getting a Rise out of Genetic Engineering

MASSIMO PIGLIUCCI

"No!" The sudden and peremptory issuing of that simple command is one of the most startling moments in *Rise of the Planet of the Apes*. Caesar, the genetically enhanced chimpanzee who resulted from the ethically questionable experiments stands up against one of his human tormentors and shouts "No!"

Should we do the same about the whole forthcoming enterprise of biological enhancement of the human race? Or should we instead embrace it to boldly go where no human or chimp has gone before?

One reason to lean toward banning enhancement may be that it is unnatural, even ungodly. The whole idea seems to violate what God or natural selection ordained for us, to be an exercise in the kind of hubris that the ancient Greeks constantly used as the underlying theme for their tragedies, of which *Rise* can be seen as a modern incarnation.

In the movie, Will Rodman, the charming scientist who works at the Gen-Sys company to develop the drug ALZ-112, is trying to cure Alzheimer's, one of the most devastating of human diseases, which he knows first-hand because his father is afflicted with it. But, just as in any good Greek tragedy, the road to hell is paved with good intentions, and Rodman's doings lead first to a revolt of a band of apes, then to death and destruction, and finally—in an obvious setup for the sequel—to the destruction of the entire human race by means of an out of control virus, originally designed by Rodman himself as a better delivery vehicle for the cure. Sophocles and Euripides would have been pleased!

But It's Unnatural, Especially for Chimps!

The "God/natural selection didn't want this" objection, however, cuts very little philosophical ice these days. The reason's the same regardless of whether you're a religious believer or not. The history of human science, technology, and medicine is a history of defying whatever constraints have been imposed on us by gods or nature, so unless you're also willing to stop cooking your food, flying on airplanes, or taking advantage of vaccines, you do not have much of a philosophical leg to stand on.

That last example (vaccines) is particularly interesting from the point of view of discussions of biological enhancement. One of the more thoughtful objections raised to the idea of enhancement is that it is somehow more problematic—ethically or otherwise—than the standard business of medicine: curing diseases. But the difference between cure and enhancement may not be quite so straightforward. As Eric Juengst has pointed out in a 1997 issue of the *Journal of Medicine and Philosophy*, getting vaccinated doesn't cure anything, it increases your chances of avoiding a future disease by enhancing the natural capacities of your immune system. Granted, this kind of enhancement—unlike Caesar's stunning intellectual abilities—is not passed to your offspring, who will have to acquire it anew by means of vaccination. But this is a distinction without much of an accompanying ethical difference.

Here is perhaps an even better way to appreciate the problem, this one proposed by Norman Daniels in his 1985 book *Just Health Care*. He compares the imaginary cases of two boys who are both destined to reach a very short physical stature as adults. In one case, let's say Peter's, this is because of a deficiency of human growth hormone, resulting from an otherwise benign brain tumor. In the second case, say Johnny's, the problem is instead caused by the fact that the boy simply has short parents, and has therefore inherited a genetic set that does not allow for much growth.

One way to look at the difference between Peter and Johnny is that solving Peter's problem requires curing a disease, in this case the tumor that is blocking the release of growth hormone. Johnny, however, will actually require a genetic engineering intervention that amounts to an enhancement, since there is no disease to cure. But there seems to be an inconsistency here:

in both cases what we are trying to achieve is a normal height for the boy in question. What difference does it make what is causing the abnormal growth? Whatever it is, we want to get rid of it to help both boys have a normal life. Whether we call it a cure or an enhancement seems to be verbal hair splitting, not a real issue.

Then again, just because one can imagine scenarios where there's no difference, or only a difference of degree, between cures and enhancements, that doesn't mean the point is moot. Consider this famous paradox, attributed to Eubulides (a contemporary, and harsh critic, of Aristotle): a man with a full head of hair is obviously not bald; losing a single hair will not turn him into a bald man; yet, if the process is reiterated a sufficiently high number of times (as unfortunately is the case for a lot of us), he will be bald.

We all acknowledge the difference between bald and non-bald men (don't we?), and yet we can't tell where exactly baldness begins or ends. The same could be true for the difference between cure and enhancement: the fact that such a difference is anything but obvious in the case of Peter and Johnny doesn't mean that the difference itself doesn't exist in principle, or that it does not matter in practice. For instance, should we one day be able to implant gills in a human being so that she can breathe underwater, there would be no disputing that the gills are a most definite example of enhancement, not any kind of cure.

As it turns out, our hero, Will, appears to be aware of the difference between cure and enhancement. In explaining his actions to his girlfriend, Caroline, he says "I designed [the procedure] for repair, but Caesar has gone way beyond that." And later on to Gen-Sys CEO Steven Jacobs, in order to convince him to back his research again after an initial failure: "My father didn't just recover, he improved." Indeed, while Will's father had been (temporarily, as it turns out) cured of the disease and then had gone beyond simple recovery, Caesar was, of course, not sick at all to begin with: genetic engineering, in his case, had made it possible for a chimpanzee to think, and eventually talk, in a way that no member of its species had ever been able to do before. Clearly a case of enhancement, if you believe that having the ability to think and talk is a good thing.

What's the Big Deal?

But, you could ask, what exactly is the problem with enhancing the human race? Having set aside concerns about violating divine or natural laws (because we do that all the time anyway), what reasonable objection can be raised?

Well, an obvious concern arises from several bits of dialogue in the movie. At one point, for instance, Jacobs, Gen-Sys's CEO, admonishes Will to "Keep your personal emotions out of it, these people invest in results, not dreams." A bit later on, Robert Franklin, a compassionate technician who works with Rodman, brings up the issue of animal welfare, saying that "There are lives at stake here. These are animals with personality, with attachments." To which Jacobs harshly responds: "Attachments? I run a business, not a petting zoo."

Or remember this bit of patronizing explanation from Jacobs to his chief scientist: "I'll tell you exactly what we are dealing with here. We are dealing with a drug that is worth more than anything else we are developing, combined. You make history, I make money." (I have to admit that it is therefore very satisfying to see, toward the end of the movie, one of the mistreated apes plunging Jacobs and the remains of his helicopter into San Francisco Bay from the top of the Golden Gate Bridge.)

In other words, a major worry about giving free rein to research on human genetic enhancement is that it will likely be dominated by greed and industry secrecy. Well, that's just capitalism, we could reply, and the system has worked well enough for all sorts of products that have enhanced our lives, from cheap and durable cars to phones that appear to be smarter than some of their users.

Still, there are a number of philosophical reasons to worry about letting the free market run amok with altering our species's genome—other than the apocalyptic end-of-the-world scenario hinted at toward the end of *Rise*. For instance, Michael Sandel, in his 2012 book, *What Money Can't Buy: The Moral Limits of Markets*, argues that we as a society ought to impose limits on what can and cannot be commercialized, perhaps including the manipulation of the human genetic heritage. While Sandel's claim may sound radical in this era of hyper market liberalism (at least in the United States), a moment of reflection will show that we already do not allow for the sale of a number of things—votes and babies come to mind—on the sole ground that we think that commercializing those things is simply ethically unacceptable. It then becomes a matter of not whether there should be restrictions, but what they should apply to and how.

François Baylis and Jason S. Robert, in their 2004 article, "The Inevitability of Genetic Enhancement Technologies," published in the journal *Bioethics*, provide an extensive list of additional objections that have been advanced against enhancement (the title of their article notwithstanding). These include: unacceptable risk of harm to human subjects (remember, in *Rise*, Rodman's father and lab tech die, and as of this writing, it's a safe prediction that there are plenty more casualties to come in the sequel, *Dawn of the Planet of the Apes*!); the possibility of a threat to genetic diversity (because everyone will end up wanting the same popular enhancements); the undermining of our genetic heritage (assuming one should really be concerned about such thing—though we're clearly preoccupied with preserving the genomes of other species to conserve biodiversity); counter-productive societal results (let's say we "cure" aging: how do we deal with the resulting population explosion, given that people will presumably still want to have babies?); the fact that enhancement may not be the best use of our resources (after all, we still have widespread famine and poverty throughout the globe); a widening of the already large gap between haves and have-nots (think of another sci-fi masterpiece: *Gattaca*); the resulting promotion of social conformity; the undermining of people's free choices (if most people are genetically engineering their children to be taller, your parents will be in a bind if they refuse to go along, since that puts you at a disadvantage); the moral worth of the means by which we achieve our goals (if all athletes are genetically engineered for top results, why give them medals, and why bother watching their performances?). As you can see, it is a long list, and although some of the items may pose less serious problems than others, it clearly shows that there are, indeed, problems to be reckoned with.

Three Primates: Kant, Mill, and Aristotle

Ethics is a way of reasoning about certain types of problems. It's a tool, just like math or logic. It starts with certain assumptions, or premises and it works out their logical consequences as they illuminate whatever moral problem we're considering. If we start with different premises we may arrive at different conclusions, and there may be no sensible way by which we can judge some conclusions right and other wrong, unless we can show that there's a problem with either the premises or with the reasoning itself.

This, however, doesn't mean that anything goes. Let's consider first an example by analogy with math. If you say that the sum of the angles of a triangle is 180°, are you right or wrong? It depends. If we are working within the axioms (which is what mathematicians call their assumptions) of Euclidean geometry, then you're correct. But if we are operating within the framework of spherical geometry then no, you would be wrong. Either way, however, if you claim that the answer is not 180° within a Euclidean space, you are most definitely wrong.

Will Rodman decides to test ALZ-112 on his father, after his research program at Gen-Sys has been shut down (having in the meantime inadvertently caused permanent enhancements in Caesar). We can look at this decision from the starting assumptions of three standard ethical theories: consequentialism, deontology, and virtue ethics, working our way from those assumptions through the ethical consequences that follow from them.

Consequentialist ethics begins with the assumption that—as the name clearly hints at—what matters in moral decision-making is the consequences of one's action. Nineteenth-century philosopher John Stuart Mill is one of the most influential consequentialists, and for him a good action has the consequence of increasing overall happiness, while a bad action has the consequence of increasing overall pain. So, for Mill it does not really matter what Will's intentions were (they were good, we assume, as he was both concerned with his father's health and with a potential cure for Alzheimer's for all humankind), what matters is what happened as a result of his action. And what happened was a disaster. Not only did his father actually die of the disease, but Will's attempt to solve the problem that led to the failure of his cure will eventually condemn the human race to extinction. That's as bad as consequences can possibly be, I'd say. There is a caveat, however. If the totality of chimp happiness outweighs the pain caused by humanity's extinction, Will may still be vindicated on consequentialist grounds. That, unfortunately, isn't going to help Will or anyone he cared for, except perhaps Caesar.

Deontological ethics is the idea that there are universal rules of conduct that govern our ethical judgments. Religious commandments are an example of a deontological moral system. The most important secular approach to deontology is the one devised by Immanuel Kant in the eighteenth century, and is based on his idea that there is only one fundamental moral rule, which he called the categorical imperative (it's not only an imperative, but no exceptions are allowed!). In one version, the imperative essentially says that we ought to treat other people never solely as means to an end, but always as ends in themselves. In other words, we must respect their integrity as moral agents distinct from but equal to ourselves.

It's not exactly clear how Kant would evaluate Will's actions towards his father. On the one hand, Will attempted the cure on his father because he was genuinely worried about the latter's health, so Will clearly valued his father as an individual for his own sake. On the other hand, if part of Will's goal was to find a general cure for Alzheimer's, then by using his father as an experimental subject, he was using him as a means toward a further end. Moreover, he did so without obtaining his father's explicit consent—indeed, he never even attempted to inform his father about the treatment before or after it was administered. For a deontologist, the consequences aren't what determine the rightness or wrongness of an action at all, so even if Will had succeeded in liberating humanity from Alzheimer's (instead of starting a chain of events that eventually leads to the extinction of the entire species), he would still have done the wrong thing. You can see why Kant was well known for being a bit too strict of a moralist.

Finally, we get to virtue ethics, an idea that was common in ancient Greece and was elaborated in particular by Aristotle. Virtue ethicists are not really concerned with determining what's right or wrong, but rather with what kind of life one ought to live in order to flourish. This means that Aristotle would consider neither the consequences of an action per se, nor necessarily the intentions of the moral agent, but would look instead at whether the action was the reflection of a "virtuous" character. "Virtue" here does not mean the standard concept found in the Christian tradition, having to do with purity and love of God. Aristotle was concerned with our character, as manifested in traits like courage, equanimity, kindness, and so on.

Was Will virtuous in the Aristotelian sense of the term? Did he display courage, kindness, a sense of justice, compassion, and so on? It seems to me that the answer is an unequivocal yes. He clearly felt compassion for his father (and for Caesar). He had the courage to act on his convictions, which were themselves informed by compassion for both humans and animals. And he was kind to people around him, beginning with his father and with Caesar, and extending to his girlfriend, among others.

All in all, then, we have three different views about Will and what he did. For a consequentialist, his actions were immoral because they led to horrible outcomes. For a deontologist the verdict is a mixed one, considering that he both did and did not use his father as a means to an end. For a virtue ethicist, Will was undeniably on the right track, despite the fact that things, ahem, didn't exactly work out the way he planned them.

Now, one could reasonably ask: okay, but given that the three major theories of ethics give us different results in the case of Will's decision, is there any way to figure out if one of these theories is better than the others? That would be a separate discussion into what is called meta-ethics, that is the philosophy of how to justify and ground ethical systems. However, remember the analogy with math: it's perfectly sensible to say that there is no answer as to which system is better, because their starting points (consequences, intentions, character) are all reasonable and cannot necessarily be meaningfully ranked.

Just to come clean here, I lean toward virtue ethics, and I suspect most viewers of the movie do too—whether they realize it or not. If you saw Will as a positive character, felt the compassion he had for his father, and shared his outrage at the way Caesar was being treated, you cannot reasonably fault him for what happened. He tried his best, and Aristotle was well aware of the fact that sometimes our best is just not enough. Life can turn into a tragedy even for the individual endowed with the best character traits we can imagine.

Is It Inevitable?

We've seen that there clearly are a number of ethical issues to consider when we contemplate human genetic enhancement, and that our conclusions about such issues depend on which set of moral axioms we begin with. But is any of the above relevant anyway? When it comes to new technologies like genetic engineering we often hear the argument to end all arguments: technological change, some say, is simply inevitable, so stop worrying about it and get used to it. François Baylis and Jason S. Robert, mentioned earlier, give a number of reasons to believe in what we might call techno-fate. Yet, holding something to be inevitable may be a way to dodge the need for tough ethical decisions, with potentially dire consequences, so it's probably wise to take a closer look.

Baylis and Robert base their "inevitability thesis" on a number of arguments.

> To begin with, they claim that capitalism rules our society, and bio-capitalism is going to be just one more version of the same phenomenon.

> Second, they quote Leon Kass as observing that the ethos of modern society is such that there is a "general liberal prejudice that it is wrong to stop people from doing something," presumably including genetic engineering of human beings.

> Third, say Baylis and Robert, humans are naturally inquisitive and just can't resist tinkering with things, so it's going to be impossible to stop people from trying.

> Fourth, we have a competitive nature, and we eagerly embrace everything that gives us an edge on others, and that surely would include (at least temporarily, until everyone has access to the same technology) genetic enhancement.

> Lastly, it's a distinctive human characteristic to want to shape our own destiny, in this case literally taking the course of evolution in our own hands.

This seems like a powerful case in favor of inevitability, except for two things. First, we do have examples of technologies that we have developed and then abandoned, which makes the point that technological "progress" is a rather fuzzy concept, and that we can, in fact, reverse our march along a particular technological path.

For instance, we have given up commercial supersonic flight (the Concorde) for a variety of reasons, some of which were economical, other environmental. We used to make industrial use of chlorofluorocarbons (in refrigerators and aerosol cans), but we have eventually curbed and then banned their production because they were devastating the environment, creating the infamous ozone hole. And we have developed the atomic bomb, but have refrained from using it in a conflict after the devastating effects of Hiroshima and Nagasaki, and indeed are trying to ban nuclear weapons altogether. (Well, okay, according to the 1968 movie we will apparently end up using it again, in the process causing our own extinction and giving the planet to the apes. But hopefully that's a timeline that does not actually intersect our own future. . . .)

The second objection to the "inevitability thesis" is that most of the attitudes described by Baylis and Robert are actually very recent developments in human societies, and are restricted to certain parts of the globe, which means that there is no reason to think that they are an unavoidable part of human nature. Capitalism is a recent invention, and it is actually managed and regulated one way or another everywhere in the world. The "liberal prejudice" is actually found only among the libertarian fringe of the American population and almost nowhere else on the planet.

We may be a naturally inquisitive species, but we are also naturally endowed with a sense of right and wrong, and the history of humanity has been characterized by a balance—admittedly sometimes precarious—between the two. Our alleged competitive "nature" is, again, largely a reflection of a specific American ethos, and is balanced by our instinct for cooperation, which is at least as strong. As for shaping our destiny, we would be doing so whether we did or did not decide to engage in human enhancement, or whether—which is much more likely—we decided to do it, but in a cautious and limited way.

The danger inherent in the sort of techno-inevitability espoused by Baylis and Robert is that it undercuts the need for deliberation about ethical consequences, attempting to substitute allegedly unchangeable and even obvious "facts" for careful ethical reasoning. This sort of capitalism-based hubris is captured in *Rise* when CEO Steven Jacobs tells our favorite scientist, Will Rodman: "You know everything about the human brain, except the way it works." Except, of course, that the (lethal) joke is on the ultra-capitalist Jacobs, since he is the one who plunges into the cold waters of San Francisco Bay a few minutes later into the movie.

Whether we are talking about human genetic enhancement (*Rise*) or the deployment of nuclear weapons (the 1968 *Planet of the Apes* movie) these are not issues we can simply deputize to scientists or captains of industry. Rather, they're the sort of thing that requires everyone to come to the discussion table, including scientists, technologists, investors, philosophers, politicians, and the public at large. The price of abdicating ethical decision making is the risk of forging a future like the one that brought Heston's George Taylor to exclaim in desperation: "Oh my God . . . I'm back. I'm home. All the time it was . . . we finally really did it. YOU MANIACS! YOU BLEW IT UP! OH, DAMN YOU! GODDAMN YOU ALL TO HELL!"

III

Ape Equality

6
Who Comes First, Humans or Apes?

TRAVIS MICHAEL TIMMERMAN

> **DR. ZAIUS:** Do you believe humans and apes are equal?
> **ALAN VIRDON:** In this world or ours?
> **APE:** In any world.
> **VIRDON:** I don't know about any world. But I believe that all intelligent creatures should learn to live and work with each other as equals.
> **DR. ZAIUS:** Silence!
>
> —"Escape from Tomorrow," *Planet of the Apes*, Season 1, Episode 1

In a turning point in the original *Planet of the Apes* movie, Charlton Heston's character George Taylor successfully steals the notepad of Dr. Zira, an ape psychologist who conducts tests on human subjects. Before being brutally beaten by a gorilla guard, Taylor manages to write "My name is Taylor" on it. Zira immediately demands his release, despite the gorilla guard's protests. From that point on, Zira does all she reasonably can to help Taylor.

Planet of the Apes could have been a much shorter film. After recognizing that Taylor is as intelligent as most (or all) apes, Zira could have simply responded with "Wow! That's strange. Oh well, he is still a *human* after all. Let's dissect his brain." But she didn't react in this way and for good reason. For one thing, we movie-goers expect a little more dramatic tension and the playing out of plot-lines before a sympathetic character can be summarily executed. More than that, though, most of us would probably agree that it seems *wrong* for Dr. Zira to respond like that. The viewer is supposed to approve of Zira's choice to save Taylor, partly because he's the star of the film and its hero, but partly because it *feels like* the right thing to do.

We expect Zira, as a rational being, to recognize what we recognize intuitively: that it would be morally wrong to sacrifice Taylor to satisfy less important ape interests, such as having human slave labor. After all, Taylor's well-being depends on things like freedom, autonomy, avoiding pain, and, let's be honest, getting a role in the sequels. None of these ends would be realized if the apes used Taylor in the same way they used other humans.

All of this should be uncontroversial, but the best explanation of *why* the audience has (or *should* have) this reaction to Dr. Zira's actions will be anything but. In this scene, and in numerous others, the audience has the intuition that Zira and George Taylor are moral equals *because* they are approximately equally intelligent beings with similar interests. The fact that they are from different species is morally irrelevant. The same goes for Caesar's moral importance compared to that of humans in *Conquest of the Planet of the Apes*, and most recently, *Rise of the Planet of the Apes*.

If the *Planet of the Apes* movie series successfully motivates the idea that species membership is not a morally relevant factor and we are to act in accordance with our moral views, then most people will need to radically alter the way they think of and treat non-human animals. Doing this will require abolishing an attitude that permeates our culture, which goes by the clumsy term *speciesism*, namely, being prejudiced against some animal (human or non-human) *because* of its species membership.

Richard Ryder coined the term *speciesism* and Peter Singer raised the public's consciousness about it with his seminal 1975 book *Animal Liberation*. Speciesists are those who allow "the interests of their own species to override the *greater* interests of members of other species." For instance, people are speciesist when they discount (or completely ignore) the interests of an animal *simply because* it is *not human*.

Most humans are speciesist, as most believe that all humans have greater moral worth than other animals. Not only do they have this belief, they also act in accordance with this belief. The vast majority of people eat non-human animals and many hunt them for sport, wear their skin, perform painful experiments on them or purchase products that have been tested on them. Some people still sacrifice them in religious ceremonies. The list goes on. Philosophers on all sides of the debate agree that most people are speciesists. But they disagree about whether there is something *irrational* or *morally wrong* with having speciesist attitudes. Contemporary philosophers such as Peter Singer and Tom Regan think speciesism is irrational and morally wrong. Others, such as Jonas Beaudry in Chapter 7 of this volume, disagree. No consensus about this complex issue has been reached, but perhaps the science fiction series that Pierre Boulle's novel spawned will allow us to make some progress in that direction.

Dr. Zaius: Fashion-Impaired Orangutan and Notable Speciesist

In spite of his five-dollar haircut and orange-or-tan suit, Dr. Zaius is the perfect antagonist. He is an intelligent, complex and almost sympathetic villain. He's also an unapologetic speciesist.

Recall that Dr. Zaius was the only ape who seemed to be aware even *before* Taylor and his crew landed, that humans had once been intelligent and, despite knowing this, he covered it up. When Taylor wrote in the dirt, Dr. Zaius erased it before anyone else noticed. He also lobotomized Landon and threatened to do the same to Taylor. Dr. Zaius reveals at the end of the film that the humans who used to live in the Forbidden Zone turned it from a "paradise" to a "desert," which might be at the root of his speciesist attitudes against humans. Egregiously, Dr. Zaius even orders that all of the human artifacts discovered by Dr. Zira and Dr. Cornelius be destroyed, then notifies them that they will be charged with heresy.

The humans (especially Taylor) have a strong moral interest in being able to avoid all of the harms that befall them as a result of the current "ape" culture. At the same time, Dr. Zaius has an interest in preserving religious myths to keep the status quo, allowing him and others to use humans for slave labor and scientific research. But to me, it's obvious that humans' moral interest (especially Taylor's) in living a good life free from suffering far outweighs the ape interest in maintaining myths about their history or treating humans inhumanely.

You might think that preserving the false, presumably comforting view of ape history outweighs the allegedly less intelligent humans' interests. But there are three responses to that.

First, Taylor and his crew might have been the most intelligent humans on Earth, but other humans were likely more intelligent than most apes thought. Once the audience gets to know Nova, she seems rather smart and consequently, has more complex interests than most apes presumably believed.

Second, when Zira, Cornelius, and Lucius discover the truth in the Forbidden Zone they find they were lied to about ape origins and wish they had known the truth all along. Wouldn't you prefer to know the truth if you were one of those apes?

Third, as the antagonist in the story, Dr. Zaius is designed to make choices that are intended to be met with strong disapproval by the audience. He appears to be intentionally sacrificing greater human interests to serve the less important interests of apes. His rationale? A prejudiced favoring of apes and distaste for humans. Pure speciesism.

Their Pain Counts Just as Much

I do not expect you to just take my word for it, of course. No, we need to ask "What is moral considerability?" and "What determines a being's moral status?" The answer, according to the movie series, is the "interests" that a being has. "Interests" are tied up with what is good for some being, or what contributes to their well-being. Every sentient being—every creature that can feel pleasure or pain—is *morally considerable* and at least has an interest in not suffering. Now, every sentient being has interests, and these interests vary depending on its intellectual capacities and abilities.

For example, you might have an interest in reading this book because it would be fun and you may learn something about philosophy. A present-day ape of normal cognitive capacity does not have an interest in reading this book simply because it cannot read. Interests depend on capabilities. Thus, Zira and Cornelius, even though they are apes, *would* have an interest in reading this book because their cognitive capacities allow them to understand it and benefit from it. Zira, if you're reading this, let me say, "Don't leave your stuff behind while you're on the run. Hasslein will find it and be able to track you down, killing you and Cornelius and the baby ape. Don't do it!" But I digress.

Beyond moral considerability, there's a related concept known as *moral status*, which comes in degrees. It is commonly accepted that all sentient beings have moral status and all non-sentient things lack it. Different moral statuses exist within a range and depend on the intensity, type and number of interests a being has. Dr. Zira and Taylor have a higher moral status than, say, a normal present-day ape, since they have a greater number of interests than this ape, qualitatively superior interests and perhaps even more intense ones. These may include: setting long term goals for the future, doing science, forming friendships with deep emotional bonds, appreciating subtle ironies, and so on.

What about when the interests of different creatures conflict? For instance, if we have to choose between relieving a human from pain or an ape from pain, how do we compare the importance of preventing each of these animals from suffering? On this point, Singer, in *Animal Liberation*, echoes the position of Jeremy Bentham, who wrote in 1789:

> The day may come when the rest of the animal creation may acquire those rights which never could have been witholden from them but by the hand of tyranny. . . . The question is not, Can they reason? nor, Can they talk? but, Can they suffer?

Singer argues for a principle of equality that he calls *equal consideration of interests. Equal consideration of interests* requires that whenever two or more different morally considerable beings, regardless of their moral status, have the same interest in something, we ought to count each of their interests equally in our deliberation.

Suppose that Dr. Zaius has to perform an emergency operation on both Dr. Zira and Dr. Cornelius, but only has enough anesthesia for one of them. Both Zira and Cornelius have an interest in avoiding pain and the strength of that interest is the same. Dr. Zaius should count both of these interests equally when deciding who to give the anesthesia to. But the same rule applies even in cases where the cognitive capacities of individuals vary greatly. If Dr. Zaius had to perform surgery on either Nova (the "primitive" companion of Taylor) or Taylor, it's not at all obvious who should get the anesthesia. Although Taylor is much more intelligent than Nova, both have an interest in avoiding pain. If the surgery would be equally painful for both of them, the pain that Taylor would feel should count for as much in our deliberation as the pain that Nova would feel.

Applying this rule consistently means giving equal consideration to the pain that Taylor would feel compared to the pain that any present-day, non-human animal would feel. If we had to perform surgery on Mark Wahlberg's character Leo Davidson from the 2001 *Planet of the Apes* or the normal chimpanzee Pericles, the pain that Pericles would feel should count for just as much as the pain that Davidson would feel (assuming that it would be the same amount of pain).

Other considerations could also apply. For example, if Leo Davidson had to undergo an operation without anesthesia, he would be intelligent enough to understand *why* he was in pain and would know that the pain would come to an end relatively soon. On the other hand, Pericles would not be able to understand this, perhaps causing extra anxiety that would not be felt by Davidson. This extra consideration could actually count in favor of giving Pericles the anesthesia over Davidson, even though the pain that each feels would count equally.

But Humans Are Smarter!

At this point, you might be asking "Doesn't human intelligence make human interests matter more than non-human interests?" Or maybe you're just wondering how awkward it was for Nova and Taylor when they rode off into the sunset together immediately after Taylor has kissed Zira on the lips. Both are excellent questions, though I can only address the first.

Even if it were true that all humans were smarter than other animals, and that human interests should be given greater moral weight than non-human interests, this argument would not give priority to human interests *because* of their species membership. Instead, it would seek to find a morally relevant property, such as intelligence, that all humans happen to have (and all non-humans happen to lack). But this property can be possessed by non-humans in imaginary worlds like *Planet of the Apes,* and some imaginary non-humans (such as Dr. Zira and Dr. Cornelius) would (if they actually existed) be just as morally important as humans according to this view, despite the fact that they are members of a different species. So even if this argument worked, it would not justify the strong sense of speciesism that many people accept.

In reality, the thinking capacities of humans vary greatly. All severely cognitively disabled humans lack the rational capacities that one would appeal to in order to try to justify giving precedence to human interests. This line of argument would entail that normal human interests are more important than the interests of any severely cognitively disabled person, even when the conflicting interests are the same, as in the case of avoiding pain. That sounds morally repugnant. For these reasons, we should reject the crude version of this argument outright.

What's that? You think that all cognitively disabled humans have the same moral status as humans of normal intelligence? If so, then you're not alone. You might accept the more sophisticated version of the argument. In order to accommodate the moral importance of severely cognitively disabled humans, some philosophers, such as Martha Nussbaum, argue that the moral weight of a group's interests depends upon what the *normal capabilities* are for that group. This often translates into the more specific idea that, as Singer puts it, "we should treat beings according to what is 'normal for the species' rather than according to their actual characteristics."

The movie series appears to expect the viewer to reject this. Consider how Dr. Zira and Dr. Cornelius were treated by humans in *Escape from the Planet of the Apes*. As soon as Dr. Branton and Dr. Dixon, the human scientists watching over them in the San Diego zoo, realize that Zira and Cornelius possess the ability to use language and are more intelligent than most humans, they immediately treat them differently. Dr. Zira and Dr. Cornelius are brought in front of the Presidential Commission, and upon the hearing of their case, are awarded their freedom. They become instant celebrities, get interviewed, go on expensive shopping sprees, eat at fancy restaurants, stay in a lavish hotel and the list goes on. Remember the extensive 1970s montage of Dr. Zira and Dr. Cornelius's newfound fame and lifestyle? Any movie with apes dressed in 1970s-style clothing is an instant classic in my book.

Yet, nothing else really changes. The rest of the apes on Earth presumably continue to be treated in exactly the same manner as they were before. They're kept in cages in zoos, experimented on in labs and some are killed to provide heart transplants for humans. But, and here's the point, *if* the moral status of a being is determined by what is *normal* for its species, then there would be nothing morally wrong with treating Zira and Cornelius in exactly the same way that all of the other apes on Earth were treated. Surely it would be absurd to think that it would be morally permissible to keep Zira and Cornelius in a zoo or, even worse, keep them in a cage in a lab to experiment on them. But, if we accept the idea that the moral weight of interests depends on what is *normal* for the species, then there would be nothing wrong with treating Zira and Cornelius in this way. Since the sophisticated version of the argument leads to this absurdity, we should reject it in addition to the crude version.

The principle of equal consideration of interests, on the other hand, can explain why it would be morally wrong to treat Dr. Zira and Dr. Cornelius like other apes. These two are unlike any other member of their species (in the 1970s) and have the same interests as humans of normal cognitive capacity. Giving equal weight to all like interests requires treating Dr. Zira and Dr. Cornelius in the same way that we treat normal humans, not normal apes.

But We Don't Live on the Planet of the Apes (Yet)

At this point you might be saying to yourself, "Of course I would treat apes who are as intelligent as humans as moral equals. That's obviously the way it should be. But the fact of the matter is that apes (and any non-human animals) on Earth are all dumber than humans. That's why all humans are more important than non-human animals and that's why we're justified in treating them the way we do."

You're right to say that no super-intelligent apes actually exist on Earth. Too bad too because it would be awesome if they did! Nevertheless, it does not follow that it is morally permissible to discount existing ape interests. There is a fair amount of overlap in the intellectual capabilities among humans and non-human animals. Humans with severe cognitive disabilities have a lower cognitive capacity than many non-human animals. In fact, there have been many cases of anencephalic babies, which are humans who lack the ability to be conscious. They have an IQ of 0. Baby Theresa is one example. She was born with only a brain stem (and no brain) and died after nine days of life. More commonly, humans are born with an IQ that falls below 70 (the threshold for being considered cognitively disabled) and many within that category have an IQ that falls below 20 (which is the threshold for being considered severely cognitively disabled). This means that for any non-human animal that ever existed, exists or will exist, there has been a human who was of equal or lower cognitive capacity than the non-human animal in question. If we grant that a super intelligent ape like Dr. Zira would be just as morally important as a human of the same cognitive capacity (such as Dr. Branton), then we should likewise grant that an ape of normal ape cognitive capacity is just as morally important as a cognitively disabled human of equal intelligence.

This may seem obvious, but here's the problem. Most people would find it morally repugnant to treat any of these severely cognitively disabled humans in the same way that we treat the vast majority of non-human animals who have the same (if not a higher) cognitive capacity. It's often said that the non-human animals' lower cognitive capacity justifies humans bringing them into existence (through artificial insemination) to live a life of constant suffering in a factory farm before being slaughtered for food.

Since species membership is not a morally relevant factor, this justification for treating non-human animals the way we do implies that it would likewise be justified to treat cognitively disabled humans in the same way. But surely it's absurd to think that it would be morally permissible to keep cognitively disabled humans confined in tiny cages for their entire lives and then kill them and eat them because we enjoy the taste of their flesh. It is sick. Likewise, the overwhelming majority of people think it would be morally impermissible to subject cognitively disabled humans to painful medical experiments. This would especially be true if the experiments were for a new cosmetic product or some other superfluous item with countless safe versions already on the market.

Holding that

1. **It's wrong to treat severely cognitively disabled humans like this**

And that

2. **Species membership is not a morally relevant factor**

forces us to the conclusion that

3. **It's likewise morally wrong to treat non-human animals in this way.**

I accept 1. as an obvious moral truth and do not feel the need to argue for it. I have argued for the truth of 2. Rejecting 2. leads to absurd conclusions and problems that I have been raising throughout this chapter. Anyone who, like me, accepts both 1. and 2., must, so as not to contradict themselves, accept the truth of 3. as well.

How Pervasive Is This Anti-Speciesist Message in the Movies?

You might be thinking to yourself something like the following. "Sure, there are a few interesting examples of anti-speciesist attitudes in the original *Planet of the Apes* film, but that's an implicitly assumed and minor point in the overall movie series." In reply, it's worth noting how important and pervasive the anti-speciesist assumptions in the movie series really are. In pretty much every film, these anti-speciesist assumptions explain not only the characters' actions, but also who we root for. Thus, speciesism actually plays a crucial role in the entire series.

Dr. Zira and Dr. Cornelius are repeat human defenders, not only in the original movie, but in the sequel, *Beneath the Planet of the Apes*, and in the short-lived animated series. Their motivation for breaking with the status quo seems to be triggered by discovering that humans can speak, as in the original movie. In the animated series, Zira and Cornelius help Bill, a human astronaut, but instead of thanking them, Bill asks why they are helping him. Their answer? "We're not really sure, but somehow I felt that killing you would be wrong" (see the episode "Escape from Ape City"). Then, in Tim Burton's film, the ape Ari seems always to have believed that humans were as intelligent (or as morally important) as apes. She zeroes in on Captain Leo Davidson, played by Mark Wahlberg, to make her case.

Is it possible that we're just rooting for the anti-speciesist attitudes when we want an ape to care about some human? I don't think so. In several movies of the series, super-intelligent apes are the minority among humans, and the humans come to fight for the apes' cause. Take Armando, in *Escape*, who adopts baby Milo (later Caesar), and in *Conquest* treats him as a moral equal, even putting his own life on the line to save him. Mercifully, he never makes Caesar wear bell-bottoms. If that's not an act of kindness, I don't know what is.

In the latest (and dare I say best?) movie in the series, *Rise of the Planet of the Apes*, James Franco (a.k.a. Dr. William Rodman) also employs inter-species adoption. Rodman comes to see Caesar not as a pet but as a member of his family, as Caesar's intellectual capabilities increase and exceed those of humans his own age. In the San Bruno Primate Shelter, more appropriately understood as the San Bruno Hellhole for Primates, we find a villain, shelter owner John Landon, who doesn't get the whole "equal consideration of interests" thing. Like Dr. Zaius, Landon wants to defend the status quo of species segregation because he benefits from being at the top of the hierarchy, one of whose perks is to subjugate and mistreat "lower" primates.

If we really thought there was nothing morally wrong with speciesism, then we could not rationally endorse Caesar's uprising against human domination in either *Conquest of the Planet of the Apes* or *Rise of the Planet of the Apes*. We could think that there is nothing wrong with the way the apes were treated in the lab in *Rise of the Planet of the Apes* and should have no problem using the apes for slave labor in *Conquest of the Planet of the Apes*. Basically, rejecting speciesist attitudes would require rooting for the bad guys in the film series instead of the good guys.

Didn't God Make Humans the Most Important Species?

At this point, you might want to say "Okay, Travis, you've made some interesting arguments about why speciesism is bad, but aren't you forgetting that God created the world with humans at the top?" Maybe your idea is that one species is more morally important because God gave them special rights. John Locke's *Essays on the Laws of Nature* is often cited as one argument for God-given rights grounded in the will of a superior authority. While Locke spoke of rights in terms of humans and human nature, he did argue in *Some Thoughts Concerning Education* that it would be morally wrong to treat non-human animals in an unnecessarily cruel way. Although many people still believe that rights depend upon God's will in some way, the majority of philosophers, both religious and secular, reject the idea of God-given rights. We'll see why shortly.

Let's begin by looking at an analogous case in *Planet of the Apes*. Dr. Zaius is a believer in God-given ape rights, appealing to their existence to justify his discrimination against humans. Now, the viewer is not expected to be convinced by this claim because, in the movie, the apes' religion is supposed to be nothing more than a myth. The broader lesson that we ought to draw from this is that in order to make the case that God-given rights exist, the burden of proof is on the believer to demonstrate:

1. **that the deity in question actually exists,**

2. **that it commanded or willed that one species is more morally important than another,**

and

3. **that the moral importance of creatures depends upon this deity's commands or will.**

This can be difficult to do for any religion, imaginary or not. Fortunately, we can sidestep the issues of God's existence by considering a point first made two and a half thousand years ago by Plato.

Appearing in the sky, God bellows "Any human interest is more important than any ape interest! Also, the Tim Burton *Planet of the Apes* is by far the worst in the series. Seriously, I am omniscient, but even I didn't see that train wreck coming from an otherwise talented filmmaker." In light of this revelation from God, we can ask *why* all human interests are more important than ape interests. Either . . .

1. **Human interests are of greater moral importance** *because* **God says they are**

or

2. **God says that human interests are more important than ape interests** *because* **of some other fact independent of God's will.**

Here's the problem. If it is option 1, then moral importance seems to be the product of an arbitrary choice by God—He could just as easily have said ape interests, or shrimp interests, etc. were of greater moral importance. Each of these hypothetical moral rules seems obviously false and most people do not want the moral rules they accept to be ones that were arbitrarily selected.

Some theists might protest, arguing that their "God is perfectly, morally wise (indeed, omniscient) and anything He says about a groups' moral importance, He says for good reason." Fair enough. But if God says human interests take precedence over ape interests, then this would be because all humans have some morally relevant properties that all apes lack. Alternatively, if God endorses the principle of equal consideration of interests, this would be because He has some independent reason to do so. Whichever view is correct, we can cut straight to the chase and look to the reasons for the view. It is these reasons, not God's say-so, that make a given view right.

The Quality of Non-Human Animal Life

In 1729, Jonathan Swift's *A Modest Proposal* was published. In one of the greatest pieces of satire ever written (think of it as an *Onion* article from the eighteenth century), Swift proposes that the problem of poverty and overpopulation could be solved by having poor adults eat their own children. Swift was happy to point out that

> a young healthy child well nursed is at a year old a most delicious, nourishing, and wholesome food, whether stewed, roasted, baked, or boiled; and . . . will equally serve in a fricassee or a ragout.

The readers, as they were supposed to, found Swift's so-called "modest proposal" horrifying. Hopefully it didn't make anyone hungry. It was clear to Swift's audience that any benefit that would result from eating poor Irish children was far less important than saving the children from undue suffering or harm. A similar satirical piece could be written using non-human animals, such as infant apes, instead of infant humans. If species membership is not morally relevant, we should find the idea of sacrificing stronger ape interests to satisfy weaker human interests horrifying for the same reasons.

The lives of non-human animals in factory farms and most labs are lives that are not worth living. It's a life of almost constant suffering, with little or no pleasure. The USDA statistics reveal that between nine and ten billion non-human animals are slaughtered each year in the United States alone. Philosopher Gary Francione describes life on a factory farm, writing that these non-human animals

> are raised under horrendous intensive conditions . . . mutilated in various ways without pain relief, transported long distances in cramped, filthy containers, and finally slaughtered amid the stench, noise, and squalor of the abattoir.

This should make you as hungry as reading *A Modest Proposal* does. Millions more non-human animals are tortured and killed in labs each year, often to test components of unnecessary luxuries, such as chemicals for a new cosmetic product. No more details are needed here. These should more than suffice to establish that it would be wrong to subject severely cognitively disabled humans to the same conditions. Once we reject speciesism, these should also suffice to establish that it is just as wrong to treat non-human animals in the same manner.

Are We Required to Change Our Attitudes and Actions?

Should we change our attitudes and actions? I think that the short answer is a resolute "Yes." We could accept the idea that speciesism is morally wrong, which could take our moral beliefs and actions in one of two directions. We could, with complete consistency, treat cognitively disabled humans in the same way that we currently treat non-human animals on factory farms and in labs, *or* we could grant non-human animals the same respectful treatment we currently afford the severely cognitively disabled, neither eating them nor experimenting on them.

If you think it would be wrong to raise and kill any human, even if it lived a good life before it was slaughtered (akin to free-range animals), then consistency would require not eating meat from any farm, even if it had free-range animals. That is, you should become a vegetarian (or perhaps a vegan).

Another interesting anti-speciesist message is contained in *Battle for the Planet of the Apes*. Caesar, the ape leader, is portrayed as possessing great moral wisdom. Among his wise decisions as the leader, he influences all apes, gorillas, and orangutans to become vegetarians.

You might still deny that speciesism is morally wrong. But there are serious costs to maintaining this view. If you hold on to the idea that all human interests outweigh the interests of non-human animals of any kind, then you must think that the humans never wronged Caesar in *Rise of the Planet of the Apes*. If we endorse this speciesist view, then it would have been perfectly morally permissible to keep Caesar locked in a tiny cage in the primate "shelter" and even kill him in the lab. Likewise, we would have to believe that it was morally permissible to kill Dr. Zira and Dr. Cornelius in *Escape from the Planet of the Apes*.

Anyone taking this line should also have no problem with the enslavement of apes and the brutally violent training methods employed by humans in *Conquest of the Planet of the Apes*. All of these acts in the film series seemed morally wrong for the simple reason that the apes had the same interests as the humans had and all similar interests should be given equal weight in our moral deliberations. Endorsing speciesism requires biting a very large bullet and accepting what seems to be an absurd view about the permissibility of killing apes in the movie series and other imagined cases.

The list of examples from the movie series and the literature on the subject could go on much longer. But I won't write everything out for the reader. Instead, I will leave it to you to think about the issue more on your own. I found that watching the *Planet of the Apes* movies through the lens of the speciesism debate adds a whole new level of complexity to a great science fiction saga. I'll end this chapter with a humble suggestion that the reader do the same.[1]

[1] I thank Amanda Lynn O'Neil Timmerman, Monis Rose, Yishai Cohen, Andrew Clapham and Kurt Blankschaen for very helpful comments on earlier drafts of this chapter. I want to especially thank John Huss for the invaluable feedback he provided at several stages.

7
Of Apes and Men

JONAS-SÉBASTIEN BEAUDRY

Four astronauts land on a strange planet where apes treat humans the way humans treat animals in our world. The tables have been turned. One of the astronauts has died during the two-thousand-year trip and the apes kill and lobotomize two other astronauts, leaving only Taylor, the hero. Taylor will discover by the movie's end that he is in fact on Earth, many years in the future from the viewpoint of the Earth he left.

What sort of hero is Taylor? There are two ways to react to the apes' domination and understand Taylor's situation. Now that humans have become the dominated species, Taylor (and the audience) can appreciate how callous humans have been toward animals,. Alternatively, Taylor can think, "Humans being ruled by disgusting brutes! How monstrous!"

Being hunted and caged does not give Taylor much of an opportunity to detach himself from his situation sufficiently to reflect upon its irony or learn from it. Maybe, below a certain threshold of comfort or peace between two groups, it's not possible for members of those groups to think in conciliatory, compassionate, or friendly terms. It may well be a vicious circle, but there's just too much at stake if they lower their guards.

That Taylor considers most apes enemies is not irrational given the circumstances. He has been shot in the neck and cannot speak until halfway through the movie, when he is captured by gorillas and snarls "Take your stinking paws off me, you damn dirty ape!" No love lost there. Much of Taylor's effort is directed at fighting apes and stating how humans are better, how everything apes have, they inherited from a superior species, how it is apes, not humans, who are supposed to smell bad and carry diseases like vermin. This human chauvinism is one form of a general type of discrimination known as speciesism.

What is speciesism? Think of racism. The term "speciesism" has been strategically used by animal rights activists from the 1970s onward precisely because of its closeness to "racism" and its nasty ring. To be speciesist is to believe that belonging to a species is in itself morally meaningful, and that the members of one species (generally, the human one) are superior to members of other species.

Speciesism can also refer to the arbitrary moral prioritization of members of one's own species. Arbitrary is the key word. Philosophers in the "anti-speciesist" camp like Peter Singer will say that a preference for one's own species is arbitrary (in the sense of gratuitous or grounded on morally irrelevant considerations, like skin color). "Pro-speciesist" philosophers like Carl Cohen, Peter Carruthers, Tibor Machan, and Bernard Williams will claim that this preference is morally justified rather than arbitrary.

Although most speciesists insist that members of their own species are intrinsically better, I don't agree. Instead I think that a moderate speciesism simply recognizes that certain within-species relationships are valuable for distinctive and justifiable reasons. This is why, in addition to the obvious value of Taylor's relationship with Zira (a chimp), Taylor's relationship with Nova (a primitive human) is also valuable. As the movies show, there's something about relations within a species that is distinctively and justifiably valuable. This is a modest and moderate speciesism that can be defended.

Taken as a whole, the entire *Planet of the Apes* franchise may be viewed as a story of moral progress, one in which the characters come to realize what's valuable about speciesism and what isn't—when belonging to a particular species matters morally and when it doesn't. Taylor can't overcome the bad aspects of speciesism and his part in the moral tale is to show us what can go wrong. In particular, his story shows us that overcoming speciesism is not an individual moral feat because of the collective and institutional dimensions that speciesism—which here becomes a symbol for racism and vicious nationalism—takes.

The movie series lays bare the individual and collective dimensions of speciesism. The moral tale continues after Taylor's death, with Cornelius and Zira traveling back in time to the 1970s, where they are the only talking apes, and their son, Caesar leading the simian uprising in the two last installments of the series, which concludes with a promising interspecies mutual respect.

Simian Superiority Is Self-Evident

The belief in simian superiority is part of the apes' "first article of faith" written in their sacred scrolls, as recited in the first movie during Taylor's "trial":

> That the almighty created the ape in his own image, that he gave him a soul and a mind, that he set him apart from the beasts of the jungle and made him the lord of the planet. These sacred truths are evident.

This reveals what the apes take to be an "evident" corollary of superior value: ape dominion over Earth. The self-evidence of these sacred truths alludes to the American Declaration of Independence which, like many other national and international legal instruments stating and protecting human rights, asserts that human beings are naturally endowed with fundamental rights such as "Life, Liberty and the Pursuit of Happiness." The ideas (generally attributed to Aristotle or to the book of Genesis) of dominion over and stewardship of lesser species has been used repeatedly by dominating groups who construe their domination as paternalistic and morally desirable rather than as a mere act of force.

Animal liberation gained momentum in the Western postreligious world when the notion of the "sacredness" of human life came under attack. Speciesist assumptions were scrutinized. Why is it "evident" that we're superior? And why would this superiority confer on us the right to infringe in such extreme ways on the welfare of non-humans?

Short of answering "because God made us so" and "because God said so," speciesists need to roll up their sleeves and start reflecting upon what exactly justifies the preferential treatment of their own species. Instead of referring to the very property of "being human," pro-speciesists refer to the great value of some capacities possessed exclusively by humans: we can speak, we are intelligent, we are moral, and so on. In other words, instead of putting a value on species in itself, these theorists give a high ranking to some particular human capacities or properties.

All Animals Are Created Equal

Peter Singer, the intellectual figurehead of the anti-speciesist movement (who, along with Paola Cavalieri, spearheaded the Great Ape Project) has a good response to the speciesist. For any capacity you show me that justifies human chauvinism, he says, I will either show you some humans who don't have it, or some animals who do have it. This goes for sentience, consciousness, sociality, perhaps even language. And yet, Peter Singer continues, you still respect humans lacking this capacity, and still mistreat animals endowed with it. What's more, your very attempts to find an exclusively human capacity reveal that you are partial to your own species: if I can prove to you that other animals are able to communicate, or are intelligent, or share some traits that we consider "moral," you will simply work harder at finding some traits that they do not have, as though the one premise that is non-negotiable is that humans are exceptionally valuable, which is precisely what is at issue. According to Singer, when people are attached to their own kind for partial, non-moral reasons, they will always try to come up with what looks like an objective, impartial ground for it.

Dr. Zaius and many other denizens of Ape City are no better in this regard. Consider Taylor's trial. The trial becomes part of just such an ideological process to rationalize and legitimize the mistreatment of humans. To start with, the President of the Assembly orders that Taylor be stripped of his clothes, like the beast he is. He says: "These rags he's wearing give off a stench that's offensive to the dignity of this tribunal." In fact, what is offensive to the dignity of apes is that an inferior species starts looking disturbingly like them by wearing clothes.

When Taylor speaks, the judge says, "Dr. Zira, would you tell Bright Eyes to be silent?" Taylor objects: "My name is Taylor." The judge orders: "Bailiff! Silence the animal." With these few orders, Taylor has been deprived of his clothes, his name, and his entitlement to speak—the first things that we give babies to welcome them into our ethical community and treat them as one of us. We immediately name them, dress them, and address them as though they could communicate even when it is unclear whether they can communicate, and even if they could not care less about being naked and nameless. We do it because some forms of treatment are symbols of community membership.

The trial turns out not to be a real trial at all: the accused is a non-ape and therefore has no rights under ape law. That he is being tried at all is "scientific heresy." Taylor is not being tried, he is being disposed of. The three judges imitate the three "wise monkeys" and block their respective eyes, ears, and mouth to highlight the obscurantist aspect of this legal masquerade: see no evil, hear no evil, speak no evil.

Later, Taylor will be threatened with lobotomy and castration if he does not co-operate. Lobotomy would deprive him of the capacities that would make him a fitting subject of solidarity and respect. Castration not only ensures that he won't propagate his kind, but also bars him symbolically from ever becoming part of a dominating elite. And of course, both treatments are degrading and would confirm that he is the sort of being not owed more respect.

Any proofs adduced by Zira, Cornelius, and Taylor are "profane," "irrelevant," and "heretical" and the artifacts found in the "forbidden zone" proving that there was a more advanced human civilization pre-existing Ape City are sealed into a cave.

Both individual and institutionalized acts of speciesism fundamentally aim at preserving superiority, as a matter of religious specialness, objective value, or social privileges. When these non-moral drives push people to be blind to evidence that some beings deserve our moral concern or consideration, they are speciesist in the bad sense of the term. These people are guilty of immoral speciesism, that is, of favoring their own species for no good reason.

A Third Way

There is certainly much truth to Peter Singer's contention that when we set our own species apart, we are merely rationalizing—and clinging to—an irrational prejudice. However, these rationalizing strategies are not the whole truth.

Some forms of partiality toward our own species are morally justified. For instance, there is value to a community whose members are in solidarity with one another, and the fact that this attachment is made possible by the capacities of the members becomes relevant. However, these capacities are then only valuable insofar as they make this valuable attachment possible. This attachment makes it morally okay to give preference to our own species, though it doesn't license mistreating other species in the ways that human beings often do.

A key flaw in the arguments of both anti- and pro-speciesist thinkers is their exclusive focus on intrinsic, individual capacities at the expense of relational aspects of morality, one example being solidarity. When these individual capacities (sentience, consciousness, rationality, speech, and so forth) are put on a pedestal, we forget that they do not matter intrinsically. We start to think of them as a sort of magical property which infuses the beings possessing them with value.

Consider the mutant human telepaths in *Beneath the Planet of the Apes* who find the capacity for speech "primitive" and communicate telepathically and have associated speech with more primitive cultures. They may come to consider the capacity for telepathic communication as a necessary condition to merit respect and be valued—but this would miss the simpler idea that telepathy is like speech: they are both ways that different beings use to communicate and create social bonds within their respective forms of life. The relational aspects of speciesism allow us to understand why speciesism, rather than being a mere prejudice, sometimes tracks morally relevant differences.

Are All Speciesisms Created Equal?

Speciesism, when it is arbitrary, can imply that another species's very existence is of negative value. This is the case, for instance, when an "inferior" species is seen as a threat to another more valuable species, or when the members of a wicked species inflict so much harm on one another that it would even be better for them to be dead.

Consider the radical ending to the sequel *Beneath the Planet of the Apes*. Taylor has been shot by an ape during the final battle between apes and human mutants and he asks Dr. Zaius, an orangutan, for help. Zaius answers: "You ask me to

help you? Man is evil. It is capable of nothing but destruction!"
Dr. Zaius deems the elimination of Taylor, and of all humans, to
be an intrinsically good thing. Taylor's lover, Nova, has just
been killed by apes, and Taylor was previously held captive by
the human mutants, who forced him to fight his best friend in
a dual to death. Dr. Zaius's refusal to show compassion is the
last straw. Taylor believes that these apes and mutants are two
wicked species whose existence should be eradicated and, con-
firming Dr. Zaius's low opinion of humans, triggers the bomb,
wiping all life off the face of the Earth. Dr. Zaius's statement is
a self-fulfilling prophecy. Had he acted more humanely toward
Taylor, Taylor would not have triggered the bomb.

The belief that it's a valuable thing for the universe if the
negative value of another species were wiped out is speciesism
at its most extreme. However, it is not necessarily arbitrary. It
could be a radical position to hold, but an impartial one. For
instance, in *Escape from the Planet of the Apes*, the US president does not think it would be fair to kill Cornelius and Zira's
baby any more than it would be fair to kill Hitler before he has
committed his crimes. Besides, he's not sure that it would be
such a bad thing if apes would eventually take control of the
world if they are indeed better creatures than we are.

His advisor, Dr. Otto Hasslein, wants to have Cornelius, Zira
and their unborn son, Caesar, dead, or at least neutered, and
asks "Do you want these apes' progeny to dominate the world,
sir?" The president answers that if the progeny turns out as
well as the parents (gentle Zira and Cornelius), "they may do
a better job of it than we have." The president cannot be said to
be a speciesist in the sense of preferring his own species. Peter
Singer would find his impartiality incompatible with
speciesism.

However I have associated bad speciesism not only with
immoral partiality, but also with a mistaken attribution of
greater "cosmic value." In another sense, therefore, the president's view is speciesist because it reflects the belief that
another species is superior (even if in this case it's not his own).
This goes to show that non-speciesists can be as unwise as
speciesists when they fail to appreciate the importance of relations within and between species. For instance, is the president
thinking morally about his grandchildren who will be enslaved
or eliminated by the future dominating apes?

Bernard Williams, in his essay "The Human Prejudice," writes about the science-fiction movie *Independence Day*:

> . . . aliens . . . want to destroy us . . . we try to defend ourselves. . . . But should we? Perhaps this is just another irrational, visceral, human reaction. The benevolent and fair-minded and far-sighted aliens may know a great deal about us and our history, and understand that our prejudices are unreformable.

Extremely similar to Dr. Zaius's statements! Williams uses this example to show where "the project of trying to transcend altogether the ways in which human beings understand themselves and make sense of their practices" could end up. In posing this rhetorical question, he does not suspect that a sort of Singerian anti-speciesist saint would bite this bullet instead of finding the theory underlying it absurd. Williams thinks that this harsh self-judgment is likely to lead to self-delusion or self-hatred. That may be true. I, for one, think that relational aspects of human lives are part of how "human beings understand themselves and make sense of their practices." But I also think that these relationships are morally significant and that moral saints ought not to transcend them. On the contrary, they are some of the most valuable things we humans know.

Is There Such a Thing as a Good Speciesist?

Speciesism sounds wicked from the get-go. After all, it's analogous to racism, and how could racism ever be good? It can't. But the properties of the members of a different species are very different from the properties of the members of a different race. Differences like skin color are of no moral significance.

The most important moral dimension ignored by the anti-speciesist camp is the relational dimension of morality. This is because they generally consider that what truly matters are the properties that individuals personally have, regardless of the relationships in which they take part. Given that these relationships are a deeply anchored fact of human life, it's not at all obvious why we should build a morality for beings who seek to morally transcend whatever pull these relations have on them—and this pull may sometimes be moral. Some aspects of species membership not only do matter, but should matter morally.

Consider reproductive capacities. Taylor is aware that some apes may be closer to him in terms of some capacities (such as speech), yet he still sees that he can only reproduce with the mute, primitive Nova. He says, "You're not as smart as Stewart [the fellow astronaut who died during the trip], but you're the only gal in town." He actually develops true feelings for her. They become lovers and companions and their companionship is different from a pet-companionship even though, as anti-speciesists would mistakenly emphasize, she would have lesser intellectual capacities than a pet (on some suspiciously narrow account of intellectual capacities).

Some relationships are not based on the many capacities that speciesists and anti-speciesists focus on: many relationships typical to the human form of life have little or nothing to do with rationality, self-awareness, or autonomy. Take two kinds of relationships central to human life: love and care. Taylor loves Nova, and we understand that he is not debasing himself because he sees that, even though she's primitive, she has human ways to respond to him. He can detect her personality, even without speech. At one point he contemplates the possibility that the speechless form of life of her "tribe" may be better than his. A speechless lifestyle may bring humans closer to happiness.

We can seriously doubt that language has brought more harm than good to humans (remember, Taylor has misanthropic tendencies), but the point is that they do not need this capacity to be attached to one another. Therefore, Nova's sexual compatibility is not the only explanation for Taylor's attachment to her, but it is still an important component. It is one of many biological facts that may be contingent, but are nonetheless inherent to human life and affect the sort of relationships that we will have with one another. We value procreation and family life. These things enrich our lives.

What if apes and humans could mate? Would that remove any moral case for species preference? In that case we would ask more questions. Regarding the value of the loving relation, we would wonder whether an ape and a human can find happiness as a couple. Would they be loyal to one another, for instance? What sort of parents would they be? Would they really partake in the good of family life? And so on. It is perhaps tempting to answer: no, no, and no. However, we may sometimes answer in the negative out of prejudice.

The apes in *Planet of the Apes* are humanoid: their form of life is essentially human. For all practical purposes, they are humans with a monkey mask. If they could procreate with humans, it seems that they could have a happy family life. But many more subtle questions surface. For instance, is it part and parcel of a caring relation to recognize oneself physically in one's caregiver? (Are white children disoriented when raised in an all-black family?) Or is it part of a valuable romantic relation to be sexually attracted to some being that resembles us?

Cornelius mentions that Taylor looks dumber when he shaves. Bernard Williams suggests that aliens might be so ugly that we just couldn't overcome our visceral revulsion. These issues are complex, notably because many of these criteria are socially constructed—and even though collectively sharing some social beliefs may in itself be valuable, the province of social construction is where prejudices breed. Morality is faced with the complex task of rooting out the arbitrary prejudices while preserving social constructions which actually serve valuable relationships.

However in some cases, the limitations to the special relationships we have with animals are not purely a matter of socially constructed prejudices but arise because of natural differences. No amount of social effort will avoid them because, contrary to what some think, truth is not a cultural construct all the way down. In the 1970s, some psychologists tried to raise chimpanzees in a human environment and teach them human sign language. "Project Nim," among similar projects, failed, but it was not for lack of trying to have "nurture" supplant "nature." Nim, because of the form of life that chimpanzees have, was limited in the way he could be integrated into a human family. And his limitations were due to his own form of life. It doesn't make sense to try to understand Nim's limitations in abstraction from his being a chimpanzee.

To say of Nim Chimpsky that he was like a mentally disabled human would be misguided. He is neither disabled by the standards of his species, nor human. The types of relationships he could have with humans were inherently limited. And the particularities of his form of life cannot be made light of. Nim disfigured and nearly killed a few human beings who acted as his primary caregivers, in a way that no mentally disabled children would (or at least, not so commonly as apes in Nim's situation would). This fact is to be taken into account when we think about the capacity that Nim has to respond to caring and to participate in a relationship of care, just as we must take other facts about Nim's form of life (such as needs, fears, and relational skills) when we reflect upon how fitting it is to enter into some kind of a relationship with him.

Some relations that depend on species-specific characteristics do matter to human life, and they are not just because of psychological preferences. They are morally warranted goals or pursuits and are part of what we humans need to be individually happy. Morality should make room for this happiness, our own and that of "others." and justice should facilitate this goal at a collective level. These "others" may include non-humans, and balancing the obligations of the various roles we occupy within different relations will be a difficult moral exercise, but one that needs to be undertaken as well as we can.

Let's Keep This Between the Species

We can have many sorts of relations with animals, including relations of companionship, which come with moral frames of their own. Yet it's a mistake to suppose that the biological facts about those animals are irrelevant. For instance, I may have a duty to preserve the natural environment so that certain wild animals can survive. I will still think it is the best moral choice to kill a lion if this means saving a baby's life, unless there is another way of saving this baby's life. My duty toward the lions would be outweighed by my particular duty of care toward a vulnerable member of my community—a ground that only extreme anti-speciesists would challenge, thinking it preferable to sacrifice a human baby with little cognitive capacities and no family than to starve a (smarter) animal who needs to feed her own offspring. This is the same extreme form of anti-speciesism that would have us, as Williams suggests, surrender to invading aliens if we thought that they had capacities that made them superior to us.

We should distinguish among human-to-human relations, within-species relations in other species, and relations between humans and non-humans. We can well recognize that a relation has value even if we do not personally take part in it, and may wish to preserve it. For instance, when Taylor realizes his friend has been lobotomized, he shouts, "You cut up his head, you bloody baboon!" and rushes Dr. Zaius in anger. Zira looks at this scene, saddened and sorry for Taylor, rather than worried for the ape he will try in vain to attack. She understands the great value of the private relation Taylor had with his friend and the fairness of his reaction. In such cases, apes and humans recognize the moral significance of relationships.

We can also realize this importance impartially, which should disarm the anti-speciesist worry about arbitrariness. Dr. Zira has done experimental brain surgery on humans, and is not judgmental of another society where apes are the ones experimented on. The problem remains that Zira or other impartial judges are still mistaken about what is acceptable to do to others, even if we're willing to do it to ourselves if we were placed in the other's situation.

A Planet to Share

As Charlton Heston tells his fellow astronauts when they paddle out of the sinking spaceship, "we're here to stay." There is no running away from this planet, no other community to join. Confronted with other species and limited resources (and other species are part of these resources) how should we act?

In all of the movies in the series, there are characters who are sympathetic to members of the dominated group—Zira and Cornelius in the two first movies, Stephanie and Lewis in the third, MacDonald in the fourth, Caesar in the final one. This is the moral stance that we must adopt to overcome the immoral type of speciesism. What conditions are necessary to acquire such a concern for other species?

These considerate characters acting as moral models are scientists trained to think objectively and humane, compassionate people. Caesar says: "MacDonald, I believe that when you grow to truly know and trust a person, you cannot help but like him. When we grow to know and trust your people, we will be equals until the end of time." This tells us that we need a certain level of security to afford empathy, compassion, or genuine concern. At the same time, we cannot give all moral concern to our own species and none to others.

In *Beneath the Planet of the Apes*, Dr. Zaius refuses to let humans live because they bring only death. Similarly, in the third installment, *Escape from the Planet of the Apes*, Hasslein, the president's science advisor, is worried that intelligent apes, given their tendency to brutality, will eventually enslave humans. It is out of solidarity for their respective groups and the relations they have with them that they need to eliminate a group of beings that has become a threat, regardless of the gravity of this threat. This utter disregard for the interests of other species will antagonize the two groups further, rather than reconcile them. It is morality's task to distinguish when, and to what extent, our relationships require that we give (only a partial and justified) priority to our own species, and when we are merely giving priority to our own species out of an arbitrary preference for "our own" and a callous indifference to others.

The *Planet of the Apes* franchise is, but for the last installment, *Battle for the Planet of the Apes*, very bleak. These films reflect two deep fears simmering in the American psyche at the time of their production. First, the fear of a great nuclear catastrophe that would end it all, wipe out all life on the planet or create mutants (a key theme of *Beneath the Planet of the Apes*). Second, the fear of descendants of slaves uniting and rising against the white oppressors (a key theme in *Conquest of the Planet of the Apes*).

It displays the tragedy of man's inability to react before it's too late to avoid ethnic wars or destroy the world and begs the question of whether men are so rotten—mainly because of their penchant for destroying other beings—that they ought to be wiped out. The movies show us humans and apes destroying one another but, thanks to time travel, bring us back to a hopeful but insecure future that looks a lot like the conflict-ridden world in which we now live. Read as a cautionary tale, they warn us we must learn to strike a proper balance between our various affiliations, loyalties, and relationships with other humans and non-humans if we are to survive.

The young apes caricaturing the "flower power" youth in *Beneath the Planet of the Apes*, sitting on the road and chanting "We want peace and freedom, not war" may have it right, no matter how unrealistic cynics may deem them to be. No true morality can come about between distrustful enemies analyzing each other objectively.

Equality doesn't have to do with strangers' respective capacities. It's a matter of recognition of the other person's intrinsic worth, rather than of some evaluation of their objective value from the standpoint of the universe. It is a matter of establishing bonds of trust and learning the ways in which we are alike. When these bonds are established, we are equals, not in the sense of possessing the same color, or height, or wisdom, or whatever, but in the sense that we are fundamentally concerned with other beings sharing our fate (or a similar fate) and our planet. We are nonetheless relational beings, capable of both a broad, universal, and a narrower, individualized concern. Such a concern may encompass various relationships which sometimes demand preferential treatment for members of our own species.

IV

Ape Spacetime

8

We Came from Your Future

DAVID L. MORGAN

The *Planet of the Apes* films are not time-travel movies, they are just movies in which people (and apes) travel through time. The original 1968 *Planet of the Apes* film, and its 1970 successor *Beneath the Planet of the Apes* rely on future-directed time travel of a sort that is entirely permissible within the confines of physics, although the mechanisms suggested in the movies are at times rather vague.

The mere fact of time travel is simply a necessary plot element that sets up the situations explored in the series. In the first movie, as Taylor is recording his final log entry before hibernation, he explains that he and his crew have been in space for six months, "by our time that is. According to Dr. Hasslein's theory of time in a vehicle traveling nearly the speed of light, the Earth has aged nearly seven hundred years since we left it."

In *Beneath the Planet of the Apes*, future-directed time travel comes with another explanation—Brent speculates that his ship must have "passed through a Hasslein curve—a bend in time." Of course no such made-up science is necessary to explain this sort of travel into the future. And no new theories, Hasslein's or otherwise, are necessary beyond Albert Einstein's 1905 Special Theory of Relativity.

Fast Forward

While Einstein's special theory of relativity does not exactly permit time travel in the sense of "skipping" from the present time to some future time, it does allow for an effect that accomplishes something similar. According to modern relativity, observers moving relative to one another do not experience time in the same way. If you are moving though space very fast—say at ninety percent of the speed of light—time will pass more slowly for you compared to a stationary observer. This allows the crew of an interstellar spacecraft to take a trip that lasts for ten years as measured by those left behind on their home planet, but only eight years as measured aboard the spacecraft. Or five years. Or one year. Or one month! There is no limit to how short the time experienced by the ship's crew can be as the ship goes faster and faster—ninety percent, ninety-nine percent, 99.999 percent of the speed of light.

We can deduce something from Taylor's description of time aboard his ship from the numbers he cites in his log entry. He claims that six months of time have gone by aboard the ship while the earth has aged nearly seven hundred years. Unless Dr. Hasslein has significantly modified Einstein's theory of relativity, we can conclude that, based on the implied time dilation factor of around 1,400, Taylor's ship is traveling at around 99.99997 percent of the speed of light.

This sort of time-travel is a well-established fact of nature. Unstable particles created by cosmic rays at the top of Earth's atmosphere live longer when they are hurtling towards the ground than when they are sitting relatively still in the lab. Short-lived particles produced in high-energy particle accelerators like the Large Hadron Collider experience this relativistic time dilation in precise agreement with the predictions of Einstein's theory.

Gravity can have a similar effect on time. Time flows more slowly for observers in a strong gravitational field than in a weak one. This means that a clock at the top of a tall building ticks a little bit more slowly than one on the ground floor. Of course the difference is measured in fractions of a nanosecond, but the difference is real, and measurable. In fact, the network of GPS satellites, which allow you to determine your location on Earth's surface to within a few meters based on timing signals received from multiple orbiting satellites, has to take these relativistic time differences into account. If the system didn't compensate for the fact that time flows at a different rate up in orbit where the satellites are located relative to our

GPS receivers on the ground, the timing signals would gradually drift out of sync, and this would cause your location to be determined incorrectly.

This means that another way to "time travel" into the future is to hang out someplace where the gravitational field is very strong, say just outside the event horizon of a black hole. Time will flow more slowly there for you than for someone located where the force of gravity is much weaker, such as the surface of a planet. If you spend a few years orbiting close to the black hole and then return to your home planet, you might find that centuries have elapsed there. Without violating any laws of physics, you would have effectively travelled into your planet's future.

A Backward Disturbance in Time

The idea that time "flows" at different rates for different moving observers seems strange to us, but it turns out that the sort of limited time travel into the future permitted by Einstein leads to no logical inconsistencies or paradoxes. Time travel into the past is another matter.

The first entry in the series that deals with time travel into the past is the third movie, *Escape from the Planet of the Apes*. The film opens with Cornelius, Zira, and Dr. Milo emerging from a spaceship that has splashed down off the California coast in 1973. We eventually learn that the three apes escaped to our time by repairing Taylor's ship from the first film, and that shortly after leaving Earth they witnessed its destruction via the doomsday bomb explosion that closes the second film. The exact physical mechanism for their time travel from the future back to 1973 is not made particularly clear. Dr. Milo simply refers to a "backward disturbance in time" caused by the shockwave of the exploding Earth.

Is such a thing possible? There's no clear consensus among physicists over whether or not the laws governing our universe might permit time travel into the past. But there are enough reasons for hope not to discount the possibility out of hand. The first reason is that the fundamental laws of physics themselves are almost entirely agnostic about the difference between the past and future. The only place the difference between past and future is apparent is on the macroscopic scale—when discussing the flow of heat, or the expansion of the universe, or the functioning of our brains.

All of the laws of physics that govern the individual interactions between individual objects at the microscopic scale are symmetric with respect to the reversal of time. So it seems as if that "arrow of time" that defines the flow of our experience from past to future is more like an emergent property of our universe than a fundamental one. If this is true, then traveling into the past might not break any fundamental laws of physics.

But how would we actually do it? How could we build a "time machine"? It turns out that Einstein's general theory of relativity, the same one which predicts the effect of gravity on the flow of time, allows certain solutions that appear to permit trajectories through spacetime that start in the present and wind up in the past. On paper, anyway. The various time-traveling solutions of general relativity involve exotic objects like "wormholes," "ring singularities," and "cosmic strings"—entities which may not actually exist outside of Einstein's equations as part of the real world. But the very fact that the laws of physics do not seem to expressly forbid time travel into the past, means that it's worthwhile examining the philosophical implications of the idea.

Paradox of *Escape*

Whatever as-yet undiscovered physics enabled them to travel back to 1973, *Escape from the Planet of the Apes* opens with the three apes (four if you count Cornelius and Zira's unborn child) present in the Earth's "present"—which for them is the past. Their subsequent interaction with modern-day humans gives rise to an apparent paradox. If the humans of the twentieth century learn the fate of their civilization, might they take action to prevent it? This is exactly what Dr. Hasslein has in mind as he tries to exterminate the apes, considering them a threat to humanity's very existence. But if this attempt to change the Earth's fate were to succeed, how would we explain the presence of intelligent apes from a future that will now never come?

The situation which arises in *Escape from the Planet of the Apes* is an example of what is often referred to as the "Grandfather Paradox." Imagine you travel into the past to a time before your mother was born, and you track down your grandfather and, for whatever reason, you kill him. With your grandfather dead, your mother will never be born. If your mother is never born, then the question arises—where did you come from?

Many sci-fi story plots run afoul of the grandfather paradox by choosing to ignore it. Take the plot of the 1984 movie *The Terminator*. Robots from the future, having nearly won the war against humans, decide to take a radical step to eliminate the remaining human resistance forces. They send a cyborg into the past to murder Sarah Connor, the mother of John Connor, leader of the human resistance. Had the Terminator, played by Arnold Schwarzenegger, succeeded in killing Sarah Connor, we would have been faced with a variation on the Grandfather Paradox—namely, if John Connor never exists, who exactly were the robots of the future trying to kill? Why would the machines of the future send a Terminator back in time to kill the mother of a person who, for them, never existed?

The scenario that arises in *Escape from the Planet of the Apes*—where Professor Hasslein's awareness of Earth's ape-dominated future seems to enable him to avert it—sets up something like a "Grandfather Paradox" for the franchise as a whole. Should he succeed in averting the rise of the apes, the entire society which gave rise to Cornelius and Zira would never come to pass.

Of course, that's not how the story unfolds. Hasslein does succeed in killing Cornelius and Zira, but their son Milo survives, switched as an infant with a circus chimp and raised to adulthood by Señor Armando. Not only does Milo (re-christened "Caesar" by Armando between the third and fourth films) survive, but he goes on to become a leader of the ape rebellion in *Conquest of the Planet of the Apes*. Not only has Hasslein failed to change the future, it seems he may have been instrumental in setting events in motion that would lead to the rise of apes and the fall of humankind. This suggests a different sort of potential relationship between the actions of past-travelers and their impact on the future from which they departed.

Escaping Paradox

The simplest way around the Grandfather Paradox is to deny that it's possible to change the past. This is not an unreasonable thing to do, given our common-sense understanding of past events. Past events have already happened, so they are "true" for all time. Thus, they cannot be changed. To do so would simply be a logical contradiction. I cannot travel back to 1930 and kill my grandfather, because it's an eternally true fact about the world that my grandfather did not die in 1930. If I travel into the past, I can only do those things that were done in the past by a time traveler. (Me!) So I cannot travel back to 1930 to kill my grandfather, but I could travel back to 1963 and assassinate John F. Kennedy. But—and this is important— only if it has always been true all along that the "second gunman" conspiracies about the JFK assassination were true, and that second gunman was myself, a time traveler from the future!

This version of time travel, where time travelers cannot change the past, but only bring about past events as they originally happened, relies on the concept of "closed causal loops." The idea is that time travel can proceed only via closed loops where past events can be *caused* by a time traveler, but are never *changed* by a time traveler. This concept can lead to compelling and paradox-free time travel stories when handled carefully. (My personal favorite is the 1995 movie *12 Monkeys*, directed by Terry Gilliam and starring Bruce Willis.)

At first glance anyway, the third and fourth *Apes* movies seem to obey the rules for past time travelers as dictated by this "closed causal loop" concept of time travel. Not only do the apes who travel back to the twentieth century not change their past, they take part in those very activities that brought about the future from which they departed.

Another Model of Time Travel

What are we to make of time travel stories in which the time traveler changes the past, thereby altering the future that they knew? Are they simply wrong? Is there any room in either physics or philosophy for the notion that we can change the past? There does seem to be room for another way of thinking about time travel into the past.

An alternative model of time travel asserts that when a time traveler changes events in the past, he or she simply creates another timeline that exists independently of the one they departed. The future they are familiar with ceases to exist, or at least exists now only in an alternate, parallel reality. Events in this new timeline unfold in a way that places no limits on the actions of the time traveler. You are free to kill your grandfather, or Kennedy, or Hitler, or whomever you wish in the past. The Grandfather Paradox is sidestepped, since the answer to the question "If my grandfather died before my parents were born, where did I come from?" becomes—"You came from the future of an alternate universe." In this conception of time travel, the traveler is more than just a traveler through time—they are a traveler between realities.

This approach to time travel is encountered frequently in science-fiction stories. One somewhat silly example comes from the 1985 comedy *Back to the Future*. When Marty McFly arrives in the past, he accidentally prevents his parents from meeting, setting up a version of the Grandfather Paradox that threatens his existence. When he tries to set the situation straight by arranging for his parents to meet at the school dance, he also changes some of the circumstances of the past, by for example convincing his father George McFly to stand up to the bully Biff. The result of this change to his past is evident when he returns to the future (his present) to find his parents as hipper, thinner, and more successful versions of the ones he left originally. By changing the past, Marty gave rise to an alternate universe with an alternate history.

A more recent movie that takes this approach to time travel is J.J. Abrams's 2009 *Star Trek* reboot. When the troubled Romulan, Nero, pursues an elderly Spock through a black hole and back in time, he sets off a whole sequence of events—from the death of Kirk's father to the destruction of the planet Vulcan—that change their past. This means that the young crew of the *Enterprise* will experience an entirely new timeline from the one described by the events of the original series. This frees the story from the implications of the Grandfather Paradox altogether. (It also frees the screenwriter and director from the requirement of appeasing demands of continuity and consistency from fans of the franchise!)

If we examine the *Planet of the Apes* movies from this angle, we can interpret the small inconsistencies between the films as evidence that the various installments of the series are taking place in multiple parallel timelines. Consider the inconsistencies that are evident between the third and fourth films in the series. In *Escape from the Planet of the Apes*, Zira and Cornelius describe the events that lead up to the fall of humankind. After a plague kills off the world's dogs and cats, humans domesticate apes as pets. "They were quartered in cages, but they lived and moved freely in human homes. They became responsive to human speech. And, in the course of less than two centuries, they progressed from performing mere tricks to performing services." And then some three centuries later, according to Zira, the apes began to recognize their enslavement and to quietly rebel. The stage was set for a full-scale revolution when a chimpanzee named Aldo was the first ape to speak. He said "No."

Contrast this story with the plot that unfolds in the next movie, *Conquest of the Planet of the Apes*. Only twenty years elapse from the birth of Caesar until the time when apes are being used in a service role by humans. And it's Caesar himself who instigates what seem to be the first battles of the ape revolution. Speaking much more than a simple "No," he delivers an impassioned speech about the coming ape domination.

What happened to Aldo and the slow, five-hundred-year process of ape advancement and growing discontent? Could it be that by traveling into their past and giving birth to the infant Milo, who would become the revolutionary Caesar, Zira and Cornelius changed their past and set into motion a series events that would accelerate the rise of the apes by centuries? As viewers, we could simply chalk up the inconsistencies as sloppy attention to continuity on the part of the screenwriters. But we might instead use the discrepancies as a case-study for the multiple-timeline conception of time travel.

There is some direct support for the multiple-timeline idea from the *Apes* series itself, through one of the few explicit statements made about the nature of time by any of the characters. In *Escape from the Planet of the Apes*, Dr. Hasslein explains to a television reporter that

> Time is like a freeway with an infinite number of lanes—all leading from the past into the future, however, not into the same future. A driver in lane A may crash while a driver in lane B survives. It follows that a driver, by changing lanes, can change the future.

He seems to be advocating for a view that allows many alternate futures to unfold, depending on the choices made in the present. This interpretation of the relationship between the certain present and the uncertain future is not far from a view espoused by a number of contemporary physicists.

The Many Worlds of Quantum Mechanics

The multiple-timeline version of time-travel may seem like something of a cheat—a way to sidestep the grandfather paradox in a way that permits sci-fi plots that are paradox-free without being needlessly convoluted. But it turns out that there may be some support for this vision of time from within modern physics, from a particular interpretation of the theory of quantum mechanics called the Many Worlds Interpretation.

One of the lasting philosophical issues facing physics is the question of how to interpret the probabilistic nature of quantum theory. In quantum mechanics, the behavior of subatomic particles is not described by a precise trajectory through space and time, the way that Newton's Laws enable us to calculate the precise path of a planet around the Sun. Instead, the behavior of a subatomic particle is described by a quantum mechanical wave-function that only gives the probability of various outcomes. The question of what actually happens when a potential outcome becomes an observed result is still the source of much debate among physicists and the source of considerable confusion within popular treatments of quantum mechanics.

The most common way to deal with this transition from probability to actuality is simply to acknowledge that when we observe a quantum mechanical system, we introduce a discontinuity of sorts into our description of the situation. Before we make our observation, the theory demands that we describe a system using a wave-function which handles all of the potential outcomes probabilistically. But after we've observed the system, only one of the potential outcomes is actualized. So the old wave-function no longer applies, and is of no use to us. This transition is usually referred to as the "collapse" of the wave-function.

There's another more exotic interpretation of this transition from probability to actuality, which is that all of the possible outcomes are actualized in separate universes. This so-called "many-worlds interpretation" suggests that every time there is a "choice" available at the subatomic level, the universe splits into multiple parallel versions of itself. Every possible outcome of the event is equally real in some parallel universe. This leads to an unimaginable number of universes branching out from our own every instant. Since these parallel universes are unobservable and undetectable from within whatever universe you find yourself, it's not quite right to call this the "Many Worlds Theory." The word "theory" suggests a scientific model which makes testable predictions, and most physicists agree that the Many Worlds idea does not. It is simply a conceptual framework designed to explain how a theory which is purely probabilistic at the microscopic scale could give rise to a universe that appears to have a single well-defined reality at the macroscopic scale. The advantage of the Many Worlds interpretation is that it de-emphasizes the role of the observer in the process, since the "collapse" of the wave-function, which seemed like something that was "caused" by the observer, never occurs in this model.

Many Worlds as Multiple Timelines

The multiple-timeline version of time travel seems to agree in its basic structure with the Many Worlds interpretation of quantum mechanics. If every choice that's made in the universe, from the subatomic level to the conscious level, can give rise to branching alternate realities, then why shouldn't the actions of a time traveler do the same?

The time traveler is just doing what we all do all the time anyway—making choices that lead to a particular future. The idea that there is only *one* such future is a side-effect of the fact that we ordinarily only get to observe one of those potential universes. But the time traveler gets to see the effect of these multiple choices directly, by traveling from a timeline where the universe unfolded in one way, traveling back in time, changing the circumstances, and seeing the universe unfold in a different way. If this picture of time travel is correct, a time traveler is as much a traveler between universes as they are a traveler between times.

Series Reboots and Multiple Universes

The idea that ours may be just one in an infinitude of parallel universes, each with its own unique history, might give some comfort to movie fans who are bothered by continuity discrepancies between the various *Planet of the Apes* movies. It can also help to sort out the place of later "reboots" of the series, such as Tim Burton's 2001 *Planet of the Apes,* or 2011's *Rise of the Planet of the Apes* (and its planned sequels), in the canon of the franchise.

What are we to make of a movie in which the intelligence of future apes is not explained in terms of years of selective breeding of apes as pets, but instead is the result of a gene therapy experiments that produce an airborne virus that causes death in humans, but enhanced brain development in apes? Rather than reject the movie entirely as being unfaithful to the original series, perhaps we can just regard this as a parallel future that exists alongside many others. If the Many Worlds interpretation of quantum mechanics is correct, perhaps every choice you make in the course of a day leads to trillions upon trillions of future universes. If so, who's to say how many different ways there are to produce a future in which man is dominated by the apes?

9
Escape from the Paradox of the Apes

RALPH SHAIN

Pierre Boulle's *Planet of the Apes* is a time-travel story. In the novel, however, we're led to believe that it's merely a story of space travel. French astronauts travel to a distant planet where most of the action takes place. In the 1968 movie, the misdirection is even more overt. Captain Taylor informs his fellow astronauts that they are on a planet 320 light years from Earth.

Yet both in the novel and film everything leads up to the revelation—the indelible moment when Ulysse Mérou returns to Earth seven hundred years later and is greeted by a gorilla in uniform, or in the movie when Taylor sees the ruins of the Statue of Liberty and realizes that he is on Earth.

Boulle's novel and the 1968 movie feature one of two kinds of time travel—travel into the future or "forward time travel." Travel into the past, or "backward time travel" occurs in the third film, *Escape from the Planet of the Apes*. There Cornelius, Zira, and Milo travel into the past—their past—back to the 1970s. The philosophical issues differ quite significantly for the two types of time travel and these differences are reflected in the way the stories are told.

Dr. Hasslein's Theory Is Right

The idea of forward time travel is conceptually unproblematic. It involves slowing down one's bodily rhythms until one is revived at some future time, akin to falling asleep or simply sitting idly as time passes. If we consider how we use the word

111

'travel', 'travelling' requires something more than the distance covered. We can imagine the slowing of bodily rhythms for future time travel taking place in a number of ways: through chemicals, coma, or freezing. The long time periods space travel requires would necessitate some such means. In the movie, drugs are used to put the astronauts into deep sleep. Taylor administers injections to others and then himself before making the voyage.

The use of drugs to slow astronauts' metabolisms may have been considered by NASA for actual use. As legend has it, explorer and author Wade Davis undertook research at the behest of NASA on zombification in Haiti, with the goal of finding the toxin used to simulate death so that the victim would "survive" burial. NASA supposedly wanted to test the toxin for use on astronauts in interplanetary space flight. Whichever means are used, this type of time-travel is a one-way trip. There's no returning to the past to catch the time that is missed.

A much more space-age possibility, well known to all science fiction buffs, is suggested by relativity theory. As Einstein showed, the rate of change is relative to your frame of reference, and slows with acceleration. If you travel fast enough—at high speeds approaching the speed of light—time slows for the vehicle and everything within it. This is the method chosen by Boulle to get his adventurers to Betelgeuse. In Part 1, Chapter 2, Professor Antelle, the scientist who organizes the expedition, explains to Ulysse Mérou, the journalist who tags along, the phenomenon of time dilation—what would be two years on board the ship would be three hundred and fifty years on Earth. Mérou slyly comments that the sole inconvenience is that if one were to return one day, he would find the planet aged seven to eight hundred years. In the movie, time dilation is exploited in addition to chemical means, but it is merely suggested and not explained.

Boulle sets the stage for the finale in the penultimate chapter, where the phenomenon of time dilation becomes a plot point. When Cornelius is helping Mérou to escape from Soror via space flight to the waiting spacecraft, Mérou announces that he will return to help the humans rebel against the apes. Cornelius reminds him that due to time dilation, this would not be for a thousand years, Soror time. This argument works on the chimpanzees, who were about to prevent him from leaving, for they realize that they and other apes will no longer exist by then.

Using relativistic time dilation for forward time travel may never be possible. No one knows how to accelerate large objects to such extraordinary speeds. But conceptually, forward time travel through time dilation is no different than through chemical means or freezing. And just as with those means, there is no way to exploit relativistic time dilation for a return trip.

The Rules of Euclid, Being Completely False, Must Be on Account of That, Universal

Backward time travel can seem in some ways to be the flip side of forward time travel. Thus the plot of *Escape from the Planet of the Apes* is like a mirror image of the original movie—instead of civilized humans from the past traveling to an ape-dominated future, civilized apes from the future travel to a human-dominated past. Yet the practical and philosophical difficulties raised by backward time travel only underscore how utterly, different it is from mere forward time travel. Let's begin with some of the practical problems.

Almost twenty years ago, I met a physicist who worked for NASA. When I told him that I worked on the philosophy of time, he asked, "Do you know the easiest way to construct a time machine? You take a wormhole and expand it until its diameter is one astronomical unit in length." I thought that this was very funny, on the order of the old Steve Martin joke about how you can be a millionaire and not pay taxes. "First, you get a million dollars." (Then don't pay taxes.)

Not much has changed in the way physicists talk about time travel—it's still about wormholes, which are tiny black holes which, if set spinning fast enough, will in theory warp space-time to such a degree that they could connect two points which are spatio-temporally very distant. No one has found a wormhole, and there is no observable evidence that they exist, but in the last twenty years, physicists have found evidence for black holes. All suppositions about wormholes and time travel are based on mathematical equations used in theoretical physics. Perhaps it was wise for the makers of *Escape from the Planet of the Apes* not to try to provide a serious explanation of Zira's and Cornelius's trip from the future.

We should be cautious in drawing conclusions about physical reality from mathematical equations alone. The formal systems of mathematics do not always provide answers which correspond to the physical world. Consider the Pythagorean theorem. The length of the hypotenuse of a right triangle is equal to the square root of the sum of the squares of the other two sides. So the hypotenuse of a right triangle with lengths of 3 and 4 for its two sides is what? The number 5 is what always comes to mind. While this is correct, it is only one of the two possible solutions to the equation. The square of −5 is also equal to 25, and thus also solves the equation. But we automatically exclude that answer because the hypotenuse cannot have a negative length.

Our feeling that mathematics always provides correct answers depends on a mental trick: the use of non-mathematical knowledge to rule out certain solutions when solving the equations. Furthermore, the Pythagorean theorem holds only for Euclidean geometry. Euclidean geometry describes space to a very high degree of approximation; such a high degree that it was taken for centuries to be absolutely exact and the paradigm of science. But with the discovery of non-Euclidean geometries and relativity theory, we know that mathematics needs to be checked against reality.

Boulle drives this point home when Mérou is trying to establish communication with Zira. In his notebook, he draws a geometrical figure illustrating the Pythagorean theorem. Mérou then recalls having discussed with Professor Antelle the use of geometry as a means of communicating with alien beings. Antelle had approved, adding that "the rules of Euclid, being completely false, must be on account of that, universal."

Another example of the problematic relationship between mathematics and reality can be taken from arithmetic. All numbers on a temperature scale function equally in arithmetical equations. If we consider Celsius, 200, 100, 0, −100, −200 all can be used in simple arithmetical equations to calculate temperatures. The same equations come up with answers for the numbers corresponding to −300 and −400. But these temperatures don't exist! There are no temperatures corresponding to these numbers because they are below absolute zero—the point at which motion ceases. Just because something is mathematically possible doesn't mean it is physically possible.

This worry becomes especially serious when it comes to time. Time is treated in theoretical physics as co-ordinated with space, as if it were a fourth spatial dimension, part of a four-dimensional space-time continuum. It shows up as a number in an equation, represented by the variable t. The possibility of going backwards in time is built into the formal system, since we can move forward or backward along the number line. Physicists tend to take the mathematics as fundamental, but it's an open question whether time is adequately represented as a space-like dimension. This is a philosophical point, and doesn't require sophisticated scientific or mathematical knowledge.

Can We Change the Future?

Here is where we need to think about the human experience of time. Thinking about the possibility of backward time travel is not necessarily an offbeat or peripheral area of philosophy, as it might seem if one approaches it by trying to manipulate the extremely complex equations for the gravitational warping of space-time by wormholes. The question of time travel converges with the most fundamental questions of the philosophy of time: Is time real? What is time? What is the structure of time? Is time a fundamental aspect of nature? Or an artifact of the perspective of conscious beings?

Trying to answer these questions is a complex and difficult undertaking, and philosophers have been discussing them since the very beginnings of the discipline. Today, there are three general philosophical views on time: Presentism, Possibilism, and Eternalism.

- **Presentists believe that only the present moment and what is occurring now have any reality.**

- **Possibilists believe that the present and the past are real, but not the future.**

- **Eternalists believe that past, present, and future are all equally real.**

These theories connect to time travel in the following way: Eternalism suggests that time travel is possible, at least metaphysically, as the past and future are metaphysically real and the present moment has no fundamental importance. Time is conceived of as a space-like dimension and we could move back and forth in time just as we can in space.

Possibilism suggests that time travel is impossible because the direction of time, from past to future, is a fundamental part of reality. No back and forth travel is possible.

Presentism, in and of itself, has no implications for time travel.

Usually the philosophy of time travel is discussed not in terms of general metaphysical theories of time but in terms of paradoxes. The standard one is referred to as the "grandfather paradox." If someone returns in time and tries to kill their grandfather when their grandfather is still a child, what will happen? If they succeed in killing him, they will not be born. If they are not born, then they will not be able to go back in time and kill their grandfather—so they will be born and will be able to go back in time to kill him.

The grandfather paradox involves trying to undo a causal sequence which has already happened. The issue raised in *Escape from the Planet of the Apes* is no different. When the scientific advisor to the president, Dr. Otto Hasslein, learns from Cornelius of the future take-over by apes, he wants to try to prevent this from happening—which involves killing baby Milo. Again, it's a matter of trying to undo a causal sequence which has already happened. It doesn't matter that the causal sequence is not in the scientist's past, since it is in Cornelius's past. Nor does it matter that Cornelius's appearance will have inadvertently undone the sequence. The question is pointedly raised by the president when Hasslein explains his plan, and the president asks, "Can we change the future?"

The parallel between *Escape* and the "grandfather paradox" goes even further, since if there is no ape takeover then Cornelius and Zira will not be scientists, and they will not be able to travel into the past. If they are unable to travel into the past, they will not be able to provide the information about the ape takeover and the takeover will not be prevented. By focusing on the contradictory nature of the actions involved, discussions of time travel seem to allow a way out. This involves the idea of a causal loop. And this is indeed the way taken in *Escape*. The ape scientists' trip to the past leads to the ape takeover—through the agency of baby Milo—which produces the ape scientists which leads to their trip to the past. A causal loop removes the contradictory aspects of the paradox. In order to permit causal influence of the past by time travel, a corollary has to be included though. Any attempt to undo the causal chain will fail. Without this corollary, trips into the past would lead to the physical impossibilities set forth in the grandfather paradox. Thus the attempt to kill little Milo in *Escape* fails because Zira has left him with the apes in Ricardo Montalban's circus.

The real issue though is the attempt to change an event that has already happened, whether or not the attempt to change it is in some causal sequence with the event to be changed. This is a matter of how the past and the future differ from one another. In all of our experience the past is fixed and the future is open. If this asymmetry is fundamental to reality, the point made by the Possibilists, then time cannot be considered a completely space-like dimension, and the solutions to equations which involve going into the past should be considered artifacts of the mathematics, just like numbers for temperatures below absolute zero. Time is of course extremely mysterious, but I will focus on this difference between past and future as characterizing a fundamental aspect of time.

Those who believe that time is not real, or is not a fundamental aspect of reality, say that reality is fundamentally timeless or 'atemporal'. Reality would then be described by atemporal laws, perhaps the laws of nature or perhaps the laws of logic. Aristotle, as the first philosopher to systematically explore logic and an early scientist, was the first to be concerned about this problem. Although he was concerned with the temporal status of both the laws of nature and the laws of logic, he discussed this issue of time with regard to the latter. The problem arose with regard to the "law of the excluded middle," the law of logic which says that all statements are either true or false. There is no problem when applying this law to the past—even when we don't know whether some statement about the past is true or false, there is no problem in assuming that it's either one or the other. But Aristotle noted that if applied to the future, the law of the excluded middle would seem to lead to the conclusion that all events are determined. Consider the following future tense statement:

An ape takeover will occur in 2600.

According to the law of the excluded middle, this statement must be true or false. We may not know which, and in fact no one may know, but it is one or the other. Let's assume it's true. If so, then nothing can be done (by anyone or anything) to prevent the takeover from occurring. And if nothing can be done to prevent it from occurring, then it will occur necessarily. Of course, it may not be true. Let's assume that it is false. Then there will definitely not be an ape takeover in the year 2600, and nothing can be done to bring one about. Same result. Since this reasoning follows for all statements about all events, it follows that all events are determined.

Many philosophers believe that there's some sort of logical error in this reasoning, but I don't think so. The reasoning is sound because it follows from considering statements about the future to have the same relation to reality as statements about the past—they describe it. Note that when we assumed that the statement is true, we are in exactly the same position as Hasslein in *Escape from the Planet of the Apes*, even though we've had no visitors from the future. In *Escape*, the statement is considered descriptive because it refers to events that have already happened with respect to Cornelius and Zira. In Aristotle's example, the statement is considered descriptive because logicians want all true statements to be descriptive regardless of whether they are about the past or future.

With regard to the future, we certainly seem to have the ability to influence events. This ability is eliminated when all statements about the future are treated in the same way as statements about the past. If we think back to the time travel paradox, we can see that it involves the same issue. When someone goes back from 2012 to 1912, the problem is that 1912 is the past (and can't be changed) and upon arrival also future (and can be changed). The problem set out by the paradox is thus not so much about undoing causal chains in a self-interfering way as about treating the future, which can be changed, on par with the past, which cannot.

No Escaping the Impossible

There is a *dramatic difference* between forward time travel and backward time travel. If we take this "dramatic difference" in both senses of the term, we can say that philosophically one is conceptually possible and the other is conceptually impossible. In the other sense, we might see the artistic differences between the first movie and the third as reflecting this conceptual difference: the first movie is a serious drama, the third movie a comedy.

The serious drama of the first film can be taken to reflect the straightforward conceptual aspects of forward time travel. *Escape from Planet of the Apes*, on the other hand, is played as a comedy, reflecting the conceptual impossibility of backwards time travel. The opening scene, where the military picks up the unknown astronauts, is treated in the farcical manner of TV shows of the period such as *McHale's Navy* or *Gomer Pyle*. The comedy culminates with the interview of the government's science expert Dr. Otto Hasslein, who the interviewer says has written "learned dissertations on the Nature of Time."

Asked to explain how someone could travel in time, Hasslein begins by saying that "Time can only fully be understood by an observer with the godlike gift of infinite regression." "Infinite regression" turns out to be the view of the cosmos which includes the observer within the view. In the movie we're shown an image of a landscape painting which then expands to take in the painter in the act of painting, which in turn expands to show the painter painting this larger picture, which in turn expands to show the painter painting this one, and so one through many repetitions.

Hasslein's "infinite regression" has nothing to do with the understanding of time. The images seem to be inspired by a Dali painting, and the comedy is emphasized by the interviewer's comment that "It's enough to drive you mad."

Hasslein, then asked specifically about time, describes it as "like a freeway with an infinite number of 'lanes'—all leading from the past into the future. But not the *same* future. A driver in Lane 'A' may crash, while a driver in Lane 'B' survives. It follows that a driver, by changing lanes, can change his future." He then goes on to say that he does "not find it hard to believe that, in the dark and turbulent corridors of Outer Space, the impact of some distant planetary or even galactic disaster 'jumped' the apes from *their* present into *ours*." This planetary or galactic disaster is left unexplained, so that Hasslein's discussion is not really meant to provide any explanation as to how time travel is possible.

Hasslein's image of time as like a freeway does not get us any further. Being a spatial image, a multi-lane freeway treats time as space-like, and thus is supposed to make time travel seem conceptually possible. The image, however, does nothing to resolve the conceptual difficulties involved in backward time travel and if thought through actually reinforces them. The idea that time is like a road raises the problem of why one can't just shift into reverse or turn around and go in the opposite direction. And it raises the further problem of whether one's thoughts and decisions, as part of the traffic within a lane, are also guided by that—whatever it is—which keeps the cars in their lanes, headed in the same direction. We end up with the same problem as the one pointed out by Aristotle—all actions including our decisions are determined. Our decisions, which seem to involve genuine choices, are themselves determined as well, raising the problem of the existence of free will.

The image tries to resolve these problems by conceiving of multiple lanes, with the decisions given enough leeway to allow us to change lanes. Let us grant for the sake of argument that somehow decisions do have such leeway, and Hasslein's scheme is able to alter the future. In this case, Cornelius and Zira would seem to have jumped back *not within the very same lane*, but rather backwards along the highway and onto a different lane. Their lane—the one containing their past—is one where an ape takeover has taken place. The lane where they've landed, though, is one where an ape takeover does not take place. *The past they visit is thus not their past, but the past of a universe very similar to theirs*. The multiple lanes should be conceived of as parallel universes, and moving from one to another is not time travel at all. Thus an image which is supposed to allow for the possibility of time travel actually makes it impossible.

The central moment philosophically comes not with Hasslein's purported explanation, but when Cornelius explains, under interrogation, how apes took over. As noted above, this story is past and future at the same time—past for him and Zira, future for the humans alive at that time (and also for him and Zira). As past it would seem to be fixed, but as future it would seem to be open, setting up the question as to whether it is open to "change." As Aristotle's argument shows, if the future is also past, then the future can't be open. And that is what the causal loop which resolves the paradox in the film illustrates. The future is not open—Milo won't be and can't be killed. The ape takeover will necessarily occur.

Destiny

At the end of the original movie, when Taylor escapes to the forbidden zone, Zira asks Zaius what Taylor will find there. Zaius replies: "His destiny." Within the film, the prediction can't fail, having an advantage that predictions outside of movies don't have: what's to come is written in the script. And in the movie, Taylor's destiny is to come across the ruin of the Statue of Liberty. He thus discovers that he has been on Earth all along, a discovery which has a huge emotional impact on him, casting doubt on the misanthropy he so proudly used to taunt Landon after landing. And this discovery shows that the entire film has been not a story of space travel, but one of time travel.

The prediction came true in another way as well. In the final scene, Taylor finds not only his destiny but, in a certain way, the destiny of the novel too. Written in French, with French astronauts who land in a future France at the end, the Statue of Liberty of course never appears in Boulle's novel. But you will find an image of a ruined Statue of Liberty on the cover of the current paperback edition of *Planète des Singes*.

V

Ape Politics

10
Banana Republic

Greg Littmann

Life's tough for a chimpanzee on the *Planet of the Apes* (1968). If anybody needs a doctor or an architect, or a blacksmith or a wheelwright, the first thing they do is call in a chimpanzee. If they need a porch swept, a load transported by wagon, or a message taken down to the laboratory, they snap their hairy fingers and send for a chimp.

Yet despite being the backbone of simian society, the chimpanzees get no say at all in how society is run. Instead, all power and authority is held in the hands of the orangutans, which is just how the officious orange bastards like it. Ape City is run according to laws set down by the orangutans, as interpreted by orangutan officials, and enforced by hulking gorillas who can snap a chimpanzee like a twig.

Chimpanzees can't even express opinions counter to those of the orangutan elite. Finally able to speak after a hundred thousand years or so of evolution, the chimps are rendered mute by the government. It's hard not to sympathize. I'm sure we all feel like little chimpanzees sometimes, trapped in an environment where the great big orangutans and gorillas hold all of the power and enjoy all of the fruit.

Just to add insult to injury, the chimpanzees are assured that society is ordered for the greater good in accordance with divine law. The orangutans insist that by holding all of the power, they are merely performing a public service in accordance with God's will and the natural order of things. They teach that an orangutan-dominated society is a *healthy* society, with everyone in their proper place, with the wisest and fittest-to-rule firmly in charge of the rest. According to the orangutans, the chimpanzees are better off with the orangutans making decisions on their behalf, and the gorillas there to keep them in line.

Is ape society a healthy society? Answering that question requires us to have some idea of what a healthy society would be like but political thinkers have come to a wide variety of very different conclusions about how society should be run. One thing that makes the ape society from *Planet of the Apes* particularly interesting from the point of view of political philosophy is how closely this science-fiction civilization resembles one of the oldest and most famous and influential conceptions of what an *ideal* society would be like. The ancient Greek philosopher Plato (429–347 B.C.E.) provided us with the earliest great works of political philosophy that we have. In his longest text, *The Republic*, he laid out his model of a well-run independent city-state.

The City of Justice and the City of Apes

Plato's aim in designing a new city-state was to ensure that it would be a *just* city. When society is just, all members benefit. Order is maintained, allowing people to pursue their work in peace, and all individuals receive their due. The just society is even good for law-breakers, since a just society will improve the law-breaker morally through punishment.

A society can only be just if it is harmonious and well-ordered, with all citizens working and living in proper co-ordination. Each individual should specialize in the work for which they are most suited by natural talent. Those most suited to being farmers should farm, those most suited to being doctors should be doctors, and those most suited to making art would be making art. Having specialized in the type of work they're most suited for, individuals should focus on their specialization and not concern themselves with matters that lie outside it— the potter should make pots and leave curing the sick to doctors, who are better qualified to cure the sick. Plato writes:

> More plentiful and better-quality goods are more easily produced if each person does one thing for which he is naturally suited . . . and is released from having to do any of the others. (lines 370c3–6)

Ruling the state, by this reasoning, should be a job performed by those who specialize in ruling, chosen from those who are best fit to rule. People who perform any other job, like farmers, craft workers, and doctors, should have no say. They should keep their noses *out* of government and simply obey. Since they don't specialize in the art of governing, they aren't qualified to make political judgments and should stick to their own trade.

For this reason, the city will be divided into two social classes, a ruling class to run the city and a producing class to do all of the other jobs in accordance with the rulers' instructions. The function of Plato's ruling class is not to benefit themselves by stocking up wealth and power, but to use their superior reasoning abilities to run society justly for the benefit of all citizens. To ensure that a manual worker "is ruled by something similar to what rules the best person, we say that he ought to be the slave of that best person. . . . It isn't to harm the slave that we say he must be ruled . . . but because it is better for everyone to be ruled by divine reason" (lines 590c7–d3). Because we can't expect the producing classes to always do as they are told by the rulers, the ideal state must also include a class of professional warriors to keep order among the producers and to protect the city from outside threats.

The three classes of citizen in Plato's *Republic* are mirrored by the three classes of citizen on the Planet of the Apes. At the top of the tree, we find the orangutans. Functioning much like Plato's ruling class, the orangutans serve as legislators and administrators and have responsibility for education, censorship, and propaganda. Why the orangutans ended up in this role is unclear, since wild orangs are no more religious than any other species of ape, nor any more drawn to administration.

Perhaps the orangutans assumed that as the most spectacularly beautiful of all primates, God clearly marked them out as leaders, bestowing on them a flamboyant orange splendor that surpasses even the athletic grace of the chimpanzee and the stately majesty of the gorilla, let alone the disease-ridden appearance of the human, afflicted as humans are with ugly bald patches over most of the body.

Enforcing the power of the orangutans are the gorillas, endowed by nature with the physical strength to impose their will. Like Plato's warrior class, the gorillas use their muscle to maintain order in ape society and to protect it from outside threats like invading humans. Right at the bottom of the barrel are the chimpanzees. Corresponding to Plato's producing class, the chimps are the ones who actually make things, grow things, and otherwise take on every job in society that does not boil down to telling people what to do or enforcing the law. Given that wild chimpanzees may use sticks and rocks as simple tools, it is unsurprising that it is the chimps who are assigned to perform the manual and technical labor. The fact that chimpanzees are smaller and weaker than orangutans and gorillas, and thus easier to push around, makes it all the less surprising to find that they are saddled with the hard work. Their function is to get on with their professional duties and do whatever the orangutans say. How can it be that the best possible city so closely resembles this simian tyranny? Let's take a closer look at the parallels and differences.

Anyone Can Become a Philosopher but Being an Orangutan Is a Gift

Plato thought that the most important task of government was to educate the ruling and warrior classes for their social roles. Nobody is born into the ruling class. At the age of thirty, new members of the ruling class are chosen from members of the warrior class who show most aptitude for the intellectual and moral demands of ruling. All young warriors are subjected to an arduous physical training, in addition to which they must master uplifting music and poetry to strengthen their moral character. In order to join the ruling class, the student must also excel in mathematics and philosophy, to ensure that they love truth and are equipped to understand it. They must also demonstrate that they are "the most stable, the most courageous, and as far as possible the most graceful . . . a noble and tough character" (lines 535a10–b1), "someone who has got a good memory, is persistent, and is in every way a lover of hard work" (lines 535c1–2). Above all, a member of the ruling class must be a philosopher, since it's the philosopher who loves truth and can best understand it.

Ape society is as hierarchical as Plato's, though there is less mobility. Plato recognized that the talents of a child often differ from those of the parents and so allowed that some children from the producing classes who show exceptional promise will be brought up as warriors and might even become rulers. On the other hand, if you aren't born to orangutan parents, you just aren't going to get a job in the administration or the church on the Planet of the Apes, regardless of your aptitude. Your species determines what you will be doing for a living. Unlike Plato's elite, the orangutans are hereditary rulers, born to power rather than chosen for their abilities.

White Lies and Orange Liars

In Plato's ideal city, the stories that young warriors hear are to be carefully screened. They must only be told inspiring tales of right moral conduct, especially in stories about the gods. There must never be stories about "gods warring, fighting, or plotting against one another, for they aren't true." On the other hand, it's permissible to tell lies about the gods as part of education, provided that the stories do not misrepresent the *nature* of the gods. The point of the lie must be to convey some deeper truth, such as that the gods always act morally and always demand that we act morally too.

What goes for the education of young warriors goes for the entertainment of the citizenry in general—any stories told in the city should be of a morally uplifting nature, with state-approved lies being propagated if they convey good moral and religious messages. To make sure that no inappropriate messages get through, Plato goes so far as to ban poetry, with the exception of religious poems praising the gods and poems eulogizing famous men of exemplary character.

Like Plato's ruling class, the orangutans try to ensure that the only ideas that get spread are those that will support the harmonious running of society under their guiding hand, even if this means spreading lies and manipulating religion in the interests of social order. The first article of faith among the apes, as related by Dr. Honorius, justifies ape rule over the planet on divine grounds—"that the Almighty created the ape in his own image; that He gave him a soul and a mind; that He set him apart from the beasts of the jungle, and made him the lord of the planet."

Plato likewise decided that the people of his city be told a myth about their own origins to make them accept the current political arrangement as the natural state of things and any deviation from it a dangerous threat. The citizens will be told that they were born out of the ground and thus that they must regard their home-ground as their mother and their fellow citizens as brothers and sisters. In accordance with their earthly origins, each of the three classes of citizen is infused with a particular type of metal. Those fit to be rulers have gold in their soul, those fit to be warriors have silver, and those fit to be producers have bronze or iron. The citizens will be warned that an oracle has predicted the destruction of the city if it should ever be ruled by someone with the wrong metal in their soul.

One particularly important orangutan myth used for political control is that of reward in a future life. Taylor accidentally eavesdrops on a gorilla's funeral, at which an orangutan minister preaches to the bereaved before a massive statue in the form of an orangutan. "He lives again! Yes, he has found peace in Heaven!" Ancient philosophers and modern politicians alike have understood just how powerful myths of heaven and hell can be.

Plato thought that it was important that the warrior class in particular should only hear stories that would make them unafraid of death, while being kept from any tales that make death look unattractive. Heroes in the stories should never feel fear, and the afterlife should only be represented as somewhere welcoming, never as a depressing or terrifying prospect. That way, soldiers defending the city wouldn't be afraid to die. He wrote "We must supervise such stories and those who tell them, and ask them not to disparage the life in Hades in this unconditional way, but rather to praise it, since what they now say is neither true nor beneficial to future warriors" (lines 386b6–c1). Likewise, modern armies come equipped with chaplains and other officials who assure soldiers that death will only open the door to a wonderful afterlife if they are in good standing with God.

The towering orangutan statue behind the minister is of the great Lawgiver, the Moses-like orangutan out of distant ape history who presented the apes with their divine law and established their society. Plato likewise approved of turning political figures into holy figures in the interests of cementing the social order, recommending that in the case of particularly outstanding leaders "the city will give them public memorials and sacrifices and honor them as demigods, but if not, as in any case blessed and divine" (lines 540b6–c2).

In Ape City, any evidence that challenges scripture is suppressed. The orangutans even forbid the teaching of the theory of evolution, recognizing that it undercuts their claim to divine authority. When Dr. Cornelius finally admits in court to being an evolutionist, it is enough for the orangutan Dr. Honorius to charge both him and Dr. Zira with "contempt of this tribunal, malicious mischief, and scientific heresy." Dr. Zaius, Minister of Science and Chief Defender of the Faith, later makes it clear that their conviction is a foregone conclusion. Likewise, the orangutans are outraged by Cornelius's announcement that he had "discovered evidence of a simian culture that existed long before the sacred scrolls were written." His discovery undercuts the myth that ape society was set up in its present state by God, and the myth that the sacred scrolls convey an accurate account of history in general.

Dr. Zaius is particularly active in destroying evidence. When Taylor writes in the dust to prove that he is intelligent, Zaius rubs it out again with his walking stick. Presented with a paper airplane made by Taylor, he crushes it in his paw rather than threaten the established doctrine that flight is impossible. When Cornelius shows him an archaeological site that proves the existence of an earlier human civilization, Zaius would rather obliterate it with explosives than admit that the sacred scrolls are wrong. The scientists may all be chimpanzees but the Ministry of Science is headed solely by orangutans, ready to make sure that the chimp scientists don't discover anything that the orangutans don't want them to.

Masters of Gorilla Warfare

The gorillas correspond to Plato's warrior class, keeping order in the city and defending it against outsiders. When human beings infest the ape's crops, or wild humans escape from the laboratories and run amok in town, climbing all over the buildings and knocking over fruit stalls, it is the gorillas who ride out with rifles and whips to kill or capture the beasts. Likewise, in the labs and stockyards where captured humans are kept, it is the gorillas, now armed with truncheons and hoses, who maintain order.

It's true, the gorillas don't seem to be particularly good at their jobs. The athletic abilities of gorillas have declined a long way from those of their modern counterparts when ten of them have trouble out-running, out-climbing, out-jumping, and out-wrestling one skinny human with no shoes and a major wound. Still, their social role is to bring force to bear on behalf of the state. They also hose down and sweep up the lab, which is work more suited to Plato's producing class, but even a soldier must occasionally sweep a floor. Serving as police as well as military personnel, gorillas provide security in courtrooms and presumably other government buildings. There can be little doubt that the prison that Zira and Cornelius are due to be sent to at the end of the film is staffed by unsympathetic gorillas.

The gorillas may understand the orangutans' mission to suppress unwanted truths. Certainly, Taylor's gorilla keepers don't want to know that he can speak, let alone hear what he has to say—"Shut up you freak!" shouts one gorilla, spraying Taylor with the hose until he yells "It's a madhouse!" At the funeral gate-crashed by Taylor as he flees his cage, the deceased gorilla is praised as a model, the orangutan minister declaring him "hunter, warrior, defender of the faith." emphasizing both his martial skill and his role as the enforcer of orangutan authority. Plato believed that in order to prevent the warriors and rulers from growing corrupt, "none of them should possess any private property beyond what is wholly necessary . . . whatever sustenance moderate and courageous warrior-athletes require . . . they'll receive by taxation on the other citizens . . . they'll have common messes and live together like soldiers in a camp" (lines 416d4–e4). Members of the warrior and guardian class were not even permitted to own money. There are no such limitations for gorillas on the Planet of the Apes, as the departed primate is ominously described as a "generous master." From the sounds of it, the gorilla had many chimpanzee servants in life and the wealth to maintain them.

On the other hand, the virtue for which the late gorilla is praised most is not his dedication to honorably performing his civic duty, but his compassion: "He was a font of simian kindness. The dear departed once said to me, 'I never met an ape I didn't like'." On the face of it, this might seem like strange praise to offer at the funeral of a warrior, yet Plato regarded it as essential for members of the warrior class to balance their toughness with kindness. They must be ferocious enough to stand in battle or to apprehend criminals, but they will be useless if they are thugs who brutalize the very population they are pledged to protect. Plato wrote "those who devote themselves exclusively to physical training turn out to be more savage than they should . . . the source of the savageness is the spirited part of one's nature. Rightly nurtured, it becomes courageous, but if it's overstrained, it's likely to become hard and harsh." It's not enough for a warrior to be as strong as a gorilla and skillful in combat. A useful warrior must love truth and honor and must be driven by the desire to do what is right.

Ordinary Working-Class Chimpanzees

The chimpanzees correspond to Plato's producing class. Like Plato's producers, they seem to form the bulk of the population on the Planet of the Apes—most of the citizens we see milling around town or gathering in angry fruit-hurling mobs are chimps. They also seem to do most of the work that doesn't boil down to administration or fighting. The chimpanzees supply society's doctors, like Zira and Galen; and its merchants, like the chimps we see working in stalls selling clothing, fabric, and fruit; and society's menial labor, like the chimps we see sweeping around the marketplace. While we are never shown who was growing the crops that the humans were raiding when Taylor first arrived, it seems safe to assume that it was hard-working chimp farmers in green overalls.

Significantly, it is the chimpanzee producers, *not* the orangutan rulers and arbiters of truth, who provide the scientists. Plato makes no special provision for scientists in the *Republic*. Living in the fourth century B.C.E., he had no conception of the possibility of scientific and technological progress as we understand it. He did believe that humanity could obtain understanding about the universe, but thought that this could only be achieved by philosophers using pure reason. Perhaps Plato would consign scientists to the producing class, which includes the doctors, craftspeople, navigators, architects, shipbuilders, and all other individuals with specialized practical knowledge. Or perhaps Plato would draw scientists from the ranks of the philosopher rulers, entrusting the search for truth to those who are supposed to love truth above all. In any case, on the Planet of the Apes, it's the chimps, at the bottom of ape society, who inherit science. It's chimps who work in the laboratories and chimp parents who take their little monkeys out to the museum to see the zoological exhibits about humans.

In Plato's ideal city, the rulers were to be the champions of truth, even though they also deceived the people in the interests of maintaining social harmony. As philosophers, their pursuit of the truth was to be their ultimate goal and desire, with their understanding of the truth guaranteeing the wisdom of their rule. On the Planet of the Apes, it is curious chimpanzee scientists like Dr. Zira and Dr. Cornelius who are the champions of truth, casting off religious dogma to ferret out reality. The orangutans are champions only of falsehood; their primary function is to prevent the truth from ever being known.

The orangutans may not respect the chimpanzees, but just as Plato's rulers understood the need for the producing class, so the orangutans appreciate the importance of the chimpanzee's scientific work. Zira explains that her research into the human brain is so generously funded because "Dr. Zaius realizes our work has value. The foundations of scientific brain surgery are being laid right here in studies of cerebral functions of these animals." Even orangutans can develop brain tumors. Plato likewise recognized that doctors have a vital role to play in his city. Even philosophers can get a bellyache.

However, all scientific research on the Planet of the Apes requires the approval of the National Academy, an organization of orangutans charged with suppressing inconvenient truths. Dr. Zaius is quick to stifle any research that threatens to contradict the written holy law. He sneers at the archaeologist Cornelius, dismissing him as "the young ape with a shovel" and warns him "as you dig for artifacts, make sure that you don't bury your reputation." Later, he makes sure that Cornelius's travel permit to the Forbidden Zone is revoked, even though the academy had earlier approved it.

When Zira asks Cornelius how he accounts for the fact that Taylor can write, Cornelius rejects the question out of fear, replying, "I can't and I'm not going to." Zira naively assumes that truth is everyone's goal just as it is hers, insisting, "If it's true, they'll have to accept it," but Cornelius has a more realistic understanding of how his society functions. When she points out that Taylor's existence might prove Cornelius's theory that apes evolved from lower primates, he asks, "Zira, do you want to get my head chopped off?" and observes that "Dr. Zaius and half of the academy declared that my idea was heresy."

When Zira demands, "How can scientific truth be heresy?" she's showing that she doesn't understand the function of heresy prosecutions as a political tool. Heresy that is also the truth is the most dangerous kind. As Cornelius observes, if Taylor were the missing link in ape evolution, "the Sacred Scrolls wouldn't be worth their parchment." Naturally, the orangutans are dishonest enough to deny that they are concealing scientifically demonstrated truths. Zaius announces, "There is no contradiction between faith and science. True science." This is an insistence that we often hear today, yet it can't be true unless "faith" is defined in such a way that having faith doesn't commit you to any claims about the origin or nature of the universe and its contents.

Taylor calls ape society an "upside-down civilization," presumably because humans are at the bottom and other primates at the top. But ape society is also upside-down in that the closed-minded and deceiving orangutans are at the top and the open-minded and productive chimpanzees are at the bottom. If the orangutans would just let the chimps get on with their scientific monkey business, the apes could gain a genuine understanding of their universe to replace religious dogma. That they also stand to gain technologies like refrigeration, painless dentistry and reliable flea-repellent, along with all of the other benefits of advancing past the nineteenth century, is just icing on the cake.

Filthy Humans

There's one last class of primate on the Planet of the Apes, a branch of the family so reviled that they are not even recognized as people, let alone citizens. The humans have degenerated almost to a level of simplicity once occupied by the apes. On the Planet of the Apes, we grow no crops, build no houses, and have even lost the art of speech—though for some reason we still make a pretty good pair of pants. The apes regard us as "beasts" and, apart from bleeding-hearts like Zira, seem to have no moral concerns about how humans are treated. Dr. Honorius, Deputy Minister for Justice, notes that a human "has no rights under ape law." Taylor is treated as humans would treat an animal today, and his fellow astronaut Landon has his brain cut up by chimps just to see what makes him tick. Dr. Zaius even says of humanity that "the sooner he is exterminated, the better."

The apes generally limit their moral concerns to members of their own society. In this, they are like Plato, who designed his ideal city to benefit the city's citizens with little thought about anyone else. Dr. Zaius's views on the need to exterminate humans even echo Plato's view that while fellow Greeks should never be subjected to "enslavement and destruction" in warfare, anything goes when fighting against barbarians (everyone who *isn't* Greek). After condemning brutality between Greek states, he concludes that the people of his city "must treat barbarians the way Greeks currently treat each other" (line 471b5).

Gorilla Girls and Other Simian Women

Perhaps the most socially revolutionary of all of Plato's doctrines is that women should be allowed to do any job that men can do, including fighting in the army and working as a member of the ruling class. Females of the warrior class should be educated right along with males since "if we use the women for the same things as men, they must also be taught the same things."

Plato did not believe in the equality of the sexes, though. He thought women were, in general, intellectually and morally inferior to men. On the other hand, he didn't think that every woman is inferior to every man. He wrote: "It's true that one sex is much superior to the other in pretty well everything, although many women are better than many men in many things" (lines 455d2–3). For this reason, Plato believed that women of unusual ability should be allowed to fulfill their potential, even if it meant promoting them to positions of power and authority over less able men.

We know a lot more about the role of women in Plato's society than we do about the role of females in ape society. We do know that a female chimpanzee, Dr. Zira, has become a respected animal psychologist who is considered by her colleagues to have "made it" and receives generous funding for her research on human beings. This suggests at the very least that it isn't impossible for a female to get ahead in the monkey-eat-monkey world of chimpanzee academia. Yet if the Planet of the Apes is like Plato's city in that it allows particularly talented females to advance, it also looks suspiciously like Plato's city in that more males than females rise to the top. We never see a single female orangutan in *Planet of the Apes*, let alone a female serving in a position of authority. The evidence is hardly conclusive since we only meet four orangutans in the film: three powerful government officials and a religious minister. Still, it seems reasonable to guess that fewer females than males rise to high office in Ape City.

Female gorillas, like female orangutans, never appear in *Planet of the Apes*. I've identified the gorillas as a warrior class, like the warrior class in Plato's city, but the women of Plato's warrior class were themselves warriors, while female gorillas don't seem to take part in warrior activities. They do not ride out to the fields to shoot down human crop raiders or wrestle with escaped animals in the market square. My best guess is that they occupy a more traditional social role than Plato's warrior women, maintaining a home and raising a family. On the other hand, maybe half of those horse-riders *are* female gorillas and I just can't tell the difference.

How Babies Are Made

One striking parallel between society on the Planet of the Apes and the society invented by Plato is their unromantic approach to the human sex act. Dr. Zira shocks Taylor by arranging for him to mate with another human, Nova. Back in twentieth-century USA, it was traditional to give a human being a say in such things. "There were women, lots of women" Taylor confesses to Nova, safe in the knowledge that she can't understand him or appreciate the implied health-risk. It's true, the American government had assigned Taylor to be one of the mates of fellow astronaut officer Stewart, who was to be the new "Eve" on a new world, but there's no suggestion that Taylor was denied the right to decline the mission, or that anyone insisted that it was his civic duty to take part.

In Plato's ideal city, on the other hand, all members of the warrior and guardian classes were expected to mate in accordance with the needs of the state, not their hearts. Plato notes that owners of dogs and horses try to breed their best stock and advises that the government make sure that "the best men must have sex with the best women as frequently as possible." To this end, his city will hold regular mating festivals for warriors and rulers at which men and women are paired up randomly by lot. In the interests of decency, the couple would be married before they got down to business, but then they would be divorced again as soon as they were done—a neat legal trick that you can't even pull off in Las Vegas today.

Any children resulting from these unions are taken to be raised together in government institutions and no record kept of the child's origins "so that no parent will know his own offspring or any child his parent" (lines 457d1–2). Plato believed that preventing warriors and rulers from forming family ties would induce them to direct their energies towards what was good for the entire community rather than to the good of their relations. To emphasize that all citizens of the warrior and ruler classes are family, they are to address each other as "father," "mother," "sister" or "brother," a practice that would many centuries later be adopted by Christian monks and nuns.

Conversely, the apes, like Zira and Cornelius, are permitted to marry whomever they choose. In fact, the apes continue to value families at all levels of society. At the gorilla's funeral, he is praised as a "cherished husband" and "beloved father." The attitude of the apes seems healthier. It isn't obvious that denying families to people will make them attach themselves more closely to society. Taylor had no family ties, but rather than making him a more civically minded individual, it alienated him, and he flew away into the distant future just to escape from his disconnected existence on Earth. Such an attitude of alienation is easy to imagine rising among generations raised by the state.

What an Ape Could Teach Plato

Plato's *Republic* remains as one of the most brilliant works of political philosophy ever written, yet the more cynical take on politics in *Planet of the Apes* shows a more realistic image of what happens when power is concentrated in a few hands. By stratifying society and giving power to a small group of people who specialize in the craft of government, Plato would be placing power exactly where it belongs, if only the rulers were perfectly rational individuals who were exclusively concerned with the common good. But people are not like that (and neither are apes, not even the greatest of them). A class holding complete power is more likely to act like the orangutans on the Planet of the Apes.

The orangutans rule ape society with an iron paw, honoring themselves and silencing all dissent. When the chimpanzee Dr. Galen complains about his lack of professional advancement (presumably, he's being paid peanuts), he reminds his colleague Zira that she promised to speak to Dr. Zaius on his behalf. She answers, "I did. You know how he looks down his nose at chimpanzees." Zaius demands to be addressed as "Your Excellency" and "Sir" by lesser primates, yet may not even acknowledge their greetings. Far from being paragons of justice, the orangutans show no sense of justice at all in their dealings with Taylor, or with the chimpanzees Zira and Cornelius, whose careers are endangered just for offering a defense of Taylor in court.

Plato's blindness to the corrupting influence of power was inflicted in part by his desire for a unified theory of justice that described both what it is for a society to be just and what it is for a person to be just. Plato claimed that a person's soul has three parts: reason, which supplies our rational abilities; spirit, which craves honor and victory; and appetite, which supplies our non-intellectual desires—our cravings for things like food, alcohol, sex, and material possessions. A person is just when these parts of the soul stand in the right relationship to one another. The rational part of the mind must be in control of the appetites, using the spirit to suppress these base urges.

Just as justice in the soul consists in the right relationship between these elements, so Plato believes that justice in a society consists in the proper relationship between people whose nature is primarily rational, those whose nature is primarily honor-driven, and those whose nature is primarily appetitive. Thus the rational people are placed in the ruling class to rule, the spirited people are placed in the warrior class to enforce the rule of reason, and the appetitive people, people who yearn for physical pleasures and material possessions, are placed in the lowest class to be ordered about and controlled by wiser individuals.

We're surely all familiar with the feeling of forces, some-thing like this, battling over our will as we decide between the right course of action and the easiest one. When Zira urges Cornelius to go public with evidence that will show the sacred scrolls to be "not worth their parchment," his prime concern is the implications for his own appetitive desires: "We both have fine futures. Marriage. Stimulating careers. I'm up for a raise." It is interesting that the last straw that finally drives Taylor into violent rebellion is likewise a threat to his appetitive life—Dr. Zaius is going to have him gelded. By this point, Taylor has already stoically endured the curtailing of his rational life, as he is left unable to communicate and confined without intel-lectual stimulation. He has also patiently suffered the subju-gation of his honor, being reduced not even to a slave but to a mere animal to be gawked at in a cage and led around on a leash. But when the monkeys come for his nuts, he finally goes berserk and fights back—only the wound to his throat that ren-ders him mute robs us of hearing Charlton Heston rage "Take your stinking paws off *my balls,* you damned dirty ape!"

However, Plato's analogy between justice in a soul and jus-tice in a society fails. The rational elements of the soul are, by definition, completely rational. But even people of a rational nature have other strong elements to their nature too. Their reason can be swept aside by greed or pride or compassion or personal attachment, or any of the other temptations that ruin our best intentions. Plato believed that the rulers could avoid believing falsehoods or falling into vice because they would be dedicated to reason. The mere fact that they are philosophers would ensure that they will never be "money-loving, slavish, a boaster, or a coward" or in any way unreliable or unjust (lines 486b6–7).

Yet *Planet of the Apes* illustrates how easily even reason can become twisted in the service of vested interests. Dr. Honorius's attempts at reasoning convince him that Taylor cannot reason at all, just because Taylor cannot recite the second article of the ape's faith or offer the traditional justifications for the beliefs that all apes are created equal and that humans have no souls. Honorius's conception of what reason dictates has become inseparable from the religious dogma on which ape society is founded. He appeals to "reason" even as he throws reason to the wind and falls back on holy law.

The temptation to be overcome by pride and to assume your own infallibility must surely be greatest when your rule is backed by divine sanction and your wisdom presented as being the wisdom of God. It is presumably the hubris of acting as spokesapes for God that drives the orangutans' authoritarian approach to government. That same hubris can be found in Plato's *Republic*. Even putting aside the fact that the rulers claim nature selected them to rule by putting gold in their souls, the very highest offices in government are only open to those who have had the experience of seeing through the ephemeral material world to the true, immaterial reality beyond it, where they apprehend perfection itself. As Plato puts it, they must be "compelled to lift up the radiant light of their souls to what itself provides light for everything . . . the good itself." In theory, this is all achieved through the application of reason, but it has more of the character of mystical revelation than reasoned argument. Having a class of officially enlightened individuals in charge of government is a recipe for blind obstinacy. How do you convince someone that they're wrong when they believe that they have glimpsed ultimate truth and you haven't?

Planet of the Humans

Plato makes some insightful criticisms of democracy. Democracy is, as Plato recognized, government by people who are largely ignorant about matters related to government. In the modern US, few members of the public have a firm grasp of international history, economic theory, ecology, or military strategy; yet it is these people who ultimately determine whether the US supports the United Nations, whether taxes should be lowered or raised, what environmental regulations will be put into place, and whether the US should go to war.

Even if we assume that the electorate is perfectly rational, they still know almost nothing about the important issues on which they must decide. On the face of it, it looks like a crazy system. Yet democracy has the great advantage that when our leaders become too oppressive to bear, we have a mechanism for removing them from office that does not require sticking anybody with iron spears. Plato was too optimistic about the ability of a small group in power to rule without favoring their own interests, but it is a fact of life that people in power often become corrupted by greed or pride to the point that they need to be replaced.

Plato can be forgiven for not having observed how useful democracy can be for keeping the worst people out of power. We have two and a half thousand years more of history to look back on. In Plato's day, democracy had been a novel experiment, and one in which the Athenian people used the power they were given to settle old political grudges and to squeeze Athens's military allies for money by turning an agreement on international naval cooperation into a protection racket. Democracy is no guarantee of good conduct, and at that point in history, had yet to prove itself as a force for good.

Arguably, democracy has *still* not shown whether it will ultimately be a force for good. The grim prediction of *Planet of the Apes* is that human civilization will wipe itself from the world, leaving only roaming tribes of mute gatherers and a half-buried Statue of Liberty to mark that we were ever there. (What did the apes make of that half-buried statue? Was it an ancient human advertisement for torches or a memorial to a heroic arsonist?)

On the Planet of the Apes, the orangutans oppress the chimpanzees, but here on modern Earth it is the appetitive souls, those who hunger for wealth and material possessions, who hold power. Plato's productive class provided the merchants in his perfect city, while the rulers, who have all political power, have no wealth. Yet wealth is political power everywhere that wealth exists and has been so for as long as wealth has existed. Plato recognized, to his dismay, that wealth rather than wisdom held sway in Athens. Likewise, in the modern world, politicians tend to be from wealthy families, and corporations donate billions of dollars to political parties to sway government policy. If making money makes you a chimpanzee, then in our own society, the chimpanzees are in charge. If we eventually find ourselves left like Taylor, standing on the beach and helplessly screaming "You Maniacs! You blew it up! Ah, damn you! God damn you all to hell!" they will have made monkeys of all of us.

11

From *Twilight Zone* to Forbidden Zone

Leslie Dale Feldman

Fear and isolation. A rocky and desolate planet. Is it the Stone Age? Just as the planet is bare, with no cosmetic shield, and the rocks comprise a dramatic, stark tableau, animal nature is played out and shown in all its ugly reality. There is nothing but the primeval—here, nature rules. But it is not a forgiving and kind nature, the nature of Bambi and the woodland nymphs. This is a state where war lurks and there is no assurance of peace, where every creature is a potential enemy to every other creature, surviving only by its own strength and guile, where there is "no culture of the earth, no navigation, no building, no arts, no letters, and worst of all a state of continual fear and danger."

In Six Months We'll Be Running This Planet

The opening scene of *Planet of the Apes*? No. This is from Chapter 13 of *Leviathan*. Written in the seventeenth century by the English political philosopher Thomas Hobbes, *Leviathan* describes the nature of humans, the origin of government, and what people are like in a "state of nature" where they have to fight for survival, punish the wicked, and in which true human nature is on display.

Humans, said Hobbes, are acquisitive, belligerent, competitive, and possessive. According to Hobbes, life in the state of nature is "solitary, poore, nasty, brutish, and short." Some time later, the Lawgiver said something eerily reminiscent of Hobbes: "Beware the beast Man, for his is the Devil's spawn.

Alone among God's primates, he kills for sport or lust or greed. Yea, he will murder his brother to possess his brother's land. Let him not breed in great numbers, for he will make a desert of his home and yours. Shun him."

A rocky and desolate scene in 3978 that is eventually revealed to be a civilization blown back to the state of nature—this is where the *Planet of the Apes* (1968) begins. But at first Taylor, an astronaut and time-traveler played by Charlton Heston, simply does not know. He is carrying a Geiger counter to measure radiation. Are there intelligent beings here? Are they ready to act on their worst instincts? Are they belligerent? Taylor asks "Does man, . . . who sent me to the stars, still make war against his brother?" Are these beings competitive and acquisitive? As one of the crew plants an American flag in the dirt, Taylor muses: "In six months we'll be running this planet."

We don't know whether Rod Serling, who wrote the original script for *Planet of the Apes*, ever read Hobbes, but he demonstrates much of the same negative view of human nature in it as he did in other work, including *The Twilight Zone* where greedy people cheat each other, there's no honor among thieves, and people are ready to believe the worst about their friends and neighbors—be they human or alien.

Fear, isolation, exploitation, and alienation are part of Serling's worldview, which explains his preoccupation with nuclear annihilation. We have only to look at such classic *Twilight Zone* episodes as "People Are Alike All Over" to see aliens acting toward Earthlings as Earthlings act toward animals in a zoo. When you see something different you put it in a cage—but unlike in "People Are Alike All Over," where Roddy McDowall was the Earthling in an alien zoo, this time he winds up on the other side of the cage as the primate Cornelius. Now it's his turn to put someone else in a cage, his turn to be the master.

This is Serling's view of human nature which, at times, is pessimistic but also, at times, optimistic. It represents an essential tension, a duality, in his thought that is demonstrated in *The Twilight Zone* and *Planet of the Apes*. "You thought life on Earth was meaningless—you despised people" Landon says to Taylor. But Taylor expresses the optimistic view that "somewhere in the universe there has to be something better than man." Both pessimist and optimist, Serling is the reluctant Hobbesian, or the hopeful pessimist.

The State of Nature

In *Planet of the Apes*, the state of nature is a state of war. As soon as Taylor and his two crew members land on the planet, and decide to take a swim, a war ensues. Their clothes are stolen and apes on horseback come with weapons and nets to scoop up and kill the natives, primitive humans, foraging for corn in the Apes' Green Belt and considered inferior by the apes. This is the Hobbesian "war of all against all" where there is a fight for resources—but more about that later.

In order to determine the origin of government Thomas Hobbes, a social contract theorist, imagined a so-called state of nature, a time before humans invented government. The purpose of the state of nature concept for the social contract theorists was twofold: to figure out how humans would act if there were no government or man-made laws, and to hypothesize the origin of government which they call the social contract. For instance, if humans were peacemakers and got along well, there would be less need for laws than if they were belligerent, competitive, and acquisitive.

But Hobbes said that if humans were acquisitive and belligerent in the state of nature then that would demonstrate their need for a government to rein in their belligerent and acquisitive impulses—that is, punish those who commit crimes. As Julius says of humans "they're natural born thieves, aren't they?" Dr. Zaius says man "is a warlike creature who gives battle to everything around him" and calls Taylor a killer.

A naturally born thieving race would require more laws and greater restrictions placed upon it by government than a naturally born altruistic race. As Plato noted in the story of the Ring of Gyges from *The Republic*: man only does right under compulsion; if two men, the "just" and the "unjust" were given a ring that made them invisible both the "just" and the "unjust" would make nefarious use of it. Therefore, according to Plato and Hobbes there are no "just" men, only those who act on the natural impulses of greed, belligerence, and fear.

In the *Planet of the Apes* Taylor and his fellow space-travelers land in a terrain which we can describe as the Hobbesian state of nature—a lawless place where there is complete freedom but also uncertainty as man has no rights under Ape law.

Human Nature?

For Rod Serling and the apes in *Planet of the Apes*, humans exhibit the same belligerent and acquisitive aspects of human nature that Hobbes and Plato described. When the apes conduct an interview with Taylor in a room that looks like it came right out of the *Flintstones* (particularly note the *Flintstones*-inspired door) they show him a map which looks like Long Island and the New York City metropolitan area. At the inquest, Taylor says that he is from Fort Wayne, Indiana. Dr. Zaius says that even in Taylor's lies there is truth: the selection of the name of a town with a Fort reveals Taylor's—and man's—belligerent nature.

Humans fight for three reasons according to Hobbes: competition, fear and glory. This sounds like the Twenty-Ninth Scroll, Sixth Verse of the sacred scrolls recited by Dr. Zaius: "Beware the beast man. . . . alone among God's primates he kills for sport, or lust or greed." This belligerence causes the state of nature to be a "war of all against all" which is demonstrated as soon as Taylor and his friends encounter the apes.

According to "reverse evolution" the apes have taken on these human traits in what Taylor calls an "upside-down civilization." Taylor competes with the apes, fights with them, accuses them of being afraid of him. He wants to prove the theory of reverse evolution so that he can have glory—the glory that humans were there first and were a superior race to the apes. But were they? Are humans generous to other creatures? Are they generous to other humans? Are they champions of equality? Are they fearless? Are they pacifists? No. Taylor asks fellow astronaut Landon why he signed up for the mission then says "oh, I know. Glory." This reinforces the Hobbesian characterization of the selfish and self-interested nature of humans.

The apes have all the negative characteristics of humans including prejudice, competition, and belligerence. The joke is that the apes are no better than the humans—but certainly no worse. Humans treat weaker creatures badly, they make war and compete with each other. For Hobbes, these traits are innate, necessitating the origin of government. Serling suggests the same in *Planet of the Apes*—the apes did not learn these traits from humans because they did not know humans. Landon says "we got off at the wrong stop" but there is one thing humans do that apes are not shown doing: they kill each other. *Planet of the Apes* depicts the apes fighting humans, but not other apes.

In addition to war, discrimination is on display in *Planet of the Apes*. The Apes wear different color outfits to signify their station and prestige—Dr. Zaius and the established orangutan apes wear orange outfits (possibly to signify orange-utan), Zira and Cornelius wear green outfits, and the military gorillas wear dark purple outfits. Zira and Cornelius mention a quota for lowly chimpanzees who are looked down upon. Other creatures, notably the primitive humans and Taylor, are put in cages, experimented on in labs, shot at, and put in the museum. Man's inhumanity to man and ape's inhumanity to man: both bespeak a pessimistic view.

Human See, Human Do

Alexis de Tocqueville, the nineteenth-century French observer of America, warned of the dangers of conformity in *Democracy in America*. He called it the "tyranny of the majority." Tocqueville said that in America, the majority would act as an invisible force that would compel everyone to agree on political and social issues.

According to Tocqueville "in America the majority raises formidable barriers around the liberty of opinion" which creates an environment that does not allow independent thinking or real freedom of speech. Tocqueville said "thought is an invisible and subtle power" that mocks all previous attempts of monarchs to suppress ideas—because with tyranny of the majority you can't have an independent thought.

This is demonstrated in *Planet of the Apes* where the evidence of human civilization in the cave discovered by Cornelius is suppressed, because that would prove the theory of reverse evolution—that ape society evolved from a sophisticated human society that existed before them. Out of pride and glory Dr. Zaius doesn't want this revealed. We see elements of this throughout *Planet of the Apes*, when Taylor writes a message in the dirt in his cage and Dr. Zaius erases it, and again with Dr. Zaius's order to blow up the cave that holds the evidence of the earlier human civilization, evidence that would support Cornelius's hypothesis.

As Rousseau said "Man is born free; and everywhere he is in chains." In the *Discourse on the Origin of Inequality* Rousseau also spoke of the practice of head binding by the Oroonoko Indians which would enable humans to retain some of their original ignorance and happiness. This is what Dr. Zaius attempts to do: keep the apes and the humans ignorant, dramatically demonstrated by Landon's lobotomy. As Tocqueville says "what remains, but to spare them all the care of thinking?" Dr. Zaius is demonstrating his power and using it to stay on top in the belligerent Hobbesian power struggle.

Zone-isms

Planet of the Apes includes several notable Serling devices that had been used in *The Twilight Zone* (1959–64) including the play on beauty and ugliness, the use of the cave as a source of magic, the Adam and Eve theme, and the twist ending that plays on the question "Which planet are we on?" Nuclear war is a political theme that also figures prominently in *Planet of the Apes* and *The Twilight Zone*.

There are frequent references in *The Twilight Zone* to men blowing themselves up via nuclear war (in episodes like "Time Enough at Last," "Third from the Sun," "The Shelter," and others) and in *Planet of the Apes* Taylor walks around with a Geiger counter imagining that the stone age world he sees when he lands on the planet of the apes perhaps came out of nuclear war. *The Twilight Zone* episode "Time Enough at Last" features Burgess Meredith who sits in a pile of rubble at a library after a nuclear war and then breaks his glasses. This scene looks very much like the terrain in the *Planet of the Apes*.

Serling was preoccupied with nuclear war in other *Twilight Zone* episodes like "Third from the Sun" where a nuclear war is about to take place so a family must leave its planet, which we assume to be Earth, and go to another planet—it's only when they are on the spaceship to the "other" planet that we learn that they are headed to "a place called Earth." This twist is echoed in the ending to *Planet of the Apes* when Taylor sees first the crown of the Statue of Liberty, then the rest of the statue, and realizes he is on Earth. There was a foreshadowing of this earlier—where the map the apes show Taylor looks like Long Island, the Hudson River, and the New York City environs.

Serling was a member of an anti-nuclear group in Hollywood in the 1950s and "Time Enough at Last" features the bomb exploding on television. Even though you don't see the actual explosion, you see the result: a pile of rubble of man's own making. In a speech at Moorpark College in California in 1968, the same year *Planet of the Apes* was made, Serling said: "I think the destiny of all men is not to sit in the rubble of their own making but to reach out for an ultimate perfection which is to be had. At the moment it is a dream. . . . But we have it within our power to make it a reality."

This points to a tension in Serling's thought. Is he a pessimist or an optimist? It's hard to tell because he switches gears and just when you think you have him figured out he pulls, as he liked to say, in the parlance of *The Twilight Zone*, "the old switcheroo."

Along with the theme of nuclear apocalypse Serling uses the Garden of Eden and Adam and Eve theme in both *Planet of the Apes* and *The Twilight Zone.* Two *Twilight Zone* episodes in particular, "Two" and "Probe 7: Over and Out," depict Adam and Eve characters who survive nuclear war and who wander off together presumably to repopulate the race. Taylor mentions that Stewart, the female astronaut who does not survive the trip because of an air leak in her protective gear (a technique also used in *The Twilight Zone* episode "The Rip Van Winkle Caper") was to be the new Eve. This is also the final scene in *Planet of the Apes*, where Taylor and Nova (reminiscent of "Norda," the name of the woman in "Probe 7") ride off on horseback along the beach. Is this a scene of optimism or pessimism? Let's think about that. . . .

The cave as a source of magic and confusion is a theme from Plato's *Republic* (see "Banana Republic" in the present volume), where the allegorical cave imprisons the ignorant and fills them with deceptive but entertaining images that distract them from reality. In *The Twilight Zone* Serling used the cave variously to depict ignorance, as in "On Thursday We Leave for Home," and wisdom, as in "The Old Man in the Cave." Similarly, in *Planet of the Apes* the action culminates in the cave, which contains the proof of previous human civilization (false teeth, eyeglasses) that could exonerate Cornelius (played by Roddy McDowall, a frequent *Twilight Zone* player) of heresy but Dr. Zaius wants to seal it up to eliminate the proof and keep the society ignorant of the doctrine of reverse evolution.

Beauty and ugliness are also in the "Eye of the Beholder," a *Twilight Zone* episode, and in *Planet of the Apes*. The "Eye of the Beholder" twists ugliness and beauty with hideous doctors performing plastic surgery on Donna Douglas, the actress who played "Elly May" on *The Beverly Hillbillies*. Wait a minute—we thought she was beautiful! Remember how Sonny Drysdale looked at her? But not in Serling's world, where prejudice against others is commonplace, conformity is essential, and beauty is relative. In the *Planet of the Apes* Zira likes Taylor and calls him Bright Eyes. Taylor says he wants to kiss Zira. She says she'll do it in spite of the fact that he's so ugly. But this is Charlton Heston—a movie star! An upside-down world indeed.

Westward, Ho*(mo sapiens)*

The westward escape of Taylor and Nova in covered wagons mimics the American pioneers going west and the theme of the New Frontier. According to Frederick Jackson Turner and the "Frontier thesis" of Manifest Destiny (which he wrote about in his 1893 essay *The Significance of the Frontier in American History*), Americans would conquer and cultivate the West. Turner said the frontier encouraged American values of independence, hard work, bravery, and common sense.

In *Planet of the Apes* Taylor is an American pioneer, re-creating the westward movement of the pioneers when he sets off with Nova on horseback to establish new territory and a new civilization. So the cycle goes: human—ape—human. Or, possibly, the humans and apes can do an "Eastside/Westside" and see who blows whom up first.

The theme of the New Frontier was popular in the 1960s because of its prominence in John F. Kennedy's speech on July 15th, 1960, when he accepted the Democratic nomination for president. In the speech JFK called for "new pioneers" on a "new frontier" that included science and technology, particularly space. Speaking in Los Angeles he said "For I stand here tonight facing West on what was once the last frontier. . . . the pioneers gave up their safety, their comfort, and sometimes their lives to build our new West. . . . Some would say that those struggles are all over . . . that there is no longer an American frontier. . . . But . . . we stand today on the edge of a New Frontier . . . the frontier of unknown opportunities and perils, the frontier of unfilled hopes and unfilled threats . . . the New Frontier."

Rod Serling was a Kennedy supporter. In 1963 he served as a "goodwill ambassador" of the Kennedy administration to Australia and the South Pacific and in 1964 was asked by the United States government to make a documentary about the Kennedy assassination. If Kennedy was an optimist (his idea of sending a man to the moon seemed "space-age" at the time) so was Serling—an idealist. Both dreamed of the "new frontier" but both also feared the Hobbesian nuclear war. It was during the Kennedy administration that Americans hunkered down in bomb shelters, echoing the time they sat in front of their TV sets to watch the classic depiction of nuclear war in "Time Enough at Last" on *The Twilight Zone*.

The Fellowship of the Holy Fallout

Beneath the Planet of the Apes, the 1970 sequel to *Planet of the Apes*, continues the theme of nuclear war with the constant rejoinder that belligerent man makes a desert of a city. Here, James Franciscus stars as the astronaut Brent, who goes to the Planet of the Apes looking for Taylor. This is perfect casting, as James Franciscus looks like Charlton Heston's younger brother and he maintains a perfect hairdo after crash landing on the planet.

The apes continue to take on the human traits of belligerence and acquisitiveness while talking about power and invading territory. Peace activists and demonstrators are locked up in jail. The "beneath" in *Beneath the Planet of the Apes* refers to the New York City subway after the city has been annihilated by nuclear war. Brent echoes Taylor's line that they "did it" and blew up Earth. But "beneath" also refers to a chapel below ground in the Forbidden Zone where mutant humans worship a nuclear bomb, which they call the weapon of peace or deterrence. Their underground worship of the bomb mimics the *Twilight Zone* episode "One More Pallbearer" which also combines nuclear war and a cave. This is the "Fellowship of the Holy Fallout" reminiscent of the themes of good and evil played beneath Toyland in Laurel and Hardy's *March of the Wooden*

Soldiers. And Dr. Zaius is right—the apes don't press the button, man does.

Landon says "We got off at the wrong stop" but there's no right stop because in two thousand years, nothing has changed. The optimism of Taylor and Nova on the horse, the pessimism of the Statue of Liberty—represent the two sides of Serling's view of human nature. But all is not lost—perhaps in place of the Statue of Liberty there'll be a "life-size bronze statue" of Taylor and Nova on their horse as the new George and Martha Washington—riding into the sunset to found a new frontier. The statue's head is still intact symbolizing hope for the future and the creativity to start again—in Tom Paine's words to "make the world over."

12
The Primate Who Knew Too Much

MICHAEL RUSE

You have to feel affection and respect for *Planet of the Apes*. How else do you regard a movie that takes the superstar Charlton Heston—he of Moses, Ben Hur, Michelangelo—and puts him in the lead role of a swaggering astronaut, and then promises his character castration in the name of scientific research?

But truly, apart from the chuckle that that always sparks, especially among those of us old enough to remember Heston in his prime, *Planet of the Apes* is the gift that keeps on giving. I show it almost every year in my Philosophy and Film course that I offer to our honors program students, and at each showing the students enthuse and I get something more to ponder. And this all apart from the fact that it is a rattling good story, moving to one of the greatest endings in the history of cinema, the discovery—I guess there's no need for a spoiler alert here—that the spaceship has in fact returned to a future Earth, one made desolate by human power and stupidity.

I'm a philosopher and as a philosopher I look at movies for what I can extract. Well, not always. I have tried to kid myself and my students that I watch my favorite zombie movie, *Shaun of the Dead*, for insights into the body-mind problem. But I'm lying really. I look at *Shaun of the Dead* for the blood and gore and whatever—although come to think of it, isn't there a philosophical problem about an aging professor like me, who never served in the military or the police, actually enjoying a movie where most of the characters go around covered in tomato ketchup from head to toe?

However, I do try to look at movies philosophically and not just those movies that cry out for such a treatment—Ingmar Bergman's *The Seventh Seal* for instance. And I find material in many unexpected places. The cowboy movie *Shane* seems to me to have the greatest portrayal I have ever seen of a figure faced with an existential crisis—"a man's got to do what a man's got to do." (Actually the line is: "A man has to be what he is, Joey. You can't break the mold. I tried it and it didn't work for me."). Of course, *Shane* is helped by the fact that it has the biggest badass in the history of cinema—black-clad Jack Palance brought to town for the ultimate shootout.

Who's on Top

But back to *Planet of the Apes*. For me as a philosopher of science, one who specializes in evolutionary theory, the obvious issues are about evolution, specifically with respect to progress and degeneration. Will evolution always push upwards? Suppose humans mess it all up and become pathetic shadows of their former selves—similar themes are explored in the movie based on H.G. Wells's story the *Time Machine*—does this mean that other organisms will move in? As it happens, this is a very hotly contested issue today among evolutionists, some (like Simon Conway-Morris, paleontologist of the Burgess Shale) thinking that we will rise again, or if not us some facsimile, and others (like the late Stephen Jay Gould, paleontologist and popular writer) thinking that degeneration and extinction are for keeps. Once we're gone, that's it.

Planet of the Apes, with its subpar humans and its intelligent apes, plunges us right into this debate. And as a bonus, there are all of the racial issues that it raises. The gorillas, the black thugs of the movie. The chimpanzees, the highstrung, intelligent, but in some respects childlike actors in the drama. And the orangutans, in charge and confident that they should be in charge. This in fact is all a bit ironic, because phylogenetically we know that orangutans are off to one side a bit and not quite as bright as the others, with chimps, gorillas, and humans all going it alone, until the gorillas go their way and then finally comes the human-chimp split. We also know that orangutans are a bit anti-social so they would not have functioned well in a society. And finally we know that the pygmy chimpanzees, the bonobos, obviously the species of this movie, spend huge amounts of their time copulating. This is how they form social bonds. Hugh Hefner would be a celibate compared to the average member of a bonobo troop. I doubt that the two chimp heroes, Zira and Cornelius, would have had time or inclination for much scientific investigation.

Dangerous Knowledge

But there are other things raised in the movie, and I want here to think about the topic of forbidden knowledge. It's one of the themes that emerges later in the movie, and, you'll remember, is focused on the Forbidden Zone, that area outside the ape-occupied territory that is under taboo and where no self-respecting primate is allowed to go. It turns out that Cornelius has already visited the Zone and in a cave found artifacts that he does not know or understand. He takes the Heston figure ("Taylor") and his girlfriend Nova to the cave, where they encounter the leader of the orangs, Dr. Zaius, who it turns out, knows exactly what's going on and what the significance of the artifacts in the cave is. As Taylor identifies and ponders over them—dentures, spectacles, a child's doll—Zaius explains that they are evidence of a long-ago human civilization that destroyed itself and its land.

The Forbidden Zone, now desolate desert, used to be a land of milk and honey. He knows this and is determined to keep it secret: the possibilities it opens up of repetition are too dangerous. As the movie ends, Zaius blocks off the cave once and for all and at the same time the truth of his claims about human madness are made apparent. Taylor discovers that humans had indeed destroyed their own world.

This whole question of dangerous knowledge, knowledge that should be banned and not explored or exploited, was not new to cinema (*Planet of the Apes* appeared in 1968). World War II, and in particular the discovery, building, and use of atomic power for weapons, hovered over a generation. It was bad enough that we in the West had such knowledge, but then the Soviets got it too (admittedly mainly through spies and traitors from the West) and that really was dreadful. As it happens, that time around, it led to the Cold War and a standoff, but it wasn't much fun. And so naturally it led to the movie theaters.

One particularly striking early movie was *The Day the Earth Stood Still*. Here the theme was not so much the use of dangerous knowledge but the threat that it posed. In this particular case, other extra-terrestrial intelligent beings decided that humans were a threat to everyone and so a stern warning was issued to Earth about the consequences if it was so foolish as to use its knowledge.

Another striking movie was the Japanese film *Godzilla*. Here atomic testing had brought about threats and destruction through the creation of a monster from the sea. Clearly a metaphor for the atomic destruction itself, Godzilla wreaks devastation on the cities of Japan, causing untold harm to the people, especially children. The monster is stopped by a heroic scientist who has discovered a way of depriving matter of oxygen. The scientist dies in the act of killing Godzilla and, as important, intentionally through his death destroys his own knowledge about his own discovery. A present and a future threat are simultaneously eliminated.

There are other examples on or around the theme. But the point is made; or rather the issue is raised. Knowledge can be extremely dangerous. Should we therefore, following Dr. Zaius, rule certain kinds of knowledge off limits? Meaning, presumably, that people should not be encouraged or should even be forbidden to follow certain lines of inquiry, and if such knowledge is acquired it should not be disseminated. It should rather be sequestered and perhaps even destroyed. Knowledge is in a very important sense a virus—not a meme, as Richard Dawkins has suggested, and thus something that infects minds—but in the sense of something very dangerous, like smallpox. It spreads and can harm. Better therefore to nip it in the bud or to contain and destroy it. Not all knowledge, obviously, like not all viruses, obviously. But knowledge and viruses that are dangers to humankind.

The Specter of Frankenvirus

I don't think this is a silly position to take. Knowledge can be dangerous. Nuclear weapons show this only too clearly. But the problem is not confined to physics. In the 1970s, molecular biology came to the fore. As Stephen Stich has discussed, the new techniques of recombinant DNA (rDNA), where one could shift genes around, shift the parts of genes around, move genes from one organism to another very different, and all of these things that came from our new understanding of the molecules of life—understanding that dates famously to the discovery in 1953 of the double helix, the structure of the DNA molecule—seemed to threaten human safety. Could some mad dictator—as I remember, Idi Amin was just then doing his worst in Uganda—run up a poison organism on the cheap, something that could go in an aerosol or be popped into the water supply? Concerns have also been raised about unforeseen and unintended consequences of gene therapy and genetic enhancement—some of which come to fruition in *Rise of the Planet of the Apes*.

As it happens, over the rDNA issue, saner heads soon prevailed. The people who delighted in running up ghastly scenarios, especially on the national evening news shows, tended to be laboratory-bench scientists. That is to say, people who had not the faintest idea about epidemiology, as Bernard Davis has pointed out. As soon as the relevant experts weighed in, it was realized just how difficult it is to make a Frankenvirus and the big worries subsided. Not that there was no danger or that the danger from biology has lessened. In 2012 there was concern about research on the bird flu virus and whether the results could end in lasting harm. Scientists agreed to pause their research for a while, although it picked up again later. As Donald G. McNeil reported in the *New York Times*, matters were not helped by the comments of one of the lead scientists:

> Some of the early alarm was fed by Dr. Fouchier speaking at conferences and giving interviews last fall in which he boasted that he had "done something really, really stupid" and had "mutated the hell out of H5N1" to create something that was "very, very bad news." He said his team had created "probably one of the most dangerous viruses you can make."

Fouchier said afterwards that his comments had been overblown and taken out of context. That is a little bit like Jerry Sandusky saying that his activities in the showers were only spurred by hygiene issues to do with boys' bottoms.

One can also think of ways in which knowledge from the social sciences can be dangerous. The 2012 presidential elec-

tion showed very clearly that those interested in polls—fore-
casting results, spotting points of weakness, suggesting moves
to improve standings—have reached a level of sophistication
never seen before. (At least, those on the winning side have
reached such a level!) One might well think that, even if your
candidate did well this time around, the knowledge acquired
could be very dangerous in the wrong hands. Manipulation of
people's intentions is easy given the right tools. The Nazis
showed us this. Imagine if a present-day Dr. Goebbels with present-day techniques and knowledge got involved in matters.

So let's agree that knowledge can be dangerous and that
this is a serious problem. I think that over the years we've
grown so used to the nuclear threat that we don't worry as
much as Rod Serling did when writing the *Planet of the Apes*
screenplay. Also the fall of the Soviet empire should be factored
in. But the threat is certainly there, and perhaps—worry or
not—even worse. It was one thing for the Soviets to have
nuclear bombs. It's a very different thing that the North
Koreans have the bomb. And if Iran gets the bomb, what price
a little flare-up with Israel?

Ban the Books?

What should we do about such knowledge? One obvious solution is that of Dr. Zaius. Stop the inquiry right now and lock up
anything we've already discovered. Just declare the topic off
limits. This was the kind of position that used to be taken by
people like Harvard geneticist Richard Lewontin in the 1970s,
as Ullica Segerstrale discusses in *The Sociobiology Debate*.
Work on areas like the sociobiology of humans, that is to say
work on the underlying, selection-fashioned, genetic nature of
humans—can only lead to prejudice and harm—Jews, women,
and blacks being declared inferior and that sort of thing—so
stop it, ban it, right now. But things are not quite this simple
and there are two immediate and obvious responses.

First, it's all very well saying that we should stop inquiry
and shut away that which has already been done, but that is a
lot easier said than done. As soon as the Americans had the
knowledge to make the atomic bomb, it was leaked to Russia,
and we have seen similar patterns since. The Pakistani scientist who gave secrets to North Korea and other countries comes

at once to mind. Especially in this day and age of the Internet and other means of instant communication, it's really implausible to suggest that anything can really be kept secret for all that long. It doesn't follow that having the knowledge means you can do anything with it, but as North Korea shows—possessing both the Bomb and intercontinental missiles—poverty-stricken, despot-ruled groups, with enough desire, can go a long way, longer than most of the rest of us would want.

Second, there are good pragmatic reasons why we might want to extend and expand the knowledge that we already have. Suppose someone has made, or knows how to make, some particularly dangerous organism. I certainly would want more research on the topic, to find out if this organism is a one-off or part of a series. I would want more research to find out whether the organism could be countered, perhaps by artificially manufactured predators or parasites. I would want . . . Well, you can see how the discussion goes. Having gone this far, the last thing I would want is a ceasing of all activity in this direction. If anything, we might make the case for increased effort, at least for a while.

New Knowledge Is Good in Itself

Simply trying to contain new knowledge, the Dr. Zaius approach, might be problematic—perhaps both impossible and undesirable. There's also the other side to the matter, whether in principle we should ever restrain the search for new knowledge, including especially new empirical knowledge. "And ye shall know the truth, and the truth shall make you free" (John 8:32). Is there not something inherently good about the search for knowledge, whatever the consequences? At a glance, I'm inclined to think that there is.

Would I want to stop a biologist looking at the reproductive behavior of a new species of lizard? Would I want to stop a mathematician deriving a new theorem? Would I want to stop a philosopher finding a new proof for the existence of God? If I were footing the bill, I might be a little wary of signing a blank check. I rather doubt that, at this stage of the debate, anyone is going to come up with much new in the God proof business—although perhaps enthusiasts for the anthropic principle would disagree. That discussion is over whether the physical

laws of nature are so exactly tuned and necessary for the existence of life that they cannot be pure chance. As best I know,
this is a fairly recent discussion—see Barrow and Tipler's 1986
The Anthropic Cosmological Principle—although perhaps it
had a precursor in some speculation by the Scottish philosopher David Hume in his *Dialogues Concerning Natural
Religion* (1779).

The Doubtful Cases

I'm not entirely sure that all search for knowledge is necessary.
Suppose somebody wanted to see if having a large nose is
genetically linked to being sharp in business. I confess I would
be very wary of this, suspecting anti-Semitism somewhere
down the line. Although perhaps the issue here is not the
knowledge as such but the search for it, and my feeling both
that (from what we know about genetics) it's highly improbable
that such a link exists and that someone engaged in such an
inquiry is motivated by less than admirable intentions. I realize however that at this point I'm walking on thin ice that may
give way to controversy.

Many gays are worried about the possible effects of
research into the genetic basis of sexual orientation—find a
gay gene and the next thing is that we're into selective abortion against such genes and gays become unfortunate people
whose parents were too lazy to get the appropriate genetic
counseling. On the other hand, we might argue that knowing
about the genetic bases of sexual orientation could be another
nail in the coffin of thinking that gay people have made a
deliberate decision not to live the life and thoughts of hetero-
sexuals: yet another reason to ignore Saint Paul's admonitions
on the subject.

My general feeling therefore is that knowledge is a good
thing and the search for knowledge is consequently a good
thing. So overall therefore on both pragmatic and intellectual
grounds I'm opposed to Dr. Zaius. But I can see that sometimes
it might be necessary to make a special case for the knowledge
search, especially if it's expensive or inconvenient and there is
no good reason to cherish whatever knowledge might be discovered. Even more is it necessary to make a special case when
there are prima facie reasons to think that a proposed search

seems unlikely to prove profitable and may well be motivated by less than seemly factors.

However there is one uncomfortable thought that does strike me. It does tie in rather nicely with what I said was part of the main message I extract from the *Planet of the Apes*.

I said that I found the movie stimulating (and fun to teach) because of the assumptions about the nature and course of evolution. Humans were clearly top dogs—or primates rather—and then they messed things up and the apes stepped into their place. Evolution is ever pushing upwards and the top position will be occupied and reoccupied as it becomes vacant. But what is the top position? Humans yesterday, apes today, who knows what tomorrow? The lurking question is whether this is the limit, the highest possible point of evolution. If the apes could move up the ladder from a lower status to a higher status, does this imply that that is the upper point of evolution? Surely not! Could not the apes, or if not the apes some other animal on the ladder, just keep climbing and so at some point in the future we will get super-beings? Isn't this at least implied or presupposed in the movie?

I think it is, but I think something else important is not so much implied as flung right in our faces. The kind of animals that humans are (or, in the movie, were) does not bolster confidence in our emotional or social stability. Humans blew up their civilization! We evolved as social beings but not as perfect social beings. We are the products of evolution which means that we are as good as we need to be, at least until a new factor intrudes. In this case, the frightening new scientific knowledge and the appalling possible technology-fired consequences. In the *Planet of the Apes*, making the fairly reasonable assumption that a perfect society would not blow itself to bits, humans' abilities to find new knowledge is balanced by—or more precisely tipped over by—humans' inabilities to function as a perfect social society.

Dr. Zaius knows this. "You are right, I have always known about man. From the evidence, I believe his wisdom must walk hand and hand with his idiocy. His emotions must rule his brain. He must be a warlike creature who gives battle to everything around him, even himself." Moreover, given Dr. Zaius's determination to suppress the dangerous knowledge, the movie rather suggests that now that the apes have taken over things are not much improved in that direction. There are still tensions and conflicts. (It is interesting to compare this with *The Day the Earth Stood Still*. In themselves the aliens may not be socially perfect, but they have put themselves under the suzerainty of robots that ensure that they will behave in a socially perfect way.)

We're Doomed Anyway

What this all suggests to me is something that I suspect is really true. The search through the galaxies for super beings is probably doomed to failure. Humanoids—human-like beings—may have evolved again and again. But the success carries the seeds of failure or at least of limitation. We have evolved big brains because biologically that is a good thing to have. We have also evolved socially because biologically that is a good thing to do. My suspicion (and this would be shared by today's evolutionary psychologists) is that the two are connected. While intelligence is very important for exploring the world around us, it's also very important for dealing with our fellow humans. And there is probably a cause and effect situation here. As I have argued in *The Philosophy of Human Evolution*, those who were better socially were brighter and the brightness led to being better socially.

However neither intelligence nor sociality is an absolute. We're as good as we need be to get along. In fact biologists point out that neither is necessarily the best in a certain situation. Having big brains requires lots of high-quality fuel, that is to say lots of protein, and getting this (in the old days at least meaning getting large chunks of dead animal) is expensive in itself. If food is scarce, you might be better off on an all-grass diet even if the cost is being intellectually challenged. In the immortal words of the paleontologist, the late Jack Sepkoski, whom I interviewed for *Monad to Man*: "I see intelligence as just one of a variety of adaptations among tetrapods for survival. Running fast in a herd while being as dumb as shit, I think, is a very good adaptation for survival."

I suspect therefore that the *Planet of the Apes* scenario may repeat itself again and again. In the universe as a whole, humanoids with the intelligence to find weapons of mass destruction may well appear on a regular basis. (I myself am not sure how often this would happen, but let's assume that in a universe big enough it does occur repeatedly.) But that is a threshold, and the social nature of these humanoids will only keep things in the air for so long. Today, tomorrow, sometime in the future, someone will use the knowledge to destroy the humanoid civilization and resting place. This will happen before there has been much more rise in the humanoid intelligence.

You think I exaggerate? In real life we have had nuclear knowledge for less than a hundred years. Already the most civilized of us all have been prepared to use it against others. Does anyone truly think that in the next twenty thousand years—a blink in the evolutionary timescale—in a world that already contains North Korea, the knowledge will never be used again? If you honestly think that within the next million years we shall not have destroyed ourselves, then let me tell you that I have a bridge for sale that might interest you.

So I see the chief message of *Planet of the Apes* as being that human civilization as we know it is not likely to survive. With great knowledge comes great responsibility and frankly we are probably not up to the task. Beneath the surface of a stirring adventure story, laced with humor—who can forget the response of Zira when she's expected to kiss Taylor: "Alright, but you're so damned ugly!"—is a grim explication of the awful human situation.

VI

Ape Ethics

13
Captive Kin

Lori Gruen

In fourth grade, I pretended to get sick the day my class went on a field trip to the zoo. For as long as I can remember, I've been drawn to other animals, but zoos made me sad. The animals seemed bored or silly or uncomfortable. They seemed to me to be misunderstood and as a child I too felt misunderstood. Sometimes I identified more with animals than with humans.

I hadn't seen *Planet of the Apes* yet when I was in grade school, I had to wait until I was a bit older. When I first saw it I was terrified by it—all of the apes, the humans, the gorillas, the chimpanzees, and the orangutans were behaving in ways that were so frightening. But I also like being scared so I saw the movie as often as I could.

Looking back, I think what scared me the most about that original movie (and also what thrilled me so much about *Rise of Planet of the Apes*, but more about that in a bit) was thinking about being locked in a cage, unable to communicate with the captors. When I imagine myself in the position of Taylor, who had been shot in the throat before he was captured and now could not communicate his desires, I feel frustrated, angry, and also really scared.

In the movie, the ape captors thought he was just a dumb animal and he had to struggle, often futilely, to try to communicate that he was somebody—with likes and dislikes, fears and hopes and plans. He had a personality and thoughts and he could suffer. Yet he was treated as if none of this was even possible, his captors seemed unable to imagine that he was anything other than a struggling specimen, sort of like a bug captured in a jar. He had to suffer all sorts of physical assaults without being able to express his pain verbally, although he obvious expressed his displeasure in other ways. He also was subject to humiliations and other indignities. But then his voice came back and through language he was able to escape his captivity.

The Harm of Imprisonment

What Taylor experienced as a captive is similar to what some chimpanzees and other apes, including humans, actually experience in captivity today—although most captives are now kept in sterile, cement and steel enclosures, not the dirt and wood enclosures from *Planet of the Apes*. To hold someone captive is to deny him a variety of goods and to frustrate his interests in a variety of ways. Though captive situations usually vary, one thing about captivity is that it confines and controls those who are captive and makes captives reliant on those in control to satisfy their basic needs.

We tend to think that being held captive constitutes a harm. We justify holding humans captive when they have done something that warrants our depriving them of their freedom. Of course, imprisoning people harms them, but it may not be wrong to do so. Some of the incarcerated people I work with understand that they are being held captive because of what they did—they committed crimes and violated the social contract so are now being punished for their transgressions. But not everything they experience in captivity constitutes rightful punishment (for example, being denied contact with their children and families or being humiliated and degraded by prison guards) particularly in those cases, and there are many, in which the people who are incarcerated didn't really have genuine options when they committed their crimes.

While denying someone their freedom harms them, certain forms of captivity can sometimes be justified. But denying freedom to one who is innocent, who does nothing to deserve the deprivation, is much harder to justify. Taylor in *Planet of the Apes* and Caesar in *Rise of Planet of the Apes* did nothing to deserve being held captive. They were confined and controlled simply for who they were.

I couldn't help but be reminded of the actual harms that captivity causes chimpanzees while watching *Rise of the Planet of the Apes*. There are currently four research laboratories experimenting on chimpanzees (they may be the only four in the world, as the US and Gabon are the only countries that still experiment on chimpanzees). In these labs, chimpanzees may be shot with tranquilizer darts from close range, causing them to then fall from their perches onto the hard floor as they start to lose consciousness, some chimpanzees experience multiple surgeries and do not have adequate pain relief after they are revived. Often chimpanzees are left with untreated serious injuries (even when self-inflicted). Sometimes some of them are housed individually and are not allowed to interact with other chimps. These chimpanzees have been in labs for decades, in fact, of the roughly 940 chimpanzees currently in labs, 180 individuals have been there for thirty or more years.

The situation Caesar and the others were in at the holding facility is not that different from conditions at some places where captive apes are held, where they don't get fresh fruit or vegetables, aren't provided with intellectual stimulation, comfort, or even fresh air and sunshine. Clearly this is harmful. But while these harms result from being in captivity, it might not be a necessary feature of captivity. The harm consists in our causing the chimpanzee to suffer, not that we are denying them freedom. Which raises the question—is there something beyond physical and psychological suffering that is wrong with captivity?

Love Across Species and Between Bars

I first began asking this question after I met a pair of captive young chimpanzees. Like Caesar they were born in research labs and then raised in a scientist's home as if they were human children. Harper and Emma are "enculturated" chimpanzees. They were working in a cognition research center in Ohio, where they were learning to use computers to match words with pictures. They also performed a variety of tool tasks.

These youngsters, also like Caesar in the beginning of *Rise of the Planet of the Apes*, were irresistibly cute and rambunctious. Unlike Caesar, fortunately, they were not given experimental drugs to boost their intelligence. They were smart, though, and they regularly gestured that they wanted to get out of their enclosures and play on the trampoline or go for a walk in the woods. They would point to the keys hanging outside of their enclosure and then would point to the lock. When they were allowed outside, Harper would run around looking for trouble. On one occasion, he opened a car door that wasn't locked, rummaged around inside, found a plastic bottle of Dr. Pepper, drank it down, and then held on to the bottle while he ran off to climb a tree in the woods. Both of the chimpanzees would do somersaults and ask to play chase or be tickled.

Sometimes little Emma would hold my hand as we walked. Once she jumped into my arms and had me carry her through the woods. Feeling her heart beating next to mine as she hugged me was an unforgettable experience. We kissed too (it wasn't anything like what happened between Taylor and Zira, but it created a bond). Spending time with the chimpanzees captivated me.

As chimpanzees grow older and reach puberty it is extremely dangerous to interact with them and they have to be confined. This was true for Emma and Harper too. They now live in a beautiful sanctuary called Chimp Haven. (The sound editors for *Rise of the Planet of the Apes* went to Chimp Haven and recorded the actual chimpanzee calls you hear in the movie.) I visit with Emma when I can. I think it's hard for both of us not to be able to touch each other. Nonetheless, we still express our affection. I bring lots of treats (nuts, seeds, dried fruit) that I tie up in socks or wrap in paper towel tubes that I can pass to her through her enclosure. Last time I saw her she picked a bouquet of weeds from inside her enclosure and handed them to me through the bars. We can exchange objects to show that we care about each other, but she will always be in an enclosure and I will always be outside of that enclosure.

That bars will always separate us led me to wonder whether there is something wrong with captivity even when Emma and Harper and the others are having a great time. They are well fed and well cared for and get all sorts of enrichment. They have room to play with other chimpanzees as well as room to get away if they need some quiet time. They engage in complicated social interactions and they are intellectually and emotionally stimulated by all sorts of interesting activities that go on at the sanctuary. But they can never be free.

Freedom

Depriving someone of her freedom, which is what captivity does, is one of the things that can make a life go badly for that individual. Captivity prevents someone from doing what they want; it interferes with their opportunities to make their own choices and to act on them. Not being interfered with in the pursuit of one's desires is important to leading a good life.

Of course, having the freedom to follow one's desires may not always, in fact, be what is best. Sometimes an individual might have desires that, if satisfied, do not actually enhance her well-being at all. Conversely, well-being might be experienced even though one is not actually free. I may think that my well-being is being promoted because I have altered my desires to fit my unfree conditions. Living a free life may contain all sorts of hardships, and being kept safe, well fed, and protected from danger may promote well-being, even while freedom is denied.

Even though keeping apes in captivity often causes them to suffer physically and certainly causes stress and other psychological harms, it is at least conceivable, that we might be able to provide an idealized captive environment for them. Chimp Haven is the closest thing to that. Since chimpanzees care about being free from physical and emotional pain, they want good food, comfort, healthcare, entertainment, stimulation and companionship. If we were to provide all these things, giving them the freedom to avoid stress and satisfy their interests, would denying them their freedom by keeping them in captivity still be a bad thing? If a chimpanzee doesn't know any better then maybe keeping him captive isn't so bad.

Am I a Pet?

Caesar knew that captivity wasn't for him, even though he had never experienced anything else. When he saw a dog on a leash in a park he signed to Will asking if he was a pet and it was clear that he didn't want to be thought of that way, he didn't want to be confined and controlled. When he realized he was a captive in the holding facility, he erased the chalk picture he had drawn on his cell wall of the window in his childhood home and began imagining a real home, free in the forests. He wanted to be in control of himself and he planned the great escape.

Caesar's escaping from the holding facility was an exercise in autonomy. Autonomous action is not just doing what you want to do, but it also involves making choices about your actions, planning and then deciding to endorse the action you engage in. Since most captive animals are not thought to be autonomous in this way, the question of whether pain-free captivity is a problem rarely gets asked.

This is a conception of autonomy that requires advanced cognitive capacities, to be sure, and it isn't clear that any non-human non-linguistic animals have precisely these capacities. Because Caesar had language abilities and was chemically altered so he could develop advanced cognitive capacities it makes sense to say that he acted autonomously, but it may be a stretch to think of regular old apes as being autonomous.

But maybe there's another way to think about what autonomous action is. All sorts of animals make choices about what to do, when to do it, and who to do it with. Many animals make plans, by making and saving tools for future use or by caching food to collect at a later time. Social animals often engage in manipulation or deception to try to get what they want and to prevent others from getting it.

One of my favorite examples of this sort of deception comes from observations of vervet monkeys in Africa. Tristan, an overly amorous male tried to "do it" with Borgia who apparently didn't have the same desires so she let out a scream. Following her scream, her family started to aggressively chase Tristan. After a short while running from Borgia's indignant family, Tristan suddenly stopped and started making alarm calls. Vervet monkeys give different sorts of alarm calls to indicate what sort of predator is in the area. Tristan must have given a call that indicated a ground predator was near because Borgia's pursuing relatives scattered into the trees. What is so interesting about this is that Tristan stayed where he was and eventually walked away unharmed as he diverted the chase.

It seems like these sorts of behaviors could be considered autonomous in the sense that animals are controlling what they do and are cleverly trying to influence the behavior of others. They certainly aren't being controlled.

It's a mistake to believe that being human or being genetically enhanced like Caesar is necessary for autonomy. Many animals, including primates, follow their own wants and desires, interests and dreams, and not simply those that are imposed from the outside or are "hard-wired" by instinct. They have distinct personalities and they express those personalities in different ways. They are self-directed, can adapt to changing circumstances, make choices and resist changes if that is what they decide, and improve their environments, often through collective action. Other animals learn from their peers and modify what they learn to suit themselves and their needs. They pursue activities that presumably they find rewarding. Not all animals in a social group do exactly the same things, eat exactly the same things, or spend time with the same individuals. They are making independent choices within the context of their biological and physical capabilities.

In *Escape from the Planet of the Apes*, there's an amusing montage in which Zira and Cornelius go shopping at pricey boutiques in Los Angeles, but elaborate grooming behaviors are not exclusively human activities. Real chimpanzees groom each other; grooming involves one chimpanzee using his or her hands to look through another chimpanzee's coat, picking out nits, inspecting for injuries, but mostly the behavior seems to provide enjoyment for the one being groomed and the one grooming.

Who gets groomed, when, and under what conditions is something that an individual chimpanzee will autonomously choose. Some species-typical behaviors involve lengthy migrations, but who leads the migration, when the migration begins, and where the group is heading will vary. Some species-typical behaviors involve remaining with the group you were born into for life and some involve leaving as soon as you're able, but the exact time you leave, where you go and with whom, are choices that an individual makes, influenced by the community.

Chimpanzees also follow social norms, in the wild and in captivity. They play important social roles, much as the various apes did in their revolution in *Rise*. And these roles will change over time. In Africa, chimpanzees are occasionally observed crossing roads that intersect with their territories. There's a video recording of chimpanzee behavior at the crossings where adult males took up forward and rear positions, with adult females and young chimpanzees occupying the more protected middle positions. The positioning of dominant and bolder individuals, in particular the alpha male changed depending on the degree of risk and number of other adult males present.

I witnessed a surprising interaction between some of my captive chimpanzee friends. Sarah likes to look at books, so when I visit I occasionally bring her children's books that can withstand chimpanzee handling for at least a few minutes. I gave Sarah her book and before she could really start "reading" it, Harper, who at this point in time was older but still mischievous, came over and took it away. Sarah didn't struggle with Harper when he took it. Then moments later, Sheba, a very smart female chimpanzee, who didn't appear to me to have noticed Harper's behavior because she was happily eating her dried mangos, went over to Harper and took the book from him. This in itself wouldn't be surprising as taking things that others have is typical among members of a group that aren't clearly dominant. What was surprising was that rather than keeping it herself, she promptly gave it back to Sarah. There were no vocalizations that I was aware of that might indicate Sarah was distressed by Harper's thievery nor that Sheba was trying to appease any distress. It just looked to me as though Sheba was setting things right. No one told her what to do— she just autonomously determined that the book belonged to Sarah.

When you spend time with chimpanzees it becomes clear what they like and don't like and what they want you to do. Some individuals will express exasperation when you don't do what they want you to and not letting them out of the enclosure is one thing that frustrates some of them.

Can We Really Know?

My experiences make me think that chimpanzees do know they are captive, like Caesar did, and if given a choice or opportunity would prefer not to be controlled by others. The chimpanzees I know point to locks and keys, they know which part of the enclosure opens and pound on it with incredible force. Spending time with captive chimpanzees can often feel like playing dodge ball—many of them will throw poop at you and wild chimpanzees don't throw poop. Maybe throwing poop isn't really a communicative act, but I can say that if I were imprisoned by aliens whom I couldn't speak to and only sometimes understood my gestures, throwing poop would be a meaningful way to indicate that I didn't appreciate being captive.

Although Caesar was able to communicate his desire to be "home" in the forests to Will with language, actual chimpanzees can't tell us what they think of captivity, if anything. Taylor initially couldn't either, but there's a lot we can understand about his displeasure without language when we look closely and try to understand.

And even with language we don't really know what someone else thinks, feels, or believes. We can be deceived by language just as Borgia's family was deceived by Tristan's alarm call. We can deceive ourselves with language too and come to believe things that aren't actually true of ourselves. Language can lead to great invention and "progress" but it can also contribute to conflict and destruction.

And language itself can be a type of enclosure—it constrains how we think and limits possibilities. But if we liberate ourselves from thinking that all we can know is through language, then it may be easier to imagine the rich, independent worlds of non-language using apes. Giving Caesar language helps us to understand his kin.

Home

If non-language using chimpanzees are autonomous, as I've suggested, and want and deserve their freedom, then isn't it wrong to deny it, even if their lives in captivity are otherwise going well?

Though Caesar ultimately escaped captivity in search of "home," that possibility doesn't exist for captive apes today. The wild places where apes live are being destroyed at alarming rates and more and more wild apes are disappearing. Orangutans, gorillas, bonobos, and chimpanzees are all endangered and some scientists predict that wild great apes will become extinct in our lifetimes. There are fewer and fewer wild spaces left and it's extremely unlikely that a captive born and reared ape could adapt to the wild if he were released. Just as Taylor discovered on his ride on the beach, their home world no longer exists as it once did.

Great ape captivity poses a real moral dilemma. It's wrong to deny them the freedom to control their own lives, but to release them would probably be a death sentence. So it looks like the best we can do is to ensure that they receive the highest level of captive care. We can provide opportunities for them to develop stable social relationships with others and let them be who they are. Respecting their wild dignity may go some way toward helping them come as close to feeling at home as is possible in a world of "maniacs!"

14

Rise of the Planet of the Altruists

JOHN S. WILKINS

Caesar's breath fogs the window of his attic room as he cries out in anguish, watching his "grandfather," Charles Rodman being harassed by an angry neighbor on the sidewalk below. The neighbor's finger jabs Rodman in the chest; his face is red with anger at his damaged car; Rodman's face is cherubic with childish innocence and ignorance. Caesar sees only a threat to his loving caregiver and leaps to his rescue.

Caesar races down three flights of stairs and attacks the unsuspecting neighbor, tackling him in the street, chasing him down the sidewalk, pummeling him with blows of decidedly chimp-like fury. Standing on the neighbor's chest, Caesar holds this man's life in his hands; he could easily smash the man's brains in and satisfy his animal bloodlust.

But Caesar doesn't kill the neighbor. Why? Is it because he sees the growing crowd of spectators eying him with social disapproval? Does he realize that killing is contrary to the moral contract of the group he lives within? Is such a realization even possible for a chimp?

Here we see Caesar the Chimp in all of his complexity: fierce animal and fierce moralist. Does such a creature, born of chimp lineage and genetically enhanced, have an intrinsic moral nature? What is a moral nature? What, for that matter, is morality? Where does it come from, where is it located, and how is it acquired? Merits of the acting and filmmaking aside, when I first saw the movie I was completely captivated by these questions, which I believe are best understood by thinking of moral behaviors as traits on the family tree of the Great Apes, humans included.

Reason and Morality

Rise of the Planet of the Apes presents an attempt to understand what morality is. Caesar is the movie's most moral agent:
he protects all primates, including humans, and acts only in
defense of those who are unable to defend themselves. The
source of his moral stance is shown as twofold: his upbringing
and his attainment of reason.

Caesar's ability to reason makes him what some would call
a *Kantian exemplar* (this has nothing to do with the Knights
Templar, even though it rhymes). The eighteenth-century
German philosopher Immanuel Kant argued that the moral
sense—the sense that stopped Caesar from crushing the neighbor's skull—follows from simply possessing rationality. If
you're capable of reason, then you must rationally assent to
what he called the Categorical Imperative, which is a little bit
like the old Golden Rule, but more universal: you must act
according to rules that could be required of everyone. This
moral imperative, or law, is the basis for any moral duty.
Kantian ethics treats other persons as moral ends, not as
means to ends, and so Kantians are respectful of the integrity
of other persons.

So, when Caesar leaps to the defense of his adoptive grand-
dad, he does not tear the neighbor apart, as a chimp could easily do. He restrains himself and stops short of brutal murder.
Compare that with the pet chimpanzee, Travis, who attacked
and seriously mauled a woman in 2009 in North Stamford,
Connecticut. Travis behaved as wild chimps do—chimps without (human) reason—attacking interlopers and killing them.
Caesar behaves in a most unchimpish fashion.

The humans in the movie, on the other hand, are shown
as mostly nasty and brutish, self-interested and exploitative,
of each other as well as the apes. The humans in the ape
holding facility, for example, behave abominably towards the
apes and sneakily towards other humans. They use their
powers of reason in a most un-Kantian way: they treat other
people as means to selfish ends, rather than ends unto themselves. These brutish humans exemplify *rational egoism*, in
which their every act, and much manipulation of others, is
calculated to serve their own interests. Popular movies are
rife with such characters, but using people without consider-

ing their wants or needs in real life strikes us as not very moral. And we all know someone who operates like this, don't we?

This somewhat bleak assessment of human nature in the movie, discussed by Thomas Hobbes in his *Leviathan* (and by Leslie Dale Feldman in this book) and the almost Rousseau-esque portrayal of the apes as "noble savages," has a long history in Western thought, stretching to at least the seventeenth century. But as far as we can tell from modern research, it is wrong.

Selfish Chimps and Caring Humans

Study after study shows that we humans, in contrast with most other primates, act with empathy and a bias towards pro-social behavior—towards treating others not merely as means but as ends worthy of care, even when we expect to receive no benefit. Non-human primates in general, and common chimps in particular, do tend to behave like the selfish traders of economic models, getting whatever they can when the risk is outweighed by the reward in predictable fashion. Chimps are known to attack and kill their fellows when it is to their benefit, as a matter of course. And even when they grant a favor, as the primatologist Frans de Waal has pointed out in one of his TED talks on YouTube, chimps are anticipating that it be returned—selfish trading at its finest.

So, if humans are the rational, morally behaving species and other primates are the selfish, opportunistic creatures, why do the *Planet of the Apes* movies, and a good deal of other literature, portray humans and other primates in this upside-down fashion?

The reason is that we have clung to an outdated view, sometimes called the Great Chain of Being, in which reason is the zenith of the living world, and moral behaviors arise out of the capacity for reason. In traditional philosophy, only humans occupy that zenith, both as moral agents and rational agents, but in the movie, the humans are clearly less rational than the apes. Are scriptwriters Rick Jaffa and Amanda Silver employing this inversion to make a not-so-subtle point about morality? Examining this Chain of Being idea will help us sort all of this out.

Primates in Chains and in Trees

Very famously, Charles Darwin came up with the idea of the evolutionary tree. Not many realize that the tree hypothesis is more uniquely Darwin's idea than natural selection, for which he is better known, though both are widely misunderstood. In the pre-Darwinian view of human nature, there was a sequence of organisms, either along a scale of increasing organization or a temporal sequence in which simple organisms shade into more complex ones over time. The historian E.A. Lovejoy called this the *Great Chain of Being*, giving it a convenient visual aspect of discrete links in a linear chain.

This chain idea was a commonly held view in the period preceding the European renaissance. Raimond Lull, a sixteenth-century humanist, illustrated the idea in his famous figure *Arbor scientiae venerabilis et caelitus*, which shows grades or ranks of being from stones through flames, plants, beasts, humans, heaven, angels, and finally God himself. Another woodcut from the sixteenth century details the ascent from mere existence to reason. During the Enlightenment, Lull's graphic ideas triggered a number of philosophers and naturalists to try and rank living things from simple and non-moral to complex and moral. Well before Kant or even the Enlightenment, to be moral was to be rational.

Through the seventeenth century and much of the eighteenth, the chain metaphor was expounded upon and embellished, but hardly challenged. It's easy to see it as blatantly arbitrary today, but the status quo was entrenched. Until Peter Simon Pallas challenged it in 1766.

Pallas came up with the idea that, rather than a single linear arrangement of kinds of living things, a better metaphor was that of a tree with two trunks, one for plants and one for animals. This new idea lined up nicely with something Linnaeus had been toying with: a nested hierarchy of species and groups of species. Every species was closely related to some other species, and less closely to even more. The tree was a good way to represent these "affinities," or sets of shared traits, as well as differences. This set up the problem that Darwin solved with the idea that a series of shared traits indicates a temporal sequence *and* common descent.

Apes in Grades and Clades

So, what does the Great Chain of Being or the Tree of Life have to do with morality? And what does any of this have to do with *Planet of the Apes*? These ideas have everything to do with the much contested, debated, and rejected notion of Human Nature. And I think we can all agree that the *Apes* films are really all about human nature.

If being rational and being moral are features solely of human beings because it is in our nature, the difference between the 'Chain' way of thinking and evolutionary tree thinking is that they will make different claims about whether or not we do in fact have a nature. And if we do, then these two schools of thought will also differ on what exactly the relations between reason and morals are.

If we adopt the Chain view of the living world, then we accept that there are objective levels (or "grades") of organization. Simple things are the least cognitive, emotive, and moral; complex things are the most. This simple view underlies almost all uses of evolution in science fiction right up to *Star Trek* and *X-Men*. I recall (but I can't find it now) a science fiction short story from the 1940s in which the protagonist traveled faster than light, causing him to individually "devolve" back down the "evolutionary scale," leaving him as a tarsier (picture a cross between a lemur and Tolkien's Gollum) when the space ship arrived, but oddly, not leaving the space ship as a rock of metal ore. Since tarsiers have never been seriously proposed as ancestral forms of human beings, the sole justification for this conceit, often found in science fiction from H.G. Wells's *The Time Machine* onwards, is that tarsiers and lemurs "represent" a "lower grade" of primate.

"Never say lower or higher," Darwin wrote in the margin of a book. For if we evolve not by rising up a chain the way Darwin's predecessors had held, but by branching outward, "higher" and "lower" have no real meaning. Everything that exists, from the simplest single cell to the most complex ape, dolphin or cnidarian (jellyfish), has exactly the same pedigree length, dating back to the common ancestor of all existing living things, whatever that was.

In a Darwinian view, change in itself is important, but not nearly as important as the branching points, the events that lead to new species. Sometimes these may bring about changes in "grade" (for example, from quadrupedal to bipedal), or sometimes they may result only in a species that's very similar to what they branched from. But it is the branching that matters.

The Enlightenment view that humans are the pinnacle of the living world rested squarely upon the Chain. So does the view of Dr. Zaius that Apes are the pinnacle of the living world and humans a lower form of primate. After we assimilate Darwin, a process we are still undergoing mentally and socially, the view that there is one superior species and below it a chain of lesser links no longer flies. For this reason, many eighteenth-century philosophers ran this argument in the opposite direction: they rejected evolution because it undercut this notion of grade. What did evolution replace this "grade" notion with, though? How does a tree undercut a grade?

All Branches, No Pinnacle

The answer is to think less of the trees we see in the real world, like the tall redwoods Caesar and his fellow primates escape to at the end of *Rise*, and think of a tree-like flow chart on a piece of paper. In an evolutionary tree, there is no "up" or "down," only "out." And while sometimes branches of the evolutionary tree will happen to evolve traits that exist elsewhere on the tree, a process called convergent evolution, mostly they will not. The earlier *Apes* films supposed that apes would converge upon human traits, like bipedalism and the ability to use their hands, but maybe that was a function of the problem of costuming, as in *Star Trek*.

So, what do tree-thinkers have to say about human nature? Well, if there is a human nature, then on the basis of evolutionary tree thinking, it must be mostly like the natures of the nearest other primate species on the tree. Human nature should be like the nature of apes, like Caesar.

Organisms were classified in a tree structure long before Darwin explained that very structure with hypothetical ancestor-descendant historical trees. The basis of this classification, then and now, is *homologies*, a term for those parts inherited from a common ancestor, no matter how much those parts may have changed in function or appearance. Go to a natural history museum sometime and look at the mammal skeletons and you'll see that they pretty much all have the same bones in the same arrangement—the correspondences (or homologies) are easy to spot. Our feet and Caesar's feet look pretty different, but they are homologous. *Homo sapiens* retains a tailbone, sans tail; birds and bats are still four-limbed creatures, even though their forelimbs can take them aloft; moles and blindfish have either eye remnants or some nerve-bundle in the place where eyes might have been. Homologies are similarities based on common origin.

By arranging organisms by homologies, we get something approaching a natural, branching classification, as opposed to an arbitrary, human-centric, linear Chain. The question to ask now is, does this translate into a classification of behaviors, too?

If several members of a branch, or *clade*, of an evolutionary tree have some trait, then it is highly likely that all members of it have that property. But some traits of organisms, like teeth, are very malleable and can be changed rather radically. Some behaviors are like that. It's not at all easy to see whether social behaviors are homologies or not. Nor is it easy to see that, because some organisms—apes—act a certain way, so must all other members of that group, including humans. To be sure that some trait or behavior is shared between humans and the other apes, you have to see that behavior in most, if not all, of the other members of the clade. Only then can you be confident that you aren't projecting human traits onto apes, or vice versa. The expectation is that if apes do something, so should we, except for our unique species behaviors.

Where does all this get us with Caesar? To answer that we have to ask what it might be for a species to have a nature. So far, we're looking at how traits are shared between species. If we know all primates are social (and they are, even orangutans when they live together), then any differences between one primate (us) and the rest must be due to our special evolution. However, we humans like very much to assert our differences from other animals. Let us instead consider our homologies.

We should predict that humans will have the kinds of social co-ordination systems that our nearest relations have, and so we do. We have social dominance hierarchies like any primate; we punish those who defect and reward those who cooperate. In other words, we establish social norms of behavior. What is rather interesting with humans, though, is that we're biased somewhat towards altruism. Our shared traits are apelike, but our uniquely moral norms are subtly different. That is our own specific trait. Would Caesar and the rest of the apes have adopted human moral behavior despite their biological differences *just because* of the retrovirus that was given to them?

Essence of Apeness

Species have typical anatomical traits. There is, however, a bit of a myth that, before Darwin, people thought species had *essences* which were invariant for all organisms within them. Since this myth was put forward in the late 1950s and early 1960s, it's become the orthodox view that species do *not* have essences, and therefore don't have natures. We can understand why people might think this: the Holocaust left everybody reeling at the implications of human groups being thought to have innate natures; each race or ethnic group or class could then be evaluated against others and some considered to be worth more or less morally.

In all the *Planet of the Apes* movies, early and recent, each species of ape has a special nature. Gorillas are warlike and aggressive; chimps are scheming and inquisitive; orangutans are clever and subtle. Humans, when not "devolved" are a bit selfish (according to the Sacred Scrolls and especially well exemplified in *Conquest of the Planet of the Apes*), and in *Rise of the Planet of the Apes*, the humans are nasty and selfish.

This is not a new problem. It goes back at least to Plato, who argued in his *Republic* that some types of people are just the best (philosopher kings, who have gold souls), some are good but not the best (the auxiliary warriors, with silver souls) and some are the least (the majority, who have iron or bronze souls). Assertions of innate natures often lead to discrimination and even genocide; scientists became most concerned about this after World War II and effectively put a ban on the notion.

But recently many scientists are claiming that race, and therefore innate natures, are real; they point out the obvious geographical variation between populations. Medical personnel need to know the ancestry of African descendants to know how to treat some diseases, for example. And some insist on immediately transferring this to behaviors: some groups (or genders, or sexual orientations) have typical behaviors, usually deemed lacking in value compared to the "best" kinds. Everything from IQ to promiscuity has been asserted to be a "nature," justifying all kinds of power relations between groups. No wonder scientists and theoreticians object to "natures" talk. It can be seriously dangerous. But is it false?

The idea that whole species have natures is equally scary. It suggests biological or genetic determinism, that each of us is forced to behave in a certain fashion because of our genes or something. So if we're to criticize and check the claim that reason forces us to be moral, or that Caesar would not be so prosocial as a human, we need first to clear up the notion of a species (especially a human) nature. And simply because it has unpleasant or unwanted consequences does not mean the notion is, in fact, false. That is a logical fallacy, one of the oldest.

Nature and Nurture Work Together

What having a nature does not mean, if we are informed by modern biology, is that we must act in a single determined fashion. We hear loose talk by journalists and occasionally by public intellectuals of the "gene for" this or that—homosexuality, religious belief, violence, rape, or alcoholism. No geneticist would ever make such a claim. Instead they would carefully qualify the claim: this gene has some role in modulating that behavior. Think of it like the claim that a certain player in a team sport had a role in winning the game. The team wins the game; the player is maybe crucial but is not the only reason they won. Moreover, even if that player is consistent, the rest of the team can lose the game next week.

Having a certain gene changes overall likelihoods, but it doesn't make certain outcomes necessary. Behaviors, like everything else biological, are distributed over a statistical curve in a population. If most organisms do something, like running at a certain speed, some will do it less and some do it more, and this will form a curve (not necessarily a bell curve, but some kind of curve). This distributed aspect of populations means that any statements about the nature of a species have to allow for variations from the mean and the mode.

So, when we say that chimpanzees show a certain behavior, we must expect there will be some chimps who vary from the "norm." It was once pointed out to me that if roughly five percent of people are "developmentally delayed," then if the distribution is normal there will be about the same number of "gifted," and that degree of difference from the mode (that is, from the most common type of person in the population) causes just as many disadvantages. It follows that a single Caesar is possible, but that it is unlikely he would do well in a population of ordinary chimps, however smart they were.

We cannot predict an individual's behaviors, and yet we can say with some degree of certainty how "typical" members of a species behave. This is as true of human beings as it is of chimps: the keepers at the ape facility in the movie are shown as selfish, aggressive, status-seeking primates, in contrast to Caesar, who is shown as pro-social and moral. That there *can* be humans like that is indubitable; that they would *likely* be that way is at best a scriptwriter's conceit. In fact, the primatologists I have met and discussed things with tend to empathize closely with their charges, and treat them as well as they can. The dramatic impact of the movie's villains is in the mismatch with our default human expectations: a contemptible villain is as important to a good story as a valiant hero.

The issue here is what we can predict about a species by observing behaviors and whether these behaviors are somehow natural. It's as much a problem with humans as with other organisms. It's not even entirely clear that behaviors can be traits. Are they inherited? Are they cultural or even convergent between species? What, exactly, does it mean for a behavior to be "natural"? Rather than saying that behaving in X fashion is inherited by ordinary members of a species or population, it is far more consistent with our knowledge of genetics, developmental biology, and evolution to say instead that the *disposition* to behave in X fashion is inherited. Dispositions are philosophyspeak for some cause that will generate an effect *in the right conditions*. Our genes don't form human beings in hard vacuums, nor in the absence of the right nutrients, which is why pregnant women take folic acid supplements to prevent spina bifida. This is also true for behaviors.

Consider so-called "feral" children, who do not learn to speak by the age of five. They never learn to speak in grammatically complicated sentences, no matter how much they're taught. We know that the developing nervous system needs the right stimuli at the right time before a "normal" behavior like speech can develop. Nova, Taylor's love interest, is an example of just such a feral child. She never learned language when her speech centers were developing, so likely never will, no matter how tenderly Taylor tutors her. Still, we can say that rats, monkeys, and humans have species-typical behaviors that ordinary members will develop *if they are given the right rearing*.

Therefore, the question of a distinction between nature and nurture so beloved of popular writers and journalists is ruled out of court from the start: it has to be and can only be *both* biological and environmental inheritances that cause organisms to behave in certain ways. And if the environmental and social resources are there, the disposition to behave in X fashion will develop.

A Chimp Like No Other

In the case of Caesar, we should be able to predict that intelligent chimps will act like their less-intelligent brethren depending on circumstances. However, Caesar had another arrow in his quiver apart from intelligence. He was *scaffolded* in his moral development by being reared in a family. The term "scaffold" to refer to cultural learning and mental development is due to the philosopher Kim Sterelny, who notes that it makes learning more stable and effective. Human scaffolding of one another in development is crucial to normal development, as in language learning. But humans also scaffold other animals, such as dogs, and in this case Caesar. Would Caesar have been so moral if not raised in that way?

Rise of the Planet of the Apes is ambivalent about this. In one sense Caesar is shown learning morality from his "family," to which he then applies his intelligence in what philosophers call "a wide reflective equilibrium"—an attempt to make all the principles and values he holds consistent. He asks his adoptive father, Will Rodman if he is a pet because he has a collar and a chain like a dog. Rodman recoils from the idea, and yet he has indeed been treating Caesar that way. Together, Will and Caesar work through the moral issues. They scaffold each other's moral development. So we can't say that Caesar would have been moral without this scaffolding.

But then consider the gorilla, Buck, who learns immediately from Caesar's example and ultimately sacrifices himself for all the apes once he, too, has been made intelligent. Buck was not scaffolded by years of enculturation, yet as a rational agent he immediately adopts the Categorical Imperative and defends the weaker apes from being killed. Well, there is no convincing answer to this in the film. Perhaps the next installment in the reboot will resolve the inconsistency, or even expound on it for even greater dramatic effect. Regardless, Caesar clearly shows us the cultural scaffolding necessary for moral development.

Defer . . . Defer . . .

We've been looking at the differences between human beings and apes, and the ways we should expect each species to behave. What do all apes have that is common in the moral realm?

When faced with a dominant chimp, other chimps lower themselves and do not stare. To do so is to make a challenge that might be met with violence. The same occurs with gorillas (the thing to do when faced with a charging silverback is to lower your head and crouch). Same goes for many troop primates such as baboons, macaques, and rhesus monkeys, although it's not always the dominant male that runs the troop or determines social rank; some species, like bonobos, are matriarchal. The same thing will occur if an artificial troop of apes or monkeys is put together in a zoo enclosure. Put a group of school-aged children in a playground and they will sort themselves into such a hierarchy, as well. This *deference* is what all primates spontaneously do when confronted with dominant individuals.

One thing that we see in *Rise of the Planet of the Apes* is the keepers at the ape facility behaving just like apes, but apes without *empathy*. And empathy is pretty much a universal trait among apes, including humans, in the right circumstances. The son of the head keeper, Dodge, treats subordinates with violence and cruelty. This is not typical ape behavior, with one caveat. Apes tend not to treat their own troop members this way—if a dominance competition is over, as we see in the movie, the rest is relatively amiable, although just as with humans there can be bad-tempered and even domestically violent apes. However, apes that encounter members of other troops, or which are challenged by a competitor for alpha status, can behave this way. Dodge may see the apes as competitors, so he treats them cruelly.

Is Dodge's behavior typical human behavior? Obviously not. Despite Hobbes's claim that "life in a state of nature" would be "nasty, poor, solitary, brutish and short," anthropologists observe that, except in cases of intertribal warfare, and often even then, humans are not typically violent, and as Stephen Pinker has recently argued, modern humans are even less violent than their ancestors, although this is most likely a cultural, not a biological, shift. In times and societies of plenty, violence is no longer a profitable activity, so we are inclined not to behave that way. This also seems to be true of chimps, as noted before. So despite the message of the film that humans lack empathy and apes are the true moralists, in fact all apes, including humans, are generally not too bad to be around except in extreme circumstances, usually involving competition between groups.

Deference, empathy, social ranks, dominance competition: that's a hefty list of common behaviors among primates. No wonder we make and consume movies about apes to better understand our own human nature!

Everywhere I Look, I See Myself

Taking Caesar as an exemplar, we come to realize that morality is not Kantian alone. A moral primate needs to have not only reason, but also the social dispositions that make morality possible; and even then, morality needs to be scaffolded by socialization and enculturation. Had Caesar never had this upbringing, he may have turned out to be more like General Thade in the 2001 movie.

Just as in the early movies of the 1970s and the first movie of the current reboot, humans are seen as the pinnacle of evolution, in a pigeonhole to which other species will evolve, as humans devolve and lose their dominance through their own mistakes. The filmmakers assume this moral superiority, then invert it to illustrate and illuminate our folly. Thinking about the surprisingly complex philosophical conundrums presented in the *Planet of the Apes* movies not only enhances our enjoyment of the cinematic experience; it helps us understand ourselves better.

VII

Ape Cinema

15
Serkis Act

JOHN HUSS

There's a guy in a spandex suit covered with polka dots. He's got some high-tech gizmo strapped to his head. He approaches a window and presses his face against it. His eyes bulge. His cheeks puff in and out. He pounds his half-open fists against the glass, and emits anguished, non-verbal vocalizations. Now that's what I call acting.

A key frame animator sits before a bank of high-powered computers, channeling performance-capture data through a computer simulation program. It produces a life-like digital image of a chimp with eyes bulging, half-open fists pounding against the window, cheeks puffing in and out. "Hey," says his boss, "can you make them a little puffier?" He emits anguished, non-verbal vocalizations. Now that's what I call animation.

Should actor Andy Serkis have even been eligible to be nominated for an Oscar for his role as Caesar in *Rise of the Planet of the Apes*? The answer lies somewhere in between these two scenes. It's easy to track down the raw and finished footage on YouTube to make the comparison yourself. Despite a campaign by Twentieth Century Fox and an impassioned blog post by James Franco, once the votes were tallied, Serkis wasn't nominated. But why? Could it be the fierceness of the competition? The nominees for Best Actor in a Supporting Role were: Kenneth Branagh in *My Week with Marilyn*, Jonah Hill in *Moneyball*, Nick Nolte in *Warrior*, Christopher Plummer in *Beginners*, and Max von Sydow in *Extremely Loud & Incredibly Close* (Plummer won).

Perhaps in the eyes of the Academy, given such a strong field, Serkis's performance was simply not Oscar-worthy. Maybe so. But I suspect that at the heart of the (perceived) snub is a performance capture quandary: the status of the art of acting in an age of digital production.

What Is Acting?

Suppose we try to decide what Serkis deserves by defining what acting is, and seeing whether the chimp performance we see on screen fits the bill. This seems reasonable. And philosophers have been asking "What is *X*?" questions for centuries. My favorite example is Socrates stumping his friend Euthyphro with the question "What is piety?" Eventually Euthyphro simply walks away crestfallen—probably emitting anguished vocalizations.

Euthyphro was onto something. Twentieth-century philosophy has taught us that we should be suspicious of "What is *X*?" questions. Just because our language allows us to ask them doesn't mean there's a meaningful answer. Ludwig Wittgenstein, the Austrian philosopher, insisted that there are no genuine philosophical problems, only confusions brought about by the questions our language allows us to ask. He felt really passionate about this point, too, going so far as to shake a fireplace poker at fellow philosopher Sir Karl Popper when Popper disagreed with him!

The problem with posing "What is *X*?" questions is that unless we're careful about it, they lead us to seek some essential definition, a set of conditions that *X*, and only *X*, must meet to qualify. For some purposes, this may be fine. In geometry, we want a definition of "triangle" that picks out all and only triangles. Real life is more complicated, and when we go all out in the pursuit of some exact criterion for acting that can be applied to the Serkis case, the real problem slips away from us. We can easily end up defining performance capture as acting or not, right off the bat, before even delving into the matter. The whole point is that with performance capture technology and computer generated imagery (CGI), the definition of acting (movie acting anyway) is in flux. You're not going to solve a problem of definitional flux by simply asserting a definition.

The Truth, Twenty-Four Frames a Second

Once you compare the raw and the finished footage of the tearful goodbye scene from *Rise of the Planet of the Apes*, you may be surprised to find that even in the raw footage, Serkis's performance as Caesar is quite believable, and it's easy to see why the studio and his co-star were moved to lobby the Academy on his behalf. Alternatively, you may be surprised to find that Serkis's performance bears only a remote resemblance to that of the Caesar we see on screen, that the artistry and the emotional connection lie not with the performance, but with what the animators have done with "the data."

I don't have an ape in this race, but obviously many people in the industry do. Blog comments to the posted footage indicate clearly that different people can look at the same footage and see very different things. People who work in animation look at the final clip and see all the marks of key frame animation, a process in which images are created frame by frame either manually or, more often, through the use of a computer program that interpolates some of the frames in between those created by the animator. The relevant question for them seems to be how much of the motion capture data was used to create the final cut. In this particular clip, apparently only data from Serkis's spine was directly used, with the rest of his movements serving as a reference for the animator (in this case Jeffrey Engel of the New Zealand visual effects studio Weta Digital).

In contrast, actors, directors, and fans tend to look at the raw footage and see in it the emotional essentials of the final product already present. They're astonished to see how chimplike Serkis's movements are. They attribute the bulk of the portrayal to the actor himself. All the rest is just "digital makeup." To many animators (and their friends and admirers), this term "digital makeup" is practically an insult. What animators do is far more involved than "touching up" the captured image.

Is Believing Seeing?

How can people look at the same footage and see something so different? I guess we shouldn't be all that surprised. Everyone's familiar with the idea that background beliefs and prior experiences influence what we see. Or is it that they influence what we *think* we see? Can these two things be kept straight? In my field, philosophy of science, it was once fashionable to draw a distinction between "seeing as" and just plain "seeing." This discussion seems to pop up every time we start comparing the perceptions of people who hold radically different beliefs (especially before and after a major scientific revolution). For example, we can imagine two people in the seventeenth century watching the sun set. Person A has read Copernicus and Galileo, and "knows" that the Earth spins on its axis once a day and is just one of several planets orbiting the sun. Person B is a little out of touch, but "knows" the Earth is stationary and that the sun orbits it once a day. So A and B believe very different things. But here's the question: when A and B watch the sunset, do they see the same thing or do they see different things? Perhaps they do see the same thing (the sun on the horizon), but each sees it *as* something else (a stationary and an orbiting body, respectively). Likewise, when Dr. Zira and Dr. Honorius watch Taylor's gestures at trial, Zira sees an attempt to communicate, whereas Honorius sees an animal's mimicry. This makes it sound as if they see two different things, but perhaps they see the same thing (Taylor's gestures); each just sees it *as* an instance of something else (communication and mimicry, respectively).

It's tempting to say that two people with different beliefs may see the same thing and interpret it differently. Sometimes this is true. If I write out "tomatoes, trout, potatoes, Shout" on a piece of paper, two people may see the same thing (a list of words) and interpret it differently (a grocery list and a poem). But it seems that most cases of seeing—and perception in general—are all-at-once processes. This almost must be true of everyday perception. Imagine if all of our perception involved taking in sensory input, followed by a separate process of interpretation. It's tough to operate in the real world in real time with that kind of two-step perceptual set-up. In a world governed by natural selection, I doubt the human race would have made it to this point.

Yet a one-step perceptual process leads to another worry. If what we already believe so strongly colors what we see, what point is there in even consulting the Serkis footage to resolve the dispute? We encounter a serious problem if we simply accept that what we perceive depends on our prior beliefs. It seems that if we went too far in this direction, we would never be able to use observations to change our minds. We'd be sentenced to a life of dogmatically held beliefs.

Use Your Illusion

Can we be trained to see things differently than we currently do? This would be a way out of the difficulty. I find optical illusions to be illuminating on this point. They can teach us an interesting lesson regarding the influence of belief on perception.

A famous optical illusion is the Müller-Lyer illusion. It involves two horizontal lines:

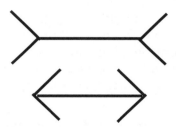

The top line looks longer than the bottom line, but in fact, they're the same length. If you don't believe me, measure them. After measuring, you should now believe that they are. But do they look it? No, the top line still looks longer. We still fall prey to the illusion despite our beliefs. In fact, as philosopher Jerry Fodor has pointed out in "Observation Reconsidered," what we believe does *not* dictate what we see.

Great! So improvements to our knowledge don't dispel illusions. This is supposed to help us trust our perceptions? How can we have any hope of figuring out whom to credit for the emotional and aesthetic hold Caesar has on us: Serkis or Engel?

Here's the problem. Throughout this discussion we have been awash in false dichotomies: either our perceptions depend on our beliefs or they don't; either the viewer's emotional connection to Caesar is due to acting or to animation. In fact, we can determine (through measurement) that the two lines are the same length, and we can learn (through discussion, through having certain visual cues pointed out to us) how act-

ing and animation *both* contribute to the emotional and aesthetic effect of Caesar. Sit down and watch the video clips with
a CG animator and an actor and you will start to pick up on
what they are picking up on.

That said, I think we may be fixating on the wrong thing
here. Is it really that important how much of what we see on
screen was simply animated and how much was digitally
processed data from Serkis's performance? Two things worry
me about this. The first is that film is the art of creating believable illusions: camera angles, editing, makeup, stunt doubles,
special effects, and so on. Even though all these things contribute to our perception of the actor's performance, we still
give credit to the actor when it is due. The second worry is that
we may be falling prey to the philosophical sin of reductionism,
reducing acting performance to the image of the character on
screen. Maybe there is more to it than that. Perhaps we should
take a closer look at the phenomenon of acting from the actor's
point of view, especially since we are wondering whether Serkis
should have been nominated for best supporting actor.

He Came to Praise Caesar

Whatever else acting is, it is a craft. Crafts have always
received a great deal of respect within philosophy. Perhaps at
some level, philosophy itself aspires to be a craft. Socrates himself spent much of his life looking for someone with craft
knowledge of virtue, someone who actually understood what it
meant to live an excellent life in the same way that craftsmen
really understand what they do: shipwrights know ship-build-
ing, or physicians know healing. Can we take the leap of believing that actors know acting? The time has come to appeal to
Serkis's co-star, James Franco. Perhaps he can help us understand why Serkis deserved to be nominated for best supporting
actor.

In his Deadline.com blog post that pimps Serkis for the
Oscar, Franco doesn't focus very much on the "How much of
Caesar is animation?" question. Rather, he emphasizes performance and especially the ensemble nature of acting. In the
olden days, he points out, a human character playing opposite
a computer-generated (CG) character would be interacting
with a tennis ball. Due to evolution in CGI technology, actors

portraying CG characters can now share a stage together. This is why in the raw footage Serkis is covered in polka dots (sensors) and a strap-on gizmo (camera). These contraptions are capturing data from his performance as he shares a stage with Franco and Freida Pinto. For actors to share a stage turns out to be crucial.

According to Franco, the transcendent performances in movies come about not so much from acting, but from *reacting* to the other actors. This is the realm of spontaneity and artistic discovery. It's unscripted. And it's very different from digitally "penciling in" a character who wasn't present on the set. The chemistry between actors is what we miss if we focus on the technical question of the origin of the image on the screen. Acting is an emergent property, dependent on individual performances, but not entirely reducible to them. If Franco is right, the whole here is truly greater than the sum of its parts.

Franco also points out that the surface realism of Caesar would be empty without the "soul" provided by the performance of Andy Serkis. Now I am completely on board with the point about the ensemble nature of acting, but when I read this little bit about the soul I was a bit dubious. What else do we see on film but what we see on film? As Andy Warhol once said: "If you want to know all about Andy Warhol, just look at the surface of my paintings and films and me, and there I am. There's nothing behind it." Couldn't a clever enough animator fool us into seeing soulfulness?

As luck would have it, I recently met someone who can answer that question. He has done a lot of key frame animation, and I was surprised when he let on how limited he thought it was. His argument was that if it were possible to achieve an emotional connection using completely CG characters without performance capture, then actors would no longer be needed to play these characters. But in fact actors still are needed.

I have to say that I'm still a little dubious. It may merely be a matter of time before clever animators can simulate "soulfulness." Hell, it may have already happened. Did not Elmer J. Fudd possess a soul? For now, I am content to let the issue rest with the fact that performance capture allows human and CG characters to play off one another.

What Belongs to Caesar

In evaluating Serkis's performance as Caesar in *Rise of the Planet of the Apes*, it is helpful to think back to the technological advance that made the original 1968 movie possible. Producer Arthur P. Jacobs had, for several years, pitched the idea for a movie adaptation of Pierre Boulle's novel without success. The holdup at every stage was the ludicrousness of human actors playing chimps, gorillas, and orangutans. Before any studio would even touch it, they needed to be convinced that the film wouldn't play as farce. It needed to be a credible work of science fiction. If the audience was too busy laughing at the "aping" on screen, the film would be a flop.

The hurdle Jacobs faced was not one of getting humans to look like apes on screen. That much was accomplished quite credibly in the same year in Stanley Kubrick's *2001: A Space Odyssey*. Rather, the challenge was to create apes that looked like apes but acted, more or less, like humans (albeit with ape mannerisms). After a screen test in which Edgar G. Robinson—in rather primitive primate makeup—played Dr. Zaius, Twentieth Century Fox gave the go-ahead, and eventually makeup artist John Chambers was brought on board to create the rubberized masks that would be worn not only by stars Kim Hunter, Roddy McDowall, and Maurice Evans, but also by all of the ape extras. While the movie made quite an impact, it's telling that its sole Oscar went to Chambers, who won an Honorary Academy Award for Outstanding Makeup Achievement. Incidentally, he had studied facial reconstructive surgery prior to going into the film industry.

If you think about it, the challenges faced by the actors playing chimps, orangs, and gorillas in the 1968 movie were very different from those faced by Serkis in *Rise of the Planet of the Apes*. These actors got up early in the morning, endured four hours of being made up, and had to subsist on a liquid diet during the day, drinking through straws. The masks were somewhat porous, but were still stuffy, and the film was shot on a hot, dry set. If anything, what is praiseworthy in those performances is the portrayal of emotion while "trapped" behind a heavy rubber mask, achieving connection with the audience all the while being handicapped in these ways.

Fast forward to *Rise,* and the actors are completely liberated. They can move and emote as each scene requires. Although some might fear that performance capture and CGI threaten the art of acting, you could argue instead that, compared to the prosthetic makeup that Chambers used, these new technologies *enabled* Serkis to perform, to emote, to ape, and yes, even to act.

So should Serkis have been nominated? That one was up to the Academy, and who knows what criteria they use, anyway? But now that we have removed the barrier to the Oscar-worthiness of performance-capture acting, it's time to give to Serkis what belongs to Serkis. And while it's too late for *Rise,* we can get a jump on *Dawn.*

A Weta Digital PETA Coda

In the long run, how important will the embrace of performance capture acting really be? We need to look at this in a societal context. From its very origins in Boulle's novel, the *Planet of the Apes* franchise has been concerned with ethical and political themes, chief among them being the oppression of "the other," brought into sharp focus by the role reversal that is the series' hallmark. Do performance capture technology and computer generated imagery have any bearing on this broader issue?

Weta Digital, the New Zealand visual effects company that has had a hand in several of Peter Jackson's movies including the *Lord of the Rings* trilogy and *King Kong,* as well as James Cameron's *Avatar* (which, by the way, won an Oscar), has found a champion in the People for the Ethical Treatment of Animals (PETA). PETA sees that through advances in performance capture technology, computer generated imagery, and performances like that of Andy Serkis (who also played *Tintin* and *King Kong* in those films), there will come a day when the use of animal actors in film will be a thing of the past. Humans will be able to supply their own entertainment needs, and the closing credit, "No animals were harmed in the making of this film," will seem oddly unnecessary.[1]

---

[1] For helpful comments I thank Joanna Trzeciak, John Marston, Sharon Cebula, and George Reisch. For helpful discussion I thank Aaron Starr.

16
It's a Madhouse! A Madhouse!

Tom McBride

If you're reading this right now, you are a human, not a simian. Of that I am certain. But what is certainty? In some notes he made towards the end of his life, collected and published as *On Certainty* eighteen years after his death (the same year human beings went to the Moon, by the way), Austrian philosopher Ludwig Wittgenstein contemplates the statement "It is certain that we did not arrive on this planet from another one a hundred years ago," and comments, "Well, it is as certain as such things *are*."

And so Wittgenstein, like Rod Serling, who wrote the original *Planet of the Apes* screenplay, was interested in planets. Following Wittgenstein's methods, if someone said she was certain we *did* arrive on this planet from another one a hundred years ago, we wouldn't respond, "No, I think you're mistaken. I think it was a hundred and two years ago." You don't correct such a person; you assume she's either kidding or crazy or hallucinating. Or writing a sci-fi novel—the next great *Planet of the Apes*. In any event, she is not "mistaken." Of that we can entertain no doubt.

Here then is a link between insanity and certainty. If a person is sure that we arrived on Earth a mere hundred years back, one explanation is that she is loony. The reverse also works: If we confront apes who act like humans and *are certain* that humans (like us!) are lowly apes, then we ourselves may become insane, or think we are. Their certainty seems insane to us, but if their certainty has the backing of a powerful social apparatus, then it is *we* who are more likely to go nuts.

In this way we forge a connection between certainty and sanity (or insanity): there are some things of which we're so certain that their falsehood strikes us as completely impossible and nonsensical. Yet what if the utterly unheard of were actually to happen? One possibility is that we would come to doubt our sanity. This linkage is the philosophical explanation for Commander Taylor's harrowing experience in *Planet of the Apes*.

Are You *Certain* You're in The Twilight Zone?

Planet of the Apes was first a French novel, but it's most famous as a 1968 movie. Rod Serling, of *Twilight Zone* fame, wrote the screenplay. He was a most appropriate choice, for by 1968 he had had well over a decade of experience in writing, for TV, precisely the sorts of episodes that are similar to those found in *Planet of the Apes*. Take the first two episodes of *The Twilight Zone*, a celebrated series on TV, radio, and comic books; the series specializes in bizarre situations that are sci-fi, or hallucinatory, or sometimes manifestly horrible.

In the first episode of the series, a man goes to a psychiatrist to report that he has recurring dreams of being in Pearl Harbor just before the Japanese attack. The man feels the dreams are so vivid that he really is there. Moreover, he warns everyone, in vain, that the harbor is going to be bombed. No one will listen. He wonders if he is time traveling. The psychiatrist is dubious. But then the psychiatrist momentarily leaves his office and returns, only to find all traces of the man gone. He later discovers that he was killed at Pearl Harbor. So who was he? A ghost? A time traveler who has come forward in time? A hallucination? Who is crazy here?

Then there's the second episode, about a man who finds himself all alone in a town where there is plenty of evidence of recent life and activity. He wanders all over, confused and disoriented, until he hits a WALK button. This turns out to be a panic button in an isolated space, for the man, it turns out, is an Air Force officer cooped up to see if he can stand such cramped quarters for a trip to the Moon. Apparently he can't. His last words, as he is taken out, quite mad, on a stretcher, are to the Moon itself. He shouts to the Moon that Man will be coming eventually. Within ten years of this episode, he was shown to be right. In another version of the same episode, the man hallucinates that he has been to a movie. It's just a crazy vision, but then the movie ticket falls out of his pocket. What are we to make of *that*?

These two typical examples from *The Twilight Zone* show that the series turns on questions of certainty and uncertainty. We usually seem certain that when we're sitting at a table writing essays on *Planet of the Apes* we're not dreaming, or that if we dream we have seen *Planet of the Apes* while sitting in a movie theater on the Moon, we will not awake the next day and find a "Moon Theater" movie ticket falling out of our pockets. But the Twilight Zone is quite different. It is an altogether alternative form of life.

Hinges and Riverbeds

In *Planet of the Apes,* after the so-called trial, there's a key scene in which Dr. Zaius tries to level with Taylor and in return wants Taylor to simply tell him the truth about his origins. The problem is that for Dr. Zaius to accept what Taylor has to say—that he arrived from outer space in a spacecraft—is simply not possible given certain certainties. For Dr. Zaius, it is certain that flight is an impossibility. It's certain that humans are from the forests near the Forbidden Zone. Within this framework, he can only conclude that Taylor is lying. Even during the trial, Cornelius, obviously sympathetic to Taylor, testifies that although intelligent, Taylor must be crazy to believe his own story.

In our form of life, we're certain that the human race didn't arrive from another planet a hundred years ago. If we believed that, then we could not believe in the existence of our grandparents. Wittgenstein furthers his understanding of certainty by stating, "I believe my name is Ludwig Wittgenstein," and adds that while such a belief is not infallible, at the same time "I could not be mistaken about it." Indeed, in *On Certainty*, Wittgenstein is at great pains to distinguish between propositions that are subject to doubt—ones we can easily envision being overturned by evidence—and those that cannot be subject to doubt—those that are so certain that if they were to be cast into doubt, everything would be up for grabs. He writes:

> All testing . . . of a hypothesis takes place already within a system. And this system . . . belongs to the essence of what we call an

argument. The system is not so much the point of departure as the element in which all arguments have their life. (section 105)

Such a system is frequently not subject to doubt if we are to get on with the testing.

Here it is vital that we distinguish between logical and empirical propositions. "I am inclined to believe that not everything that has the form of an empirical proposition *is* one" (section 308). There is a vast distinction between "I think my arm is broken" and "I think I spent last night on the Moon." While an appropriate response to the person who thinks his arm is broken might be, "No, it is just sprained," the appropriate response to the person who says he spent last night on the moon would not be, "No, you were on Neptune." "My arm is broken" is an empirical proposition and hence verifiable or refutable by inspection. But the element in which the argument "my arm is broken" has its "life" is something like, "My arm exists." Wittgenstein thought that if we looked at the contraries of these two kinds of sentence, we would see that there is something importantly different about them. We can entertain uncertainty about "my arm is broken." If it turns out to be false—a sprain not a break—we can live with it. We were simply mistaken. We cannot entertain any uncertainty about "my arm exists." To say "my arm does not exist" while holding up one's arm is not to say something false, but to say something nonsensical. We'd have to question whether whoever said it really meant it, understood what they were saying, or was sane. For if it such a statement could be true, it would throw both our language and our logic, our entire basis for making empirical judgments, into disarray.

Wittgenstein wrote, "My life consists of being content to accept many things." He thought there was a difference between "riverbed" or "hinge" propositions, about which we are certain, and what we shall call non-hinge propositions (or non-riverbed propositions) about which we may entertain doubts. The hinges make sure that the door can be open or shut, and of it's being open *or* shut we have no doubt. But we may doubt whether the door is open or whether it is shut until we see for ourselves. The riverbed of certainty allows us to be uncertain whether or not our friend slept in his room last night, but it does *not* allow us to be uncertain about whether or not he slept on the moon, or on the Planet of the Apes in 3974, the year when Taylor and his crew crashed there.

Without such guiding systems—or hinges or riverbeds—we could not have certainty *or* uncertainty. We could, suggests Wittgenstein, doubt everything and hence be unable to doubt anything: "A doubt that doubted everything would not be a doubt" (section 450). And while no organized living, including that in Ape City, can succeed without certainty, neither can it succeed without doubt. Thus it is crucial, he adds, that we know what kind of proposition we're considering: whether it is a systemic, hinge proposition, such as "External reality is made up of material elements," or empirical ones such as "It is cloudy today." And "this is my hand" (or on the Planet of the Apes, "this is my paw") is not an empirical claim but a logical one. It is like a hinge, not like an assertion that the door is open.

Life is for Wittgenstein a series of language games—in which what we can say is of a piece with what we can do and what we can think—and some doubts are prohibitive: "If he calls *that* in doubt—whatever doubt means here—he will never learn the game." What was of philosophical interest—he would call it "logical" interest—is not what we can know but what we cannot seriously doubt, regardless of its ultimate fallibility or infallibility. Furthermore, what seems to be maximally certain and beyond doubt can change. I am certain that Taylor is certain he is on some distant planet other than Earth until he encounters Lady Liberty half-buried on the beach. At that point he becomes unhinged.

George Taylor, Meet G.E. Moore

Taylor is rather like Wittgenstein's philosopher friend and colleague, G.E. Moore. Both of them are captured, one in a legendary film, the other in Wittgenstein's philosophical speculation. Let's take Taylor and Moore in turn.

Given his appearance and the wound in his throat that keeps him from speaking, Taylor is immediately judged upon his capture to be sub-simian, or human. He eventually recovers his voice and—as a benefit of having traveled 2006 years in just eighteen months at the speed of light—is unusual among sub-simians because he is still able to speak: "Take your stinking hands off me, you damn dirty ape." It is a shocking thing for him to have said, for a foundational, hinge, riverbed principle of this planet's society is that humans or humanoids are themselves grunting, stinky, filthy, inferior creatures.

Wittgenstein mused in *On Certainty* about "What if something really unheard of happened?" such as the cattle standing on their heads and laughing and men turning into trees and trees into men. Well, something unheard of on the Planet of the Apes has happened. A foundational principle has been breached. A form of life has been fractured. A hinge proposition has been loosened, and now the whole Planet of the Apes may become *un*hinged. A riverbed has been breached; a flood may ensue at any time.

Wittgenstein: "But what could make me doubt whether this person here is N.N., whom I have known for years? Here a doubt would seem to drag everything with it and plunge it into chaos." We can dismiss a man who says he slept last night on Pluto. Simian society on the Planet of the Apes cannot dismiss a stinking human who acts as though *he* is a simian—and can back it up with language and authority. He creates doubt that "would seem to drag everything with it and plunge it into chaos."

As for Moore, whose "capture" we will momentarily investigate, he was famously the inspiration for the work Wittgenstein did in *On Certainty,* for it was based on a paper given by his Cambridge colleague Moore, who wrote, "Here is a hand" (holding up his hand) and "Here is another" (holding up his other hand) and saying that there are simply no reasonable grounds on which to cast any philosophical doubts upon such assertions. Wittgenstein admired the forthrightness of Moore's commonsense assertion and agreed with it. But, following the brilliant trail we have already traced, he thought Moore erred because he did not identify what sort of proposition "Here is a hand" really is. It is not an empirical proposition, like "Your arm is broken" or "I spent last night in Beloit, Wisconsin." Rather, it is a logical proposition, the sort of hinge assumption on which so much in daily life depends and about which we cannot entertain any serious doubt if we are to live our form of life.

If you can't believe that your hand is your hand, you can't fetch a book. You can't drive a car. You can't be sure that it is you who is typing a letter. Here we arrive at the paradox inherent in the professor's classroom request, "Those of you who do not believe that your hand is your hand, raise your hands!" Or: "Those of you who do not believe you are simians, raise your paws." Believing that your hand is your hand is rooted in the assumption that you're not hallucinating. It's based on the assumption that the hand has external reality apart from your mere perception of it: that it does not vanish when you are not looking at it, or that it disappears for a while but your friends haven't quite had the heart to tell you about it.

There may be contexts in which the statement might make more sense, such as in an anatomy class in which the professor holds up a detached hand and says, "Here is a hand," or if a person has a brain lesion and says, "I am making progress. I now know that this hand is a hand and that it is my hand." But "this is my hand" is not in the same category as "this is my broken arm." Rather, it is such a bedrock proposition that it compares favorably with "In 2012 it will take us 2,006 years to get to the year 4018," even if, by year 4018, it may be possible to say, along with Commander Taylor and hinge-like certainty, "I can travel 2,006 years in three months."

But suppose the forthrightly common-sense philosopher, Professor Moore, were captured not by an advanced simian society but by "a wild tribe" convinced that he had come from somewhere between the Earth and the Moon. Wittgenstein asks, how would Moore convince them otherwise? Unlike Commander Taylor, he cannot *show* them anything by speaking the unspeakable. Unlike the simians on the Planet of the Apes, this wild tribe has no knowledge of physics. And it may have some fantastical ideas about "the human ability to fly."

Could Moore insist that he has never been to such a place as they say he has come from? But even if he did, what compelling grounds would he communicate to them that would be convincing? He could say he "knows" that there is no such place from which he is said to have come. But Moore is not up against an empirical disagreement with this wild tribe. He is contesting a logical disagreement. And they are playing an entirely different language game from his.

As Wittgenstein says, the language-game is "not reasonable (or unreasonable). It is there—like our life." The language game of the "wild tribe" is not based on something it "knows," any more than a child "knows" that milk exists. "Does a cat know that a mouse exists?" Ways of life via language are not based on "knowledge" or "experience" but on "acting." And the wild tribe's form of life, its daily and routine actions, is based on those things which it can never seriously doubt, or even consider doubting, if such a form of life is to function. Thus Professor Moore *must* have come from somewhere between the Earth and the Moon. We ourselves, along with Moore, might think of the wild tribe—as well as simians everywhere, on whatever planet—as "primitive beings," but here Wittgenstein gives us a timely warning: "I want to regard man here (i.e., in language games) as an animal; as a primitive being to which one grants instinct but not ratiocination—as a creature in a primitive state. Any logic good enough for a primitive needs no apology from us. Language did not emerge from some form of ratiocination."

Thus Moore, himself a primitive, is up against an equally primitive—but wildly different in its assumptive form of life—wild tribe. There's nothing he can say other than, perhaps, "Well, where I come from we do things differently." Wittgenstein would say that Moore should not say to the tribe, "I know I don't come from there," but rather "It 'stands fast' with me that I do not." It is not a matter of knowledge but of what simply cannot be borne—something that we just cannot have, any more than a "primitive" squirrel can entertain the notion that nuts are not for collecting.

Commander Taylor is, in a way, luckier. In addition to his ability to demonstrate the validity of alternatively logical foundations—what might be demonstrated to *us* the day a gorilla rides a horse and orders us about in perfect Shakespearean English—he also has two simian scientists, Zira and Cornelius who are ready to allow empirical investigation to trump logical social foundations, and thus permit an empirical process to transform a hinge proposition into a door one, and to metamorphose what was once the river bed into the stream (as happens, presumably, in geological phenomena as well). The planet's philosopher king, Dr. Zaius, has been promulgating some parallel to Plato's "Myth of the Metals" in *The Republic*, by which the members of an ideal society are convinced to do, via second nature, what they are told.

Though he knows there is evidence in a cave that the simians evolved from the despised humans, Dr. Zaius feels it is better to keep the simians in the dark. He gives them instead an origin myth justifying their permanent superiority, for if humans can devolve into apes, then apes can always devolve into humans—a dangerous idea. Wittgenstein observed, "The propositions describing this world-picture might be part of a kind of mythology. And their role is like that of the rules of a game. And the game can be learned purely practically, without learning any explicit rules." Wittgenstein's insight is also a key to why Dr. Zaius' origin myth is so flimsy. If it must be based on an *explicit* rule—Do not enter the Forbidden Zone or its cave— then it has not yet been woven implicitly or powerfully enough into the warp of the planet's society. Rulers who have to insist on rules are not potent. Dr. Zaius is reduced to having to destroy the evidence. His desperate powerlessness is also a lucky break for Commander Taylor's getting his humanness validated.

Thus Taylor (maybe until he sees the sunken Statue of Liberty and discovers to his horror that the Planet of the Apes is Earth itself) is a far more powerful foundation breaker than poor Professor Moore. Dr. Zaius is a far less powerful foundation upholder than is the chief of Moore's "wild tribe." "Take your stinking hands off me, you damn dirty ape" is far more effective, in saying what no human was presumed to be able to utter, than poor Professor Moore's "That I do not come from a place between Earth and the Moon holds fast with me." Taylor can suggest an empirical line of investigation that can shake social foundations. Moore can only confess that *his* logical foundation—*his* form of life—is not the same as that of his captors. He would be like a cat explaining to us that in its form of life, eating mice is a steadfast practice, never to be greeted with any form of skepticism. But if a cat could speak we could probably not understand him, just as Moore's captors cannot understand him.

Controlled Hallucination

Planet of the Apes represents a new type of fiction in which certainty is overturned without necessarily driving us insane. What's the aesthetic appeal of this type of fiction? Does it not reside in the play between logical and empirical propositions, between hinges and doors, or between rivers and riverbeds?

The science-fiction writer Bruce Sterling suggests that there is an emerging genre that is not strictly science fiction or speculative fiction. He calls it "SF," and says it is "a contemporary type of writing which sets its face against consensus reality . . . which makes you feel very strange: the way that living in the late twentieth century makes you feel, if you are a person of a certain sensibility."

Margaret Atwood has recently published a series of essays on the subject of what she too calls "SF" and also "thought experiment" fiction. She herself prefers to write not about things unlikely to occur, such as an attack by Martian lizard men, but about things more likely to occur, just as Jules Verne did when he wrote about submarines before there were submarines. At another point Atwood calls SF "a controlled form of hallucination."

A "controlled form of hallucination" means the difference between saying, "I am going to the store to buy a bottled baby" (hallucination without control) and "*Suppose* we could all go the store and buy the bottled baby of our choice" (hallucination under control), as in Aldous Huxley's *Brave New World*.

In *Planet of the Apes* we can live in a hallucinatory world and enjoy its freedoms while always feeling secure that we are in control. We can go through crazy doors that nonetheless swing on safe hinges; swim in wild rivers that nonetheless have stable beds. We can be as certain as we want that humankind lost the Earth to simians while being just as certain that they did not, at least not yet. This is a liberating beauty indeed.

17

Inside the Underscore for *Planet of the Apes*

WILLIAM L. MCGINNEY

Most audiences probably accept that film music can convey meanings about the mood or setting of a movie scene if for no other reason than because film music has been treated this way throughout its history. But where do the meanings brought by the music come from? Are they inherent in the music itself?

If the music has lyrics, we might say that meaning comes from the words. Indeed, as far back as the fifteenth century, the words of vocal music were considered the principal source of meaning in music. But most movie music is instrumental music, with no words to carry meaning. Yet, movies use music, assuming that it brings meaning to the film. Are there inherent meanings in instrumental music that movie music taps into? How and why does music seem to carry meaning, and where do those meanings come from?

There are actually two questions at work here: 1. whether "pure" music (that is, music without words) possesses inherent meanings, and 2. whether pure music can carry meanings, inherent or not. We can explore these questions by considering a highly original musical score such as that for *Planet of the Apes* that doesn't resemble more traditional styles of film music. Because of the score's unique nature, audiences might not expect it to convey meanings normally carried by film music. Despite this, most fans of the movie would probably argue that the score adds meaning to the film, although they may not be able to say what meanings it adds or how it adds them.

We might first confirm our sense that the score for *Planet of the Apes* carries meaning by imagining the movie without its music. We would still have the spectacular performances from Charlton Heston, Kim Hunter, Maurice Evans, Roddy McDowell, and the other cast members. We would have the dialogue and story, the remarkable prosthetic makeup and the settings that bring the world of the apes to life. But would the alien and desolate landscape of the Forbidden Zone seem quite so desolate without the music? Would the apes seem more or less alien (or human) without the music accompanying their activities? Would the film's pointed social commentary be as biting without the musical score?

Certain Young Cynics Have Chosen to Study Man

Planet of the Apes was a movie ripe with meaning for audiences in 1968, which allowed for the possibility and even the expectation that the music would carry meanings. *Planet of the Apes* appeared at the beginning of a cycle of science-fiction films that featured a dystopian future as a vehicle for critique of the present. This trend lasted into the mid-1970s and included all the movies in the original *Apes* series.

Planet of the Apes was also part of a broader movement in American cinema that saw filmmakers experimenting with existing film genres even as they used their films for social criticism. Although initially promoted as an action film, *Planet of the Apes* has since been widely discussed as an allegory for race relations and as a broader commentary on the place of "others" within Western society. It also includes pointed statements on the relationships between science and religion, the distinctions between "primitive" and "advanced" cultures, and the degree to which technology and progress mitigate humanity's own aggressive tendencies.

The meanings carried by *Planet of the Apes* resonated with several cultural currents coming together at the time of the film's release. The Vietnam War, the Civil Rights Movement, and environmental concerns all posed challenges to existing social and political values that became the subtexts for films and other artistic works of the period. The newly achieved artistic self-consciousness of American cinema enabled it to engage these social questions even as it explored and manipulated film conventions in ways that film audiences found meaningful. When considered in this social and cultural context, what would the unique score for *Planet of the Apes* bring to the table? Could it satisfy traditional functions of film music while also reinforcing other ideas?

The ability of instrumental music to convey meaning by itself has been debated since the flowering of instrumental music in the seventeenth and eighteenth centuries. Although composers and critics acknowledged that instrumental music could suggest emotions, they had greater regard for vocal music and its ability to convey specific ideas through words. In his *Critique of Judgment*, Immanuel Kant summed up this secondary status given to instrumental music when he called it "more pleasure than culture."

The status of instrumental music rose significantly during the nineteenth century, largely due to the influence of Romanticism, which placed great value on emotional experience. Questions of meaning in music stood at the center of debates between advocates of absolute music, which focused almost exclusively on form and thematic development (such as the instrumental music of Johannes Brahms) and a "poetic music" that sought to create meaning by combining music with poetic subjects (as in the program music of Franz Liszt and the operas of Richard Wagner).

The rise of modernism in the years after World War I saw composers rethinking fundamental attributes of music, especially harmony and form. In his autobiography of 1936, Igor Stravinsky famously wrote that he considered music to be "by its very nature, essentially powerless to *express* anything at all, whether a feeling, an attitude of mind, a psychological mood, a phenomenon of nature, etc." His statement resonated well into the second half of the twentieth century as modernist composers emphasized music's separateness from the idea of expression and celebrated musical works as autonomous aesthetic objects.

The music of *Planet of the Apes* sounds very much like the works of these composers as they explored new ways of creating and organizing music. But if the film's score was modeled on music that is assumed to carry no expressive content or outside meaning, how could the score do its job? Could it still carry meaning anyway, and where would that meaning come from?

For the More Ancient Culture Is the More Advanced

The significance of modernism generally lay in its break with the artistic practices of the past and the critique implied by that artistic break. Critics like Theodor W. Adorno frequently wrote about the "stylistic ruptures" at the heart of modernism and how those ruptures brought our attention to conventions, whether artistic or social, that were so common and familiar that they were treated as "natural." Modernism's advocates praised its austerity and intellectual purity over the commercialism and sentiment of popular culture.

During the Cold War, modernist art, with its implied critical stance, was promoted as an example of the freedom of expression available in the United States and the West. Its abstraction and emphasis on formal organization contrasted sharply with the overt appeals to sentiment and nationalism found in the state-sanctioned socialist realism of the Soviet Union and other communist countries.

As the most prestigious examples of modernist music, the severe and intellectually rigorous works of composers like Milton Babbitt, Roger Sessions, and Pierre Boulez took their places alongside the visual artworks of Jackson Pollock and Willem de Kooning as pillars of high art in the West. But this elevated status also conferred on modernist art and music the very sort of political and social associations that their austerity and abstraction sought to deny. Modernist art and music inadvertently stood for the Western values actively promoted by the United States, with its pervasive mass culture, its economic and military power, and its technological superiority. This music even symbolized the space program that, in the context of *Planet of the Apes*, would send Taylor and his crew on their fateful journey.

Reactions to modernism as part of the broader turmoil of the 1960s brought about a new artistic prestige for cinema that made movies like *Planet of the Apes* possible. Young, up-and-coming directors in the US banded together into a "New Hollywood" and explored familiar movie genres like westerns and science fiction to give critical perspectives on current events and conditions.

These filmmakers took an unfavorable view of Cold War politics and values and the ways that these shaped American society. By adopting recognizably modernist features into their films, such as the musical style used in *Planet of the Apes*, the filmmakers turned the critical power of modernism back onto the Western culture that was its chief patron and advocate. In the case of *Planet of the Apes*, the score's modernist style implicated Western culture as the cause of human self-destruction even before the movie revealed that Earth is the Planet of the Apes.

A Gorilla to Remember

By "modernist" music, I mean music that deliberately avoids the traditional practice of consonant functional harmony that informs most film music, popular music, and most familiar classical music. The music of *Planet of the Apes* is marked by unusual and exotic instrumentation, frenetic and relentless rhythms, eerie and off-kilter melodies, and unsettling atonal harmonies, all reminiscent of modernist concert music from the middle third of the twentieth century. These features were comparatively rare in movie music up through the 1960s, which encouraged their associations with that concert music and, by extension, its associated ideas.

Unusual timbres and instrumentation supply some of the most striking qualities of the music for *Planet of the Apes*. In addition to the standard orchestra, the score features a ram's horn, a slide whistle and a variety of exotic percussion instruments including log drums, scraped gongs, metal mixing bowls, and a Brazilian cuíka. Many of these sounds simply contribute to the oddness of certain settings. The agitated rhythms beaten on the mixing bowls create a bizarre sound that underscores the surreal barrenness of the Forbidden Zone as Taylor and his companions hike across it. Likewise, the scraped gongs add to the sense of arid, open space in these scenes. (The struck mixing bowls can be heard beginning at 16:19 and 26:01 on the Fox Home Video DVD. The scraped gong produces "whooshing" sounds that start at 15:42 and can be heard throughout scenes in the Forbidden Zone.)

The slide whistle and cuíka allude to the apes more directly by evoking simian vocalizations. The slide whistle, heard during the main titles and intermittently throughout the score, gives a soft hooting sound. The sounds of the cuíka are more animated, suggesting anything from short squawks to bellows and whoops. The cuíka's sounds appear during scenes of ape violence and aggression, notably Taylor's first sight of the marauding gorillas during the hunt (32:13 on the DVD), Taylor's escape and capture in the ape city (57:01 and 59:08), and the ape soldiers' ambush of Taylor's party in the Forbidden Zone (1:31:07 on the DVD).

The ram's horn, log drums, and similar instruments carry cultural associations with their striking and distinctive timbres. The log drums and other exotic percussion heard throughout the score sound reminiscent of instruments from non-Western cultures that in the past would have been called "primitive." Similarly, the rough, shrill timbre of the ram's horn has an almost primal sound that intensifies the war cries it emits during the scenes of the hunt and the ambush at the cave in the Forbidden Zone (33:10, 35:04, and 1:47:06 on the DVD).

Unusual rhythms abound in the score. Many musical passages rely on *ostinati*, or incessantly repeated rhythmic and melodic fragments. Other passages use syncopation, or emphasis of "off-beats," sometimes to the point where any clear sense of a regular meter or time signature is lost. The hunt and Taylor's first escape both feature rapid ostinati churning under a succession of punctuated chords (31:09 and 54:47 on the DVD).

Although these incessant ostinati and syncopations sometimes obscure the music's meter, they still emphasize the underlying pulse of the music. That pulse has a visceral, almost primal quality to it that can connote notions of "primitive," "non-civilized," or even "savage" to whatever the music is accompanying. When used to accompany scenes featuring apes, it marks the apes as "primitive."

He Keeps Trying to Form Words

Many composers of modernist concert music would have had little interest in cultivating these types of associations, preferring instead to think of these sounds as materials for abstract music. But John Cage was one composer who worried less about the construction of music and more about the experience of music. Although Cage took positions that some considered extreme (he regarded *any* sound experience as musical), he did allow for the possibility that music could carry meaning. For

Cage, however, any meanings related to music lay primarily with the listener and the listener's musical experiences.

Cage's ideas resonated with those of sociologists, musicologists, and other composers who increasingly saw music as a medium capable of *carrying* meanings even if it held no *inherent* meanings. These individuals understood music as a communication system that's much like language and able to convey meanings in similar ways. Comparisons between music and language were themselves nothing new; even Kant's contemporaries wrote of the importance of using language as a model for creating music with internal coherence. What was different about this newer thinking was its focus on how music is received and perceived rather than on prescriptions for composition.

Jean-Jacques Nattiez is one of several musicologists who include music among other "symbolic forms" that can carry meaning using words, pictures, "sound-images," or other *signs* that can refer to objects or concepts. Drawing on the works of pioneering linguists such as Ferdinand de Saussure and Charles Sanders Peirce, Nattiez describes "meaning" as the result of an individual's receiving signs and using them to understand and make sense of his or her existence. These signs possess meaning only in relation to other signs, and they are able to possess and convey meaning only because and only as long as we collectively agree on the references and associations that they carry.

Just as words and other signs acquire meaning through repeated association with objects and concepts, music can take on meaning through repeated association with a particular context or experience. Listeners learn that certain musical gestures can carry particular associations by hearing those gestures used multiple times in similar contexts. Because the musical score for *Planet of the Apes* sounds like modernist concert music, it recalls that music for listeners who are familiar with those sounds.

Traditional Hollywood movie music, music of the "Classical Hollywood style" from the 1920s through the 1950s, is replete with associations like this, carried by music. Beginning with silent films and continuing through the early years of sound films, Hollywood composers developed an extensive stockpile of gestures, styles, and other "codes" that they regularly used to evoke moods, settings, and characterizations, all to enhance the film being accompanied. Hollywood cultivated these associations because it assumed the ability of music to convey the meanings implied by these musical codes. Noel Carroll has called this movie music "modifying music." Carroll compared the functions of film music to the ways that adjectives and adverbs modify and give information about nouns and verbs in a sentence. Similarly, movie music works in tandem with other film elements such as image, story, and dialogue, contributing its own associations to the meaning of the whole.

None of these elements, including the music, has any inherent meanings. However, all of them carry associations accrued from the broader range of cultural experiences that audiences bring with them. It's the interaction of these associations with the audience's cultural knowledge that produces meaning in a film and in its music.

What I Know of Man Was Written Long Ago

In the case of the music for *Planet of the Apes*, the musical features that make it unique—the sounds of specific instruments, the rhythms and harmonies used, and even the compositional techniques used by the composer, Jerry Goldsmith—all carry their own distinctive associations. These allow the music to modify the images, story and dialogue of the film with ideas associated with those styles. In turn, those ideas affect how we receive the characters and understand the story based on our understanding of the cultural implications of the distinctive musical features of the score.

Angular, jagged melodies and discordant harmonies are features of the score that are probably most recognizable as "modernist." All of these materials are essentially *atonal*, meaning that there is no primary pitch or tonic that provides the music with a harmonic resting point. Because all of the melodies and harmonies in the score are non-conventional, they don't convey pathos, triumph, humor, or other moods in ways that are readily perceptible to the audience. Perhaps the most immediate and consistent impression that a listener might get is one of unease; otherwise, the music may seem dispassionate, with no sense of mood.

Jerry Goldsmith created the melodies and harmonies in *Planet of the Apes* using methods of twelve-tone composition, a modernist technique that contributes to the score's unsettling dissonance. The film's main theme juxtaposes wide leaps and closely spaced intervals to avoid any suggestions of a more traditional melody. This theme appears prominently in the movie's main titles, sounding successively by the flute, oboe, and clarinet, all while being accompanied by ostinati in the strings and piano. Versions of this theme also underscore scenes in the Forbidden Zone, where the slow tempo and widely spaced accompanying chords emphasize the desolate and open space of the setting (22:29 and 1:48:45 on the DVD among others).

"Twelve-tone methods," or "Composition with Twelve Tones," was a means of creating music using the atonal sounds often found in modernist music, but in a methodical way that brought coherence and unity to the otherwise unfamiliar and frequently discordant harmonies. The Viennese composer Arnold Schoenberg first wrote about the practice in the early 1920s and is credited with the concept, although other composers adopted and used a variety of individualized versions of these methods. Goldsmith self-consciously chose to use twelve-tone methods in the score, describing the process as "not avant-garde anymore; it's sort of old hat, but for film it is still sort of new."

Essentially, a composer using twelve-tone methods first creates a "tone row" from the twelve pitches of the chromatic scale (C, C-sharp, D, E-flat, E, F, F-sharp, G, G-sharp, A, B-flat, B). The composer then manipulates the row in a variety of ways to generate the melodies and chords used throughout a given piece. In *Planet of the Apes*, Goldsmith used a complete tone row to create the movie's main theme and used fragments of the row to create melodies and ostinati elsewhere in the score. The rapid piano figuration accompanying Taylor's escape in the Ape City derives from the main theme's tone row. Other short, percussive piano gestures, such as those heard in the opening titles, also have their source in that series.

Because a primary goal of atonal music is to give all tones equal emphasis, there is usually no contrast between consonant and dissonant sounds to create a sense of harmonic tension and release. This gives the harmonies and gestures in atonal music an abstract quality comparable to works of abstract expressionism such as the paintings of Jackson

Pollock. As with modern art, most mainstream audiences found such music puzzling and unsettling because of its unfamiliar, dissonant sounds and its cerebral aesthetic. However, they could accept sounds like those of twelve-tone music more easily when they were included as part of a movie score, especially for a horror or science-fiction film like *Planet of the Apes*. The startling, disturbing, and uncanny scenes and subjects from these films provided a context that gave meaning to the otherwise bizarre and disconcerting musical sounds.

Part of Goldsmith's purpose in creating his twelve-tone score was to characterize the strangeness of the setting and story with some suitably strange music. But by using these methods throughout the score, he left no room for any heroic or triumphant music. How does this affect his underscoring of the movie's hero, Taylor? And how else might Goldsmith's use of this culturally charged method affect the perception of Taylor as a heroic and sympathetic figure?

The Ape Evolved from a Lower Order of Primate

We've already mentioned the evocative timbres in the score that mark the apes as primitive: the cuíka and slide whistle that both produce sounds like ape vocalizations, the ram's horn that sounds almost like a barbaric war call, and the other exotic percussion that is suggestive of instruments from non-Western "primitive" cultures. Although novel and unique in themselves, these sounds fulfill a traditional function of movie music by using their associations to give the audience information about the setting and characters. They not only mark the apes as "primitive," but also mark the apes as "others" distinct from Taylor.

The unusual instruments, timbres, and other devices don't suggest notions of "primitive" solely from their sonic character. Take the prevalent ostinati and syncopations throughout the score. These features recall Igor Stravinsky's once-scandalous ballet, *The Rite of Spring*. Stravinsky's ballet depicts a human sacrifice conducted by an imagined prehistoric tribe to appease the gods of spring. The music features ostinati and syncopation along with dissonant harmony and fragmented, modal melodies to reinforce the primeval nature of the tribe and its rituals. Goldsmith's music for *Planet of the Apes* achieves a similar effect by using similar devices. Its resemblance to Stravinsky's famous work also highlights the score's own modernist features and thereby evokes the cultural associations of modernism.

Part of what makes these characterizations effective is how they interact with the oppositions between "human-ape," "advanced-primitive," and "civilized-barbaric" present in the movie. In addition to being very articulate, the apes have power and control, even though the music and visuals mark them as crude and uncivilized. The music becomes an integral part of the film's deconstruction of the notion of "primitive."

Traditional Hollywood movie music practice usually dictates that a film's protagonist will be accompanied by distinctive music, but as we noted earlier, this isn't really true of Taylor and his companions. They tend to be accompanied by atonal music that is mildly or moderately dissonant and provides little in the way of traditional cues for mood. Much of this music is either atmospheric or emotionally "flat" and dispassionate, as in the music accompanying the treks across the Forbidden Zone or even Taylor's pairing with Nova (heard at 42:18 on the DVD).

As the hero of the movie, Taylor should be the figure that the audience identifies with, but as Eric Greene has noted in his book, *Planet of the Apes as American Myth*, their identification with Taylor goes beyond just his character and includes the culture and civilization that Taylor represents. Yet, he has no heroic theme, fanfare, or any especially agreeable music. Even though Taylor is the movie's central character, the music *doesn't* perform one of its intended functions here, which is to encourage the audience to develop a strong emotional attachment to him. It's almost as if Taylor, despite being the protagonist, is somehow not a very likeable figure, and we sense that through the music.

Greene cites several critics who point out Taylor's alienated and even misanthropic nature, evident in his disaffected log entry at the movie's beginning, his goading and needling of his crewmates, his assumption of the inferiority of the apes he encounters despite their articulateness, and his ruthlessness and even brutality in taking Dr. Zaius hostage and tying him up. Much of Taylor's reaction is a response to his own harsh treatment at the hands of the apes. Still, after having earlier stated his desire to find a species or culture more compassionate than man, Taylor maintains an air of superiority toward Cornelius and Zira even as they help him escape. He seems unable or unwilling to acknowledge the depth of personal and professional sacrifice they have made in recognizing him as essentially an equal.

Taylor is a classic anti-hero, and the music's dispassionate and non-heroic nature captures his stance as a cynical outsider. But is that the whole story? What about the cultural meanings behind the twelve-tone methods that Goldsmith used to create this dispassionate music? Could they allude to ideas and values that go beyond Taylor, implicating the Western culture that he inadvertently represents as somehow responsible for bringing about the Planet of the Apes?

That Was the World We'd Made

Anti-heroes like Taylor were just the sorts of figures that filmmakers of the New Hollywood used as part of their social commentary. If Taylor is both an anti-hero and a de facto representative of Western culture, it's not hard to pick up on the commentary implied in this relationship. The music's style has its own connection to Western culture that strengthens the film's critique of Western culture through Taylor.

As an astronaut and scientist, Taylor is among the elite of Western technocratic society. Goldsmith's music, following the twelve-tone method, reminds us of Taylor's ties to the contemporary Western culture he shares with the audience by recalling the modernist concert music championed as the high art music of the West at the time. These associations invoked by the movie's twelve-tone music score are ironic, of course, because, in the story, *that* contemporary Western society is gone and its last surviving member is regarded as an animal by the newly dominant apes.

The score's twelve-tone passages take on a further measure of critique when that musical style's association with Western values—nominally democracy and freedom—are considered alongside other, less positive attributes of the West that Taylor displays, such as arrogance, aggression, and self-superiority. We could also add other forces shaping the West at this time that would have been fresh in the minds of the film audience: anti-communism, the arms- and space-race, and segregation. The disagreeable surface of the music provides its own commentary on the West's role in creating the Planet of the Apes.

Taylor's aggression and insistence on de facto leadership mirror that of the United States during the 1960s and its tendency to take actions in the Third World that not only contradicted its expressed regard for peace and equality, but also disregarded the wishes of indigenous populations. The war in Vietnam was easily the most visible example at the time. Such actions implied a belief by the West in its superiority over non-Western cultures due to its technological power and political ideology, both of which are evoked by the modernist musical style that the West promoted.

Taylor laughs at Landon's gesture of "claiming" the planet by planting an American flag at their landing site. Yet, Taylor's own thought on first viewing the native humans ("If this is the best they've got, we'll be running this planet in six months") suggests his own tendency to dominate rather than co-operate, even if his thought was expressed half-seriously. Again, Taylor's assumption of his superiority reflects that of his culture despite his culture's professed values of democracy and freedom that are supposed to be symbolized by modernist music.

Finally, Taylor's vocation as an astronaut places him at the center of the technological advancement that contributes to his society's self-destruction. Modernist music resonated with the highly rational, logical and scientific aspects of Western society that allowed technology such as space travel to reach the level of sophistication that it achieved. Modernist music also represented the values of democracy and freedom that, together with its quasi-scientific thinking, led to the West's cultural, technological, and economic superiority. But, as a product of Western culture, it was also the music of atomic bombs, ICBMs, and brinkmanship that, in the movie, overwhelm all of the positive attributes of Western culture and contribute to the demise of humanity. Despite their scientific advances, humans succumbed to their own primitive impulses and destroyed themselves, making the rise of ape culture possible.

None of this is inherent in the accompanying music, of course. The score acquired these meanings by evoking the ideas related to modernist concert music that it resembled. Indeed, the modernist concert music that was Goldsmith's model acquired its own meanings from its cultural reception during the twentieth century, first as an intellectually pure practice, then as an example of elite high culture, and finally as a political symbol. Goldsmith engaged all of these meanings through his use of twelve-tone methods and other modernist devices that permeate the movie's score. Even though these meanings don't originate in the music, they strongly affect our experience of *Planet of the Apes* due to the weight of the associations that they carry.

The mechanics for carrying these associations are much the same as in any movie music; the musical "adjectives" characterize and modify the filmic "nouns" and "verbs" of Taylor, the apes, and the movie's plot. The film's cultural environment allows those associations to point beyond those filmic nouns, however, and emphasize the subtext of *Planet of the Apes*.

What About the Future?

Subsequent movies in the *Planet of the Apes* series all used newly composed music, but they continued to use the modernist style of the first film. The composer Lalo Schifrin even preserved Goldsmith's particular modernist idiom in the title theme and underscore for the short-lived television series. The persistent use of this general style throughout all the incarnations of the *Planet of the Apes* films from the 1970s shows the extent to which it became part of the identity of the *Planet of the Apes* franchise.

Other science-fiction films released soon after *Planet of the Apes* also drew on the critical capacity of modernist music to inform their scores. Stanley Kubrick's *2001: A Space Odyssey* used portions of actual concert works by the contemporary Hungarian composer György Ligeti as part of its score. Over the next eight years, *THX-1138*, *Soylent Green*, *Zardoz*, *Rollerball*, and *Logan's Run* all followed suit, underscoring cautionary stories with modernist music to emphasize the dystopian aspects of their respective visions of the future. As in *Planet of the Apes*, part of the power of the music for these movies came from its invoking the cultural significance of modernist concert music for contemporary Western society, which was implicated as the source of each movie's depiction of a future gone wrong.

In the decades since the first release of *Planet of the Apes*, the modernist style that the score draws on has lost much of its cultural weight. Like other styles of movie music, it's become something of a commodity, sometimes accompanying uncanny and terrifying scenes in science-fiction and horror films as it has in the past. With the release of *Star Wars* in 1977, science-fiction movies became less critical and more escapist. They made little use of modernist music, returning instead to more traditional musical styles or relying on scores made up of pop and rock songs.

The music from *Planet of the Apes* may seem noteworthy today only for its uniqueness and the breadth of imagination that it shows. We have to use our own imaginations to reconstruct the associations it could have carried at the time of the movie's release, to understand how "modern" this music would have sounded to an audience in 1968, and to appreciate what that "modernity" would have meant then.

VIII

Ape Identity

18
Caesar's Identity Crisis

CHAD TIMM

> **CAESAR:** Am I a pet?
> **WILL:** Are you a pet? No. You're not a pet.
> **CAESAR:** Who is my father?
> **WILL:** I'm your father.
> **CAESAR:** What is Caesar?

"What is Caesar?" With this question begins an identity crisis that sparks a global ape revolution. Throughout the movie *Rise of the Planet of the Apes*, Caesar, who inherits increased intelligence from his mother's exposure to the experimental drug ALZ-112, struggles to know himself. Faced with conflicting images and societal expectations he goes from trying to *be* human to waging war *on* humans.

In order to have an identity crisis, however, Caesar first needs to have an identity. But what does it mean to have an identity? How do we come to know who we are in relation to the world around us? And what role does language play in the formation of a person's identity?

Rise of the Self

One approach philosophers have taken in accounting for the self is to establish a subject-object relationship. This approach holds that we essentially control our destinies and exist in an inner world where our thoughts are our own. According to this view our inner world contrasts with the world outside, including those objects that we perceive and come into contact with. René Descartes (1596–1650) went so far as say that everything can be doubted except his own existence when he proclaimed *cogito ergo sum*—"I think therefore I am."

Jacques Lacan (1901–1981) broke from this tradition by contending that we can't ever fully know ourselves. Lacan claims that a portion of our thought is always occurring somewhere else. This "somewhere else" is the unconscious, which operates parallel to the "self," or ego, and influences our thoughts, actions, and beliefs without our full awareness. We want to believe that we can fully know who we are, but according to Lacan that's impossible: a part of our thought is always occurring beyond our awareness.

The self, according to Lacan, is the result of the interplay of three interconnected "registers," what he called the imaginary, the symbolic, and the real. Each person's identity, or sense of self, arises out of the images we see (imaginary), the rules, laws, and expectations of our society (symbolic), and that which we can't symbolize or represent in words or language (real).

Think of this in terms of Caesar completing the Lucas's Tower intelligence test: being images, the shape and color of the disks—they could just as easily be flat squares—represent the imaginary register. The rules of the test, that only one disk may be moved at a time and that no disk can be placed on a smaller disk, represent the symbolic register. All of the unconscious thoughts that have yet to be put into words and all of the factors that are unknowable or unpredictable, like whether a fire alarm will suddenly sound or if a disk might inadvertently slip out of Caesar's hand, represent the real. The relationship we develop with these three registers dictates our sense of self and determines who we are.

He's Not a Monkey! He's an Ape

Compared to most other animals, human beings are all born prematurely. As infants we can't control our bodies, care for ourselves, or survive on our own. It's during this period of infancy that the child encounters the Lacanian register known as the real. From birth to about six months of age the child experiences life with no beginning and no end in something of a sea of stimuli.

Imagine all of your visual images blending together in a distortion like when looking into a circus mirror. The infant can't tell where it ends and the parent begins because there is no reason to believe it is a separate entity. After all, the child is basically attached to the parent, being fed, cleaned, consoled, and played with continually. This is even true of Caesar. During the short time he spends with his mother, Bright Eyes, in her cage in the lab she nurses, cleans, and grooms him as she holds him close to her. In Caesar's mind he has no individual sense of self, as he and Bright Eyes are *one*, his existence limited solely to the sea of stimuli in the real.

It's during the Mirror Stage, however, between six and eighteen months of age, that a child begins developing a sense of self after seeing its own image for the first time. Lacan describes this experience through the child's encounter with a mirror, but it could just as easily see itself through a reflection in its mother's eyes or even by watching other children at play and identifying with them. Through seeing itself in the mirror and encountering the reflected images the child leaves the real and enters the imaginary register. The night Will brings Caesar home, for example, he is confronted with the imaginary as Will rocks him to sleep. Caesar looks at Will, smiles, and we can imagine him seeing his own reflection in Will's eyes.

In his *Écrits* (Writings), Lacan states, "The function of the mirror stage thus turns out . . . to be a particular case of the function of imagos, which is to establish a relationship between an organism and its reality." These experiences are imaginary because they are comprised of images, what Lacan calls imagos, and these imagos are illusions because they are reflections. My reflection in the mirror isn't really *me*; it's merely a reflection of *me*, and therefore an illusion. Even though the images are illusions they are essential to the child's development as this entry into the imaginary is imperative for the child if it is to acquire a sense of self separate from his primary caregiver. In the domestic scenes in *Rise*, we see this process unfold with Caesar.

I'm Looking at the Man (er . . . Chimp) in the Mirror . . .

When Caesar stares into the lens of the camera as he plays chess with Will or sees his reflection in the attic window while watching children ride their bikes, he's captivated by what he sees. While Lacan found that normal chimpanzees quickly realize their reflection is an illusion and lose interest, this is not the case for the human child. "What demonstrates the phenomenon of recognition, implying subjectivity, are the signs of triumphant jubilation at the playful image starting in the sixth month." For Lacan the belief that you are the reflection in the mirror is a sign of a fledgling self-awareness, a quality shared by Caesar, a genetically enhanced chimpanzee.

The mirror stage is actually a metaphor because the child doesn't have to be looking at itself to see its reflection. For example, while looking out the attic window and watching children play, Caesar sees himself in them, reflecting back an image that he identifies with. Because he identifies so strongly with the children they *are* Caesar, and he *is* them. It's like an infant who cries when she sees a sibling or other infant injured. Identifying so fully with the mirror image, she struggles to differentiate the reflection from herself.

Parents and even grandparents also help give the child their self-image by affirming what the child sees in their reflection. During Caesar's first night with Will, Charles, Will's father, makes comments like "He's a cute little guy, isn't he?" and, quoting from Shakespeare's *Julius Caesar*, "But as for Caesar, *Kneel down, kneel down*, and *wonder*." These comments and others like "That's my boy" help Caesar internalize the images he sees and form the core around which his whole sense of self develops. According to Lacan, "This form would, moreover, have to be called the 'ideal-I'." Lacan calls mirror images "ideal-I" because these are the idealized images that we spend the rest of our life aspiring to be. Because they are imposed from the outside and are never really *us*, we can't ever fulfill our drive to be them.

They're Not People, You Know

While these images were necessary for Caesar to begin the process of creating an identity, they were also alienating because they came from outside. Caesar's budding sense of self, based on the images that represent him and who he will aspire to be, were the images of his own reflection and of children, both of which were *not* him. According to Lacan "The mirror stage is a drama whose internal pressure pushes precipitously from insufficiency to anticipation . . . and to the finally donned armor of an alienating identity that will mark his entire mental development." Mirror images are alienating because they are both outside of us and are inevitably inverted. When you look in a mirror your right becomes your left and your left becomes your right. This inversion creates the inevitability of misrecognizing what you see, what Lacan referred to as *meconnaissance*, which roughly translates as "misrecognition." Furthermore, the bodily integrity seen in the mirror is an illusion, especially given that the child at this age lacks complete control over motor functions.

For example, Caesar sees his mirror reflection in the children at play but the fact that he isn't in control of his body in the way they are and he can't control his voice the way they can results in tension. Caesar's mirror images contradict his physical self, a tension that was painfully obvious when he ventured into the neighbor's garage in an attempt to ride bikes with the children only to be chased out by a bat-wielding Hunsicker. Although there is a definite misrecognition in the images he sees, the mirror image—of being a human child—nonetheless becomes the goal to which he will aspire, but will never achieve.

The mirror stage is not merely a developmental phase that we grow out of—in fact, it remains a reference point for the self. The image we have of ourselves, our ideal-I, is constantly confronting the image reflected back to us from others. Our identity, therefore, is always in conflict with our notion of how we are perceived. Throughout his life Caesar comes back to this ideal-I as a goal but in order to enter into community and the symbolic order he must break from his sole relationship with the imaginary.

Your Ape. He Spoke

While the mirror stage represents the first encounter with the self, we come to know others through the second alienating moment in our lives: our entry into language. Will says "By eighteen months Caesar was signing up to twenty-four words," and we see Will and Caesar sitting at the dinner table while Will teaches him the sign for "home." Caesar begins acquiring language and for Lacan accepting language is the way we enter into the rules, laws, and customs of the society in which we live. This usually begins at about eighteen months of age and through language we encounter the third and final Lacanian register making up our reality, the symbolic order. Lacan referred to the symbolic as the *Other* because it is *"Other"* than us or outside of us. Whereas the image in the mirror represents our ideal-I, the symbolic represents what we think society expects of us. Our acceptance of language is necessary in order to break with the imaginary but further alienates us because we are never able to fully say what we mean or *be* what we think the *Other* wants us to be.

You Can Sign?

Lacan's philosophy of the self is heavily informed by linguistics, or the scientific study of human language. He was especially influenced by Ferdinand de Saussure (1857–1913), considered by many to be the father of twentieth-century linguistics. Saussure contended that we don't simply give names to the objects we encounter in the world. Instead, language is more of a sound and symbol system paired with the concepts they represent. In other words, there is what we mean, called a signified, and what we say or try to communicate, called a signifier.

For Saussure, what we say and what we mean are two sides of the same coin; they are linked together into what he called a "sign." The notion of the sign is especially relevant to Caesar and Maurice, given that they communicate signifiers through sign language. In this case hand gestures represent the signifier while their intended meaning represents the signified, as when Maurice signs to Caesar "Hurt bad?" and Caesar, surprised, replies "You can sign?"

Because we see objects in the world that we don't have words for, we don't understand, or that have multiple meanings, Lacan claims it's too difficult to completely represent them. Language is far too inadequate to fully express meaning, and because of the ambiguity of representing what we are thinking we are never able to fully say what we mean. Instead of a signifier representing a signified as Saussure contends, Lacan argues that signifiers are instead forced to refer to other signifiers in an endless chain of signification called metonymy. Think of it this way: Have you ever looked up a word in the dictionary only to find the word itself in the definition, or reference to another word that you have to look up as well? Looking up the word "tree" in the *American Heritage Dictionary*, I find: "a usually tall woody plant, distinguished from a shrub by having comparatively greater height and, characteristically, a single trunk rather than several stems." In other words, we don't find a real tree; rather, we find other words (signifiers) that describe the tree, some of which, such as shrub, we may even need to look up and whose definition may even contain the word "tree" (in fact it does). Not only that, but each of these words has multiple meanings beyond the "primary" one. Seemingly, we must rely on words to represent other words, never truly getting to the heart of what we actually mean.

There are a number of examples in *Rise of the Planet of the Apes* when language fails to help Caesar express what he means. When Will taught Caesar the gesture for "home," he could be referring to any place of residence, to a specific place of residence for Caesar's family, or to the process by which an animal instinctively returns to its territory. This metaphorically represents how all of language works: it never fully tells the whole truth.

In a pivotal moment in the movie Will, Caroline, and Caesar are walking through the park and Caesar is confronted by an aggressive German shepherd dog on a leash. Caesar is visibly upset, realizing he was also on a leash. Distraught, he signs to Will, "Am I a pet?" To this Will responds, "No, you're not a pet." In this instance the sign language gesture "pet" is what Lacan calls a signifier over-stuffed with meaning. The signifier "pet" can't hold all of the meaning being attributed to it. What is a pet? A pet can be an animal I own and care for, it could be someone I am particularly fond of, or it can be an action as well: I can even pet my pet!

It's a Madhouse! A Madhouse!

But what happens to all the meaning we are unable to express? It is forced into our unconscious. While Freud claimed the unconscious was all about biological instincts, Lacan asserts "It is the whole structure of language that psychoanalytic experience discovers in the unconscious." Because signifieds are over-stuffed with meaning and there is always more to what we say than we can express, the meaning that's left over is pushed into our unconscious, or repressed, and operates beyond our knowing. The result is a sense of self, an identity, which is split between the conscious, or what we are aware of, and the unconscious which is beyond our knowing. In the unconscious we essentially talk to ourselves without even knowing it!

The significance of the unconscious from a philosophical perspective is that the unconscious guarantees that we can never fully know ourselves. To return to Descartes's famous *cogito*, "I think therefore I am," his claim is that when we think we *are*, we become fully aware of ourselves. Descartes could doubt everything except his own thinking. For Lacan, the unconscious lies beyond doubt and as a result we can never fully know it. Lacan counters Descartes with "I am thinking where I am not, therefore I am where I am not thinking." To think we must use language. Language is unable to fully convey what we mean. Therefore, the more we think about our self the less we really know. Lacan's point is that the self exists as much in the unconscious as the conscious and maybe even more!

Bow Down to the Master Signifier!

So how does anyone understand anything we say? If meaning completely evaded us we wouldn't be able to communicate at all. If I say, "That's a beautiful sunset," you would understand that I'm expressing a certain feeling about the sunset, even though we may have different ideas about beauty. This is because there are certain signifiers that help to briefly link signifiers to the signified, what Lacan calls *points de capiton*, or the button-ties in a quilt that keep the stuffing from moving all over. These button ties are master signifiers, or signifiers that help organize and hold together all other signifiers and form meaning. Imagine two strings lying parallel to each other, one representing what we say and the other what we mean. A loop tied around the two strings bringing them closer together at certain points represent a master signifier. All societies have master signifiers that serve to represent a subject for other signifiers, like democracy, gender, or ecology.

In *Rise of the Planet of the Apes*, the master signifier that provides coherence to the flood of signification early on for Caesar might be *Family*. *Family* links together language, safety, community, play, clothing, and friendship for Caesar in a particular way. *Family* itself has no universal meaning, which allows it to quilt other signifiers together in much the same way that different people might define a "traditional" family. The clothes Caesar wears, the longing for human companionship, and his play with Will and Caroline in the attic or park reflect meaning that is "buttoned" in place by the signifier *Family*. Despite master signifiers helping to momentarily hold meaning together, when our idealized image formed in the mirror stage is contradicted by the way we are perceived by the *Other*, the result can lead to an identity crisis.

Am I a Pet?

To exist is to experience a lack, a hole in the center of our "self," because visual images are projected onto us and our own language can never fully convey what we mean. This lack, therefore, comes from the fact that we know something is missing but we can't quite put our finger on it because there are always elements of the *real* that haven't been symbolized through language. At certain moments in life we are confronted by gaps in the symbolic and we unexpectedly come face to face with bits of the real. For Caesar, an encounter like this begins an identity crisis that threatens his sense of self.

Seeing the dog in the park and identifying with it as a pet traumatizes Caesar because up to that point his identity has been completely wrapped up in his ideal-I. He's a chimpanzee that walks upright, wears clothes, and lives with a human family, all of which are in harmony with the idealized image he developed in the mirror stage. When Caesar realizes that to the Other he is merely a pet he is exposed to the real in a way that traumatizes him. When Caesar asks Will "Am I a Pet?" and "What is Caesar?" Will is unable to express through language what Caesar *is*.

Even though his sense of self wavers, his former image tries to come back, a flicker of his ideal-I, drawing Caesar back to the mirror. Caesar stands before the mirror shaking his head in disgust and looking at himself in confusion. Although still fascinated by his former self-image and trying to maintain a grip on it another event further compounds his identity crisis. Upon admission to the primate shelter he is confronted and assaulted by other chimpanzees. Not only is he not accepted into the human community, he isn't accepted by his biological community either. Caesar comes face to face with the void and realizes his entire sense of self is an illusion. As we've already learned from Lacan, the self *is* a void because it is a complete fabrication from the outside, but encountering this void is so traumatizing that Caesar teeters on the verge of a breakdown.

Apes Alone, Weak. Together, Strong

Since Lacan was most interested in developing a philosophy of the self to aid in the practice of psychoanalysis, he probably would have sat Caesar down on his couch and tried to help him symbolize some of the elements of the real that were stuck in his unconscious. If our identity, however, is formed through our ideal image interacting with the symbolic order, we also need to question what forms the symbolic order itself. Slovenian philosopher Slavoj Žižek (1949), a self-proclaimed Lacanian-Marxist, claims that ideological fantasy forms the symbolic which in turn impacts our sense of self.

Because language brings us into the symbolic order and can't say all that we mean, there's always something left over, like the remainder when you divide an odd number by an even one. The remainder makes us feel as if we're missing something, and Žižek calls this feeling the traumatic kernel of the real. Typically we cope with this by unconsciously creating fantasies where we try to fill the lack with things we think we want like sports cars, techie gadgets, or even world peace.

When our fantasies rest on the idea that there is some universal truth that is missing in the world, such as how a traditional family should be defined, whether we support unlimited gun control, or if humans should experiment on animals in order to find a cure for Alzheimer's, they become ideology. In *The Sublime Object of Ideology*, Žižek tells us, "The function of ideology is not to offer us a point of escape from our reality but to offer us the social reality itself as an escape from some traumatic, real kernel." So, ideology is a fantasy working through our unconscious that hides the two moments of alienation in the Lacanian subject. Just as the young Caesar mistakes the mirror image for himself, the adult misrecognizes ideological beliefs as the source of some universal truth.

It's a Question of Simian Survival

Caesar's identity crisis leads him to construct a fantasy of ape liberation. While fantasizing about taking the apes to the forest he signs to Maurice, the former circus orangutan, "Apes alone weak, together strong." Maurice's response, "Apes stupid," encourages Caesar to memorize the door code, escape the facility, and steal the remaining ALZ-113 from Will's refrigerator in order to increase the other apes' intelligence.

While leaving Will's house Caesar stops and looks at himself in the mirror. He doesn't see the same ideal-I that initially formed the core of his sense of self. Instead he sees a new Caesar, redefined in light of his confrontation with the real. His encounter with the absence of a universal self forces him to begin the process of re-establishing an identity he can live with. For Caesar, his new identity is rooted in the fantasy of being free and returning the apes to their home in the forest. *Freedom* becomes the new master signifier tying together Caesar's social reality.

Fantasy is essential in helping us cope with the lack that is a fundamental part of being human, but when fantasy takes the form of an ideology that claims there is some ultimate truth ordering the universe it becomes dangerous. To every ideological fantasy there is a positive and negative component. While our ideological fantasy contains a positive vision for a better world based on our particular viewpoint, it also contains the feeling that there is an *Other* lurking in the shadows plotting to destroy our fantasy. This belief in the evil *Other* can lead to horrific persecutions and atrocities. For example, in a 2001 interview, Žižek describes the way the ideological fantasy of solidarity and community in Nazi Germany led to the Holocaust. According to his argument, "Eichmann himself didn't really have to hate the Jews; he was able to be just an ordinary person. It's the objective ideological machinery that did the hating; the hatred was imported, it was 'out there.'"

Although freedom in the forest is Caesar's ultimate goal in *Rise of the Planet of the Apes,* the ideological fantasy of ape liberation also includes the underlying belief that the human species is a savage, oppressive *Other.* In later movies in the series the apes eventually take this ideological fantasy to its terrifying conclusion and return the oppressive favor by capturing, imprisoning, and treating humans as animals in the way apes once were. Just as capitalist, consumerist, or religious ideology forms the symbolic order into which American citizens develop identities, the ideology that humans should be subservient to apes is the ideology that structures the new symbolic order depicted in the 1968 movie *Planet of the Apes*.

This, therefore, is the real danger of ideology: it serves to form the symbolic structures that in turn dialectically form our "self." Society's rules, laws, and expectations play a pivotal role in our identity because when we use language we accept those rules and laws. When those rules and laws are formed by particular ideological understandings our identity gets wrapped up in this ideological fantasy imposed upon us by the symbolic.

What Would Žižek Do?

Žižek calls for us to work to disrupt the symbolic order and destabilize the ideologies that determine our reality. This destabilization, what Žižek calls traversing the ideological fantasy, involves confronting the void in what he refers to as an Act. As he wrote in 2010, "An act is more than intervention into the domain of the possible—an act changes the very coordinates of what is possible and thus retroactively creates its own conditions of possibility." We can do this when we consciously recognize the way ideology tricks us into believing there is a universal reality.

Confronting the real, coming face to face with the illusion of reality, invokes trauma but also has the potential for re-positioning and/or reforming the ideal-I. In seeing how we are being played on the puppet strings of the symbolic through ideology we can restructure or redirect our desire into a new fantasy that is more our own. This is the key: by traversing the ideological fantasy we won't all of a sudden see the Wizard behind the curtain, or reality for what it truly is. As Žižek says in a 2000 essay, "In an authentic act, I do not simply express/actualize my inner nature—rather, I redefine myself, the very core of my identity."

This is exactly what Caesar does when he confronts the trauma of his own identity crisis. Given that he was not a human being or even an ordinary chimpanzee, but something entirely different, Caesar recognizes that what he thought was his identity was actually a fiction. He embraces the void and the absence of a universal self and cuts ties with the symbolic order and its oppressive ideological rules of conformity. Thus Caesar completes the Žižekian Act, inhabiting a space in between chimpanzee and human being, and seeks to reformulate the symbolic order free from ideological control. No longer traumatized, Caesar finds peace in this space between spaces, and when approached by Will in the forest who tells him "Come home and I will protect you," Caesar leans forward and defiantly proclaims "Caesar *is* home."

19
Aping Race, Racing Apes

Jason Davis

It's one of those stories that's the stuff of legend. Soon after *Planet of the Apes* was released, Sammy Davis, Jr., the black entertainer, thanked and congratulated Arthur P. Jacobs and Mort Abrahams, the movie's producer and associate producer, for making the best film he'd ever seen on US black-white race relations. And Jacobs's response? He had no idea what Davis was talking about. End of story.

But the legend also says something about the nature of knowledge of race and race relations. And it's less about what Davis sees in *Planet* than what Jacobs doesn't see. After all, the original movie has a lot to say about race relations in America. A "racial" caste system divides social roles, power, and opportunities. There is a "quota system" for advancement among the ape species, with dark-skinned apes furthest from the fields of science and law, which are dominated by light-skinned orangutans.

So it's not so much whether Davis's take on the movie is merely a personal or subjective view that was never the explicit intention of the white producers. It's more the producers' cluelessness that a black person would see the movie's ape-ing of racial conflict and violence through their own experiences and knowledge of a racist country. The race relations played out in the science-fiction world of *Planet of the Apes* reveal what Planet Hollywood could never say directly—not even to themselves apparently—about the lived reality of black America. In both art and in life, it illustrates how white privilege depends upon a self-sustaining blindness to racism, suffering, and white domination. To put it a bit more strongly, this obliviousness by white folk to race and racism exemplifies an epistemology of ignorance.

Epistemology is concerned with how humans gain knowledge about themselves and the world. So looking at how ignorance affects knowledge means not just detecting what is lacking in someone's understanding or knowledge. It's also about how ignorance determines the knowledge a dominant group can have about themselves and others. This might sound as if it's describing the orangutan religious/scientific elite of the first two Apes movies, who deny and even destroy evidence and, therefore, knowledge of human civilization, and the human origins of apes. But that kind of ignorance is more a willful suppression born out of fear of humans.

A better example is the human reliance on and enjoyment of the slave labor of apes in *Conquest of the Planet of the Apes*. The human benefit, both in terms of pleasure and profit, from ape slavery is facilitated by not knowing the torturous cost of ape "training" provided by the benignly named Ape Management. It's more than just not knowing what it takes to have your non-carcinogenic cigarette lit by Frank or roasted quail flambéed by ape with cognac (or maybe that one-percent burger with Kobe beef braised by the ape bus boy, with foie gras, gold leaf, and Grey Poupon). It's also not knowing the experiences of other humans involved in the daily labor of making apes more servile (obviously other than investors in ape slavery services).

This deliberate ignorance of class distinctions and inhumane treatment and class becomes part of the justification for ape slavery. Practices and beliefs are a ritualized form of willful human ignorance, naturalizing a deficient, even distorted, understanding of the order behind the existing state of things, including the privileged place of humans in such an order. And this ignorance shows up in the need not to know otherwise, not to think beyond what's experienced. What the epistemology of ignorance tells us about a dominant group is that they benefit from seeing the world wrongly.

Aping the Makeup of Race

Aping humans. That's *Planet of the Apes* scholar Eric Greene's take on how apes got their ideas for their own "racially discriminatory society: they copied it—aped it—from human beings." There's another way the movies ape human thinking about race, namely our ontology of race: our operative concepts of what race is, and the ways it exists in the world.

To inquire into race is to inquire both into human attitudes and into the makeup of reality. And makeup very much makes up the racial world we see in the *Planet of the Apes* movies. Hair and skin color, facial features, size, and build are physical differences distinguishing the ape castes into species. Likewise, behavior and intelligence reflect what role each sub-species can have in ape society. That's how the movies get us to think about racial identity and discrimination. That's also one of the ways race has been understood in reality, as a visible way of putting people into different groups according to shared physical traits and behavioral characteristics. So in a way, the films are relying on a perceived biological realism about race. To be a biological realist about race is to hold that race exists independently or outside of human minds or consciousness, and that scientifically racial categories are more like natural phenomena, than something socially constructed.

Moreover, with apes and humans perpetually in conflict with each other, and the three ape species displaying characteristics that set each group distinctly apart, there's another aspect or dimension to the apes' world: biological essentialism. For those apes controlling military power and scientific truth, humans are inherently destructive, ruinous, and incapable of civilization. Even chimpanzees see humans as a species uniquely disposed towards violence against each other.

Apes, on the other hand, define themselves as categorically different from humans because of their lack of ape-on-ape violence. Within ape society, the essential differences between the species are played up. Members of each species share intellectual and behavioral qualities that the other species don't. So to be a chimpanzee in the world of the *Planet of the Apes* movies is to be pacifist, open-minded, and book-smart. That such qualities aren't part of the ontological makeup of gorillas ought to be worrying. Is biology destiny for a segregated ape society? Are gorillas literally "being all they can be" in the army? Are chimpanzees destined to be always marginalized and disenfranchised in ape society no matter how many times Cornelius and Zira travel back into ape pre-history and beget the chimpanzee liberator of apes from slavery?

It's the last movie of the original series that suggests some answers. In *Battle for the Planet of the Apes*, the last prequel of the series (and yes, if you think about it, the films after *Beneath the Planet of the Apes* are all prequels), there are changes to the nature of apes and the social order of things— biology is not destiny. A chimpanzee is in power, orangutans work for peaceful co-existence with humans, and friendships exist between the ape species. Go figure. Apes also become "more human."

The species-defined divide between apes and humans has ended. Unfortunately, so has the innocence of Caesar, with the traumatic breaking of the cultural prohibition against ape killing ape. And ape-human relations are recast, with humans integrated into ape society as servants and workers under "ape management." So we get a shakeup, but not a complete upending, of both essentialism and biological determinism of apes and humans: for gorillas, the more things change, the more they know their AK-47s better than their ABCs.

Nevertheless, *Battle for the Planet of the Apes* introduces us to social and historical differences in how apes can co-exist with each other as well as with humans. This suggests that not all influences on identity and behavior are biological.

Race and the Point Zero One Two Percent

Is race biologically real then? Ironically, just as science is employed in *Planet of the Apes* and *Beneath the Planet of the Apes* to perpetuate the myth of humans as primitive pestilence, science has also been used to make claims about the biological nature of race among humans.

The idea, originating in eighteenth-century Europe, that humans can be classified into distinguishable subgroups that reflect biologically real racial differences based on physically visible traits is about as scientifically valid as Zaius's claim that humans never possessed the capacity for speech. The 'scientific' claim that physical characteristics, such as the color of human skin, eyes, hair, as well as the size of lips, hair texture, height, and build are the result of naturally occurring racial divisions has been discredited by developments in late-twentieth-century science, such as population genetics and biological anthropology.

How? Take MacDonald and Governor Jason Breck. Comparing their DNA would show no more than 0.2 percent difference between their individual genetic material. And as for the genetic makeup of the racial differences between them, that only amounts to 6 percent of that 0.2 percent. That means race accounts for about 0.012 percent of all human genetic material. And let's not forget the genetic comparison that would shock both Breck and Caesar, that ninety-nine percent of a chimpanzee's functionally important DNA is identical with that of a human. Look who's occupying the genus *Homo* now.

From a biological perspective then, racial classification tells us very little about the genetic diversity of humans. As the authors of *How Real Is Race?* explain about genetics research published the same year as the cinematic release of *Conquest of the Planet of the Apes*, the racial categories we've inherited based on geographical differences were not only "biologically virtually meaningless" when used for studying human genetic diversity; they also hampered efforts to further understand such variation. Racial categories are made up of recognizable markers that are only a very small part of visible biological variation in humans. And the greatest amount of human genetic variability is invisible to us as it occurs beneath the surface of human bodies. Just as Cornelius challenges the accepted, naturally occurring reality paradigm about humans as the backward, mute creatures the Almighty Ape always intended them to be, the biological reality of race is also something that shouldn't be taken as a naturally occurring, observable reality.

Not everyone agrees that racial categories have no biological basis. For example, Robin Andreasen has argued that there are breeding populations within the human race, each traceable to a distinct ancestral population, and that these breeding populations are races. One difficulty with this view, besides the fact that lots of interbreeding has gone on and still does, is that the identified breeding populations do not match recognized races. Thus, even if we defined race in this way, it would undermine, not support, our accepted racial categorizations. Moreover, defining race in this way would also undermine any expectation of shared race-wide traits, as each breeding population continued to diverge from its founding population.

Can a Planet Long Endure Half Human and Half Ape?

Depending on which side of the twenty-first century you are on when reading that tagline from a poster for *Beneath the Planet of the Apes*, you might've answered: For as long as there are sequels or prequels and reboots. But it's also suggestive of something more than a cynical answer.

What if it also means something half-human and half-ape, like a child born of interspecies sex? Would this new species pass for ape, or human, or neither? If you're a *Planet of the Apes* fan, you'll know that an ape-human hybrid character now exists in that universe full of other abandoned and unused ideas for the *Planet of the Apes* series that never made it into the finished movies. Because of the association of interspecies with interracial sex, the ape-human child was too controversial to risk losing the family film rating the studio wanted for *Beneath the Planet of the Apes*.

After all, it'd been only three years before, in 1967 that the US Supreme Court had done away with anti-miscegenation laws. These were laws that made marriage illegal between whites and non-whites. That a fictitious, half-ape, half-human child would invoke fears about real interracial coupling and sexual relationships tells us something about the limits of what even the *Planet of the Apes* movies could show about US race relations. Then there are the 'what ifs' had such a character been included. Would a child born of ape and human be ape enough to keep the 'divine spark' that separates apes from humans? Or would the child be human enough for Governor Breck to grant it freedom from slavery?

But even without this symbolic child, the ape society of the movies reflects pretty much what anti-miscegenation laws were created to keep in place: a racial caste system. It's not so much that we don't get to see the ape version of the protection of 'racial purity' with laws that refuse to recognize the legitimacy of children from apes and humans. What's being played out in the ape societies is a social order, where *who* gets to do *what* is based on the visible physical differences between apes. What if chimpanzees and orangutans, or gorillas and orangutans, had children? Would those "interracial" children be enough like one of their parents to be permitted or prevented from entering the National Academy of Science? Deciding how dark or light an ape's skin or fur color has to be to pass as orangutan or chimpanzee, or determining if an ape of mixed parents is behaviorally more chimpanzee than gorilla to be an officer in the ape military, sound like more "humanizing" twists of ape society's racial politics.

But these 'what ifs' are closer in kind to the questions about changes in ape nature and racial identity that *Battle for the Planet of the Apes* raises. After all, having brown fur and skin in one ape population could have the same ape regarded as 'just black enough', or even as light-colored in another ape community. And even where an ape thought of herself as belonging to one caste, social enforcement of what counts as membership is a reminder that subjective or individual choices about racial identity collide with institutionalized racial categories. To ape race a bit more, apes visually test apes with parents of different ape castes to see who's more gorilla than chimpanzee. This is a good example of how the ontology of race is made up of social constructs such as laws, practices, and shared beliefs, rather than-biology. As *Battle* shows, the ontological makeup of race can and has changed for social reasons and will continue to change.

Black, White, and Read All Over

The original movie's iconic use of the Statue of Liberty brings to mind how racial categories in the US have changed. You might not think twice about Italian- and Irish-Americans today being as white as Charlton Heston, but as nineteenth-century immigrants, Irish and Italians were regarded by many Americans as not white. Likewise, someone categorized as black in the United States might be classified as brown, 'colored', or even white in the Caribbean, South Africa, or Latin America, as Charles W. Mills has pointed out.

Philosophically, this gets us away from racial realism, which argues that racial differences reflect natural kinds of human differences, and into metaphysical thinking about race as socially constructed. For philosophers such as Charles W. Mills, Sally Haslanger, and Lucius Outlaw, race, racialism, and racial identity are social phenomena. And arguing that such social phenomena don't exist independent of human beliefs isn't denying that race has an objective reality. The social ontology of race is very much bound up with social institutions, such as political, educational, and legal systems, as well as what has been inherited from human history. The basic social reality of such things, how they endure or get reproduced, challenged, and changed, stems from their objectivity outweighing what individuals think. Social objectivity is a shared or intersubjective construction. Mills sums up the social ontology of race, and some of what *Battle* tells us too, with three things that race isn't:

> **Race is not foundational: in different systems, race could have been constructed differently or indeed never have come into existence in the first place.**

> **Race is not essentialist: the same individuals would be differently raced in different systems.**

> **Race is not 'metaphysical' in the deep sense of being eternal, unchanging, necessary, part of the basic furniture of the universe.**

But reactions to the *Planet of the Apes* movies also show other aspects of the social ontology of race. For one thing, Hollywood is part of the social ontology of race. Mort Abrahams and Arthur P. Jacobs's cluelessness at Sammy Davis, Jr.'s challenging read of a movie where the only black guy doesn't even survive to buddy-up with the white male lead points to how Hollywood has, and mostly hasn't, contributed to the wider society's challenging of social exclusion of non-whites. In the *Journal of Personal and Social Psychology*, research into mental associations between Blacks and apes has been identified as symptomatic of American society's "broader inability to accept African Americans as fully human."

Black comedian Paul Mooney flips white folks' long-standing racial association of apes with blacks by drawing on the social ontology of race. Mooney notes how the thin lips, straight hair and light skin of the chimpanzees and orangutans of the *Apes* movies look more like whites' interpretations of how blacks see them.

And the Lawgiver said, Let There Be No More Talk of Race

For philosophers such as Kwame Anthony Appiah and Naomi Zack, what comes out of arguing for the non-existence of race is the need to eliminate the use of racial references as labels for people because they're misleading about what is actually being referred to. Can the same argument be made for the *Planet of the Apes* films? "No More War" and "No More Arms Race" are slogans capturing the anti-war and anti-nuclear-war political messages of the first two films, but can the films also be said to say "No More Race"? Do they have something to say about what we ought to do with "race talk"? If the terms or concepts used to describe or refer to people as "Black," "White," "Hispanic," or "Asian" don't refer to a natural kind or racial essence in the world, do the movies give us better terminology?

You mightn't have thought about the *Planet of the Apes* movies as having much to say about race. For one thing, it doesn't sound anything like what the films' racial politics was aiming at. The race war and annihilation of both apes and humans at the end of *Beneath the Planet of the Apes* makes it pretty clear that an end to the use of racial categories or types as a social solution in the real world is ruled out. But interrogating the movies is one way of seeing where we stand today on the social construction and implications of race.

To view the movies as racial allegory presents a problem if you're skeptical of race and racial identity in the first place. Racial skeptics like Appiah and Zack, who argue there's no reality behind the racial terms used to refer directly to racial phenomena in the world, wouldn't be so accepting of the *Planet of the Apes* films as a form of "race talk." They'd see the movies as contributing to more of the racial concepts and terms that we ought to stop using. But for philosophers like Charles Mills, the social reality of race, both as racism and as a positive form of cultural racial identification by individuals, is very much at the heart of issues, such as social justice and social membership, that define human identities.

Black to The Future of the Planet of the Apes

There's no denying that comedy and humor have given the original *Planet of the Apes* movies an afterlife. From *The*

Tonight Show Starring Johnny Carson to *Saturday Night Live* send-ups; from *The Simpsons* musical spoof to stand-up comedy, such as Dana Gould's alternate-world Americana involving the channeling of Maurice Evans's original Dr. Zaius doing Hal Holbrook's Mark Twain: ("When I was a boy in Hannibal, Missouri, my comrades and I had but one goal: The destruction of the vile pestilence known as man . . . and to be a steamboatman").

But leaving the films as "campy fun" forgets how they invoked race and racial politics when other science-fiction movies left such issues off the screen. The original *Planet of the Apes* movie with a black astronaut showed us how white the future was back in *2001: A Space Odyssey* (cue Gil Scott-Herron's "Whitey's On The Moon"), while in our year 2001, Tim Burton's remake has a simian Lincoln Memorial conjuring up past racist caricatures of Abraham Lincoln as "Abraham Africans I" and "the original orang-outang."

Even the iconic ruins of Lady Liberty Forever remix the US history of immigration, anti-miscegenation, and racialism: "Give me your tired, your poor, your huddled masses yearning to breathe free. . . . Just keep your dirty, stinking paws off our white women." Or compare *Conquest of the Planet of the Apes* with its black characters and simian replaying of black America and slavery with the question a *Village Voice* writer quoted from a young black kid taken to a screening of *Star Wars* when it was first released: "Where are all the black people?" The same could be asked of *Blade Runner* five years later.

The *Planet of the Apes* movies reflect Black America. And what better ape-philosophers of race than Caesar and Cornelius? They're Roman names, after all, from a time in human history when race as a category didn't exist.

20
Rise of Being-in-the-World

SHAUN MAY

An ape walks into a bar and orders a beer, passing the barman a $10 bill. The barman, thinking the ape wouldn't know how much change to expect, gives him $1 in return. "You know, we've never had an ape in here before", says the barman. "I'm not surprised," the ape replies, "At these prices you won't get any more!"

There are hundreds of jokes like this, featuring an animal that's more humanlike than the people around it expect. In *Rise of the Planet of the Apes*, the central character Caesar slowly becomes humanlike—but what exactly does that mean?

Consider the scene about thirty minutes into the movie in which Caesar corrects Charles, afflicted with Alzheimer's, who is holding a fork incorrectly at the breakfast table. This isn't the first sign that Caesar's intelligent, but it's an important one which demonstrates the main thing that philosopher Martin Heidegger argues distinguishes humans from other animals.

According to Heidegger, man is a 'being-in-the-world'. At first this seems blindingly obvious—aside from the crazy guy at my local bus station, I can't think of anyone who would deny that we live in a world. But Heidegger's point is a bit more subtle than this—for him, we're not in the world in the same way that Jelly Beans are in a jar. It's more like being in love or in the army. If I say, 'General Aldo's in the army', I don't mean that he can always be found at a particular place such as the barracks, but that he's committed to a certain activity with the skills and equipment that go along with it.

I'm in the world in the same sense—I have projects that matter to me and equipment and skills that enable me to do them. At the moment, I'm writing a chapter for *Planet of the Apes and Philosophy*, using a dusty old laptop and my touch-typing skills. Earlier this afternoon, I used a different skill-set to make myself a grilled cheese sandwich using two knifes, a chopping board and George Foreman grill. I'm not telling you this to boast (although I have to say, I do make a mean grilled cheese sandwich) but to draw out Heidegger's main point—human life is defined by the huge array of projects, equipment, and skills that underpin everything we do.

When Caesar corrects Charles, he demonstrates this practical understanding, and Heidegger claims that this sort of understanding is what distinguishes humans from other animals. Although other animals might use sticks to get termites from a mound, humans have constructed millions of tools, including tool-making-tools, which pervade every part of our lives: from breakfast table to bathroom, tools are involved in even our most basic bodily functions.

Returning to the example of Caesar correcting Charles's use of the fork, what does it mean to use a fork 'correctly'? Growing up in England I was taught to hold the fork in my left hand, but if I'd been raised in Boston I might have been taught the opposite. As an adult, I don't often get told off for using the fork incorrectly, but I do sometimes have the embarrassment of asking for a fork in a sushi restaurant because I suck at using chopsticks. Different cultures have different rules about what, where, and how you should eat but there aren't any human cultures that have no rules about eating. The chimp, by contrast, doesn't keep hold of the stick long enough to develop rules about how to use it—as far as we know, no chimp has been shouted at by his mother for fishing for termites using the wrong hand.

When Caesar corrects Charles's use of a fork, he demonstrates that he knows the rules we are taught as we grow up, a knowledge that isn't found in other animals. These rules are what distinguishes a human sitting at the table from a parrot being in the same place. Like 'being-in-the-world', sitting at the table means more than being in a particular physical space—it requires a certain skill-set and an understanding of the rules and norms surrounding the equipment that we use. Although most of these rules are unspoken we usually know when we have broken them from the tuts and glares we get from other people. (The fact that they are now largely unspoken is probably a sign of progress—in the 1950s, English schoolchildren were frequently beaten for writing with their left hand!)

When we arrive at the ape civilization in the original Charlton Heston movie, we find the apes living in a world as complex as ours. They have an operating table that they use to treat Heston's character, Taylor, and they have a range of surgical equipment that they use with precision. As with human doctors, the apes that use the scalpel have trained for several years before wielding it, something for which there isn't any equivalent in the rest of the animal kingdom.

All of this might seem to be stating something trivial or obvious, but for Heidegger this means that the understanding that humans, Caesar, and the other 'worldly' apes have is completely different from the sort of understanding most animals have of objects. For us, the chair is understood as 'to be sat on' and the table is 'to be sat at'; the scissors are 'grippable' and 'to be used for cutting paper'. All of this is governed by (mostly) unsaid rules which keep everything going smoothly. In physical anthropology, it's often said that what distinguishes us from other primates is our opposable thumbs, meaning that we can form a range of grips that no other animal can. The fact that we're in a world with millions of man-made tools which we can grip easily and without thinking means that we are the 'handy animal'. But this isn't the only difference between us and other animals, another obvious one being language.

He Spoke

In both the original movie and the recent prequel, the iconic phrase "Take your stinking paws off me, you damned dirty ape" is prominent. In the first movie, the apes react with shock as Taylor uses something that they thought was unique to their species, language. In *Rise of the Planet of the Apes*, we see a reversal of that—the phrase is uttered by Dodge Landon, a cruel caretaker who's being dominated by Caesar, and Caesar surprises him with a cry of 'No!'.

It's not an accident that language is so prominent in both movies—often language is said to be the distinguishing feature of human life. A fantastic documentary that explores just this is *Project Nim*, which was released a week after *Rise of the Planet of the Apes*. This film follows a research project at Columbia University that attempted to raise a chimp, dubbed Nim Chimpsky as a cheeky nod to the linguist Noam Chomsky, in a human environment in which he learned American Sign Language.

The success of the project is hotly debated, with the project's leader eventually declaring that he thought it was unsuccessful. One of the main things that came out of the experiment is that Nim was unable to learn what's known as 'syntax'—the change of meaning created by word order. So, for Nim there is no distinction made between "Nim eat banana" and "banana eat Nim." For us and the apes in the *Planet of the Apes* series, there is.

In the tribunal where Taylor is tried, Dr. Zaius states that "The Almighty created the ape in his own image," echoing the well-known Christian doctrine. Here, syntax is really important—claiming that 'the ape created the Almighty' means the exact reverse of what is being argued. Dr. Zaius demonstrates a grasp of language far more sophisticated than what Nim or any other chimp we've studied is capable of.

In a rather mystical manner, Heidegger claims that if we want to say that the lizard lies on the rock, the word 'rock' ought to be crossed out, as it smuggles in too much of our human understanding. What he means by this is that the words that we use are deeply tangled with our practical use of things. As I mentioned earlier, we understand scissors primarily as 'grippable' and 'to be used for cutting paper', and when we use the word 'scissors', its use and handiness is what we're referring to.

When I say that Taylor holds the rifle, his holding it refers to more than just having it in his hands—it involves him understanding what it's for and how to use it. In *Rise of the Planet of the Apes*, Charles holds the fork incorrectly but Nim wouldn't 'hold' it in the same way at all, as holding something involves a sense of how you 'ought' to hold it and what you would normally use it for. So, if we say 'the lizard sits on the desk', (crossing out the word 'desk' as Heidegger insists that we should) what this means is that it sits on the thing that we call a desk, but it doesn't understand it as a 'desk' because it doesn't know what it is for and how to use it.

What about the simplest example of language use—pointing and naming something? In *The Planet of the Apes*, Taylor points out where he landed on the map, but that involves a complex representation of geography. Instead, think of the simpler act of pointing at an object and giving it a name, such as 'tree'. This act, called 'ostensive definition' by some philosophers, is more complicated than it seems as it's actually quite ambiguous. If I'm sitting with my niece and point to a tree in the window, how can she be sure that the word 'tree' refers to the object rather than the color or the way it sways in the wind? In fact, how does she know that I'm pointing at something beyond the pane of glass immediately in front of us? We can only make sense of such pointing because we are already in the world with each other—there's a sort of tissue of things that we both take for granted, including the practice of pointing (which, it should be noted, we aren't born with—we learn it like many other practices).

There's a lot of evidence to suggest that chimpanzees are unable to understand pointing, and although some researchers have suggested domesticated dogs can understand it, I think the jury is still out on that one (Raymond Tallis's book *Michelangelo's Finger* looks in depth at the act of pointing, and it's well worth a read if you're interested). Returning to Taylor pointing to the map, this is a practice that we acquire socially much like using a fork or learning to speak. Most of us have become so good at reading maps that we take map-reading skills for granted. It's important to remember that it is a practice that we each have to learn as individuals and developed collectively at some point in our history, and the same is true of pointing. Not wanting to belabor the point, it's a practice that we learn on the back of our already being in the world with others.

Now, it's probably worth adding that there are loads of philosophers who disagree with both me and Heidegger on many of these points. But I think one of the big advantages of Heidegger's view is that it avoids a common trap in discussing the difference between humans and other animals—trying to guess what other animals might be thinking. Precisely because we can't have a chat with them, we really can't know. Some philosophers, such as Descartes, have suggested that animals don't have minds at all, whereas others have just suggested that we can't know if they do. I think the way around this is to focus almost entirely on observable practices out here in the world. Although both humans and Caesar are probably smarter than other animals, I think what's really important are the abilities that that leads to—using tools and sharing a language. These abilities allowed a cultural evolution which works much faster than a biological one, and I suspect that this explosion of culture is the real difference between us and other animals.

Is That the Time?

I was pulled over for speeding today. The officer said, "Don't you know the speed limit is 55 miles per hour?" I replied, "Yes, but I wasn't going to be out that long.

—Steven Wright

Okay, so that joke had nothing to do with apes or language, but if you can think of a better segue into a discussion on time than a Steven Wright joke, then I'd like to hear it. Anyway, Heidegger's point about time is that just as we are in the world, we're in time. (Although, again, don't think of "in" the way you think of Jelly Beans in a jar). We have a grasp of our past and an eye on our future, and this is something that is shared by the apes in *Planet of the Apes*. Cornelius says to Zira, "We both have fine futures—marriage, stimulating careers. I'm up for a raise."

This sort of 'projecting' into the future is not found in other animals. My dog might expect me to come home tonight but he doesn't have plans for next Tuesday. All our lives are structured by time—I might commit several years of my life to getting a degree, or I might try to work my way up through the ranks at McDonald's, but either way this plan is structured by time. Although Caesar doesn't discuss the future as explicitly as Cornelius (after all, his language skills aren't as developed), I think that towards the end of the movie he does show similar abilities in forward-planning. When he escapes from the primate sanctuary, he goes to Will's house to steal some canisters of the new 'smart drug', then returns to the sanctuary and releases it to increase the intelligence of the other apes. Only once they're as smart as him does he lead them all to freedom. This requires foresight that, as far as we know, no other animals possess and in *Rise of the Planet of the Apes*, we see the other apes develop this previously uniquely human trait.

What about looking back in time? Returning to the dispute between Cornelius and Zira, the subject is whether or not Taylor provides proof of Cornelius's theory of evolution. The main conflict between the ape characters in that movie arises because Dr. Zaius insists that this theory of evolution is heresy, mirroring equally absurd creationist debates in some parts of the US and elsewhere.

Regardless of whether either is correct, we should note the remarkable fact that they are having such a dispute about their origins. Human societies have strong senses of their shared history and creation myths seem to be present in every culture we know about. This is simply not found in other animals—just as they don't make a five-year plan for the future, they don't have the animal equivalent of the Book of Genesis or Gibbon's *Decline and Fall of the Roman Empire*.

Humans are born into a world which already has a history, a shared sense of 'what we do' and what to use when doing it. The fact that we understand our past and plan for the future means that, unlike other animals, our lives are similar to the narratives that you find in books and movies. In fact, because we're aware of the stories that we're writing with our lives, we're uniquely able to decide what sort of story that should be. This is basically what Heidegger is getting at when he starts talking about 'being authentic'.

We've all watched a movie or read a book which doesn't seem to be going anywhere and the whole thing seems a little slapdash. This is kind of what an inauthentic life is like—Bob flits from one thing to the next without ever figuring out what really excites him and, as a result, never pursues it. There isn't really a sense of him doing anything with his life—or at least, nothing that really matters to him—and so when his life ends, rather than the satisfying conclusion of a life well lived, his final days are filled with regret.

On the other hand, Caesar's story is closer to authenticity, in which the person realizes that their story will definitely end some time and tries to ensure that their life is a meaningful whole in which they pursue the things that truly matter to them. Caesar finds himself in a world in which humans (with the exception of the few nice characters that raise him from birth) treat apes like crap, and the ape uprising is an attempt to change this.

Put another way, the rise of the apes is a movement towards 'being-in-the-world'—both individually, as Caesar is raised into the human world by Will, and collectively, as the apes stage a revolution which will lead to a whole new type of civilization. Once this happens, the apes' lives are something that they own—they can decide what sort of lives they want to have and, ultimately, what sort of world they want it to be. Will they get it? To find that out we'll have to wait for *Dawn of the Planet of the Apes*.

IX

Planet

21
The Last Man

NORVA Y.S. LO AND ANDREW BRENNAN

Fantasies about the sublime uniqueness and special moral status of the human being are neatly undermined by Pierre Boulle's 1963 novel, *The Planet of the Apes*. The story is cunningly framed in a way that shocks readers out of their natural preconceptions. The narrative itself is told in a manuscript found in a bottle by two intrepid space sailors, Jinn and Phyllis. Only at the end is it revealed that the couple reading the story are themselves chimpanzees, who regard the story as a practical joke, declaring that no human would have the wit to write such a tale.

In the first of the movies spawned by Boulle's novel, Franklin Schaffner's *Planet of the Apes* (1968), the shock factor takes a new form. In the memorable closing sequences disoriented, time-travelling astronaut George Taylor (played by Charlton Heston) discovers with sickening certainty that his vessel did not land on some remote planet far from the Earth. Instead, he's home, on Earth, an Earth transformed by nuclear war. It's 2,006 years in the future, and the dominant species is now apes, not humans.

On this future Earth the apes talk and the humans are mute, apes are hunters and humans are game. The apes have technology, including some simple weapons, and their religion identifies humans as the source of wickedness, greed, cruelty, and destruction. The apes' sacred scrolls show that humans are the source of devilry and degeneration: "Beware the beast man, for he is the Devil's spawn"—so says Cornelius the chimpanzee archaeologist reading from the scrolls, going on to intone:

"Alone among God's primates, he kills for sport, for lust, for greed. Yet, he will murder his brother to possess his brother's land. *Let him not breed in great numbers, for he will make a desert of his home and yours.*"

From the simian perspective, then, it's as well that apes are in charge. Rebelling against his captivity among the apes, and despite the humane treatment shown by the chimpanzee academics Zira and Cornelius, Taylor escapes from the Ape City into the Forbidden Zone, the zone which was once a paradise before human beings turned it into a desert. There, in the shocking climax to the movie, Taylor discovers the ruins of the Statue of Liberty, convincing proof that he is not on some far-away planet, but back on a frighteningly unfamiliar Earth devastated by nuclear war.

At the time when the *Planet of the Apes* franchise got underway in the late 1960s, the study of primate language learning was already well advanced, very often in ways that look amateurish by modern standards. Prolonged studies were carried out on two signing chimpanzees, who became minor celebrities at the time. Their names were Washoe and Nim, and their stories are compassionately described in *Next of Kin* by Roger Fouts and *Nim Chimpsky* by Elizabeth Hess.

The dominant view in those days was that possession of language is the defining condition of higher intelligence, and hence of reason and self-consciousness. If a creature had language, or could learn it, then it could aspire to the same intellectual and moral status as human beings. The importance of language is neatly reflected in the very first *Planet of the Apes* movie. Early in the film Taylor, being generally disappointed with mankind, declares that there has to be—somewhere in the universe—something better than man. But in the upside down society of Ape City, he finds nothing better, only a repetition—suitably inverted—of the human prejudices of racism, classism, and speciesism. The apes themselves are clearly delineated by species, so that warrior gorillas, bourgeois orangutans, and academic chimpanzees each fulfill different roles in the society. Below all of them are the humans—who, since they are mute, can give at best only the appearance of intelligence. They can mimic ape behavior, but since they cannot use language, they cannot be truly intelligent, hence they are regarded as being of inferior intellectual and moral status.

Taylor seems to go along with the idea that to be mute is to be lacking in reason and intelligence, hence speechless beings are not fit candidates for being treated with the levels of respect and dignity shown to humans. He treats the humans with no language in an arrogant way—even though he falls in love with the mute but physically attractive Nova. When she is killed in the sequel, *Beneath the Planet of the Apes*, Taylor's appetite for destruction is whetted. For the most part, Taylor's conception of value is tied to a theory of intelligence, consciousness, rationality, and mind that is—like that of the chimpanzee scientists—a reflection of the dominant view of the time. While some people nowadays still hold a similar view, a lot has happened in the meantime. Animal rights advocates such as Tom Regan have urged that we owe moral respect at least to some animals, and maybe to the species, ecosystems, and systems of life that make the Earth the only living planet in the solar system, as has been argued by environmental philosopher Holmes Rolston III.

Planet of the Apes can be said to have paved the way for The Great Ape Project in which a number of scientists, philosophers, and other activists advocated for claims on behalf of the great apes as holders of moral and political rights. Clearly, the original movie and its sequel raise questions about natural value and destruction that were key to the development of the new environmental ethic that was to blossom in the 1970s and 1980s. They also raise a puzzling question about Taylor himself—does he go mad, or is he simply evil?

As if to drive home the points made in the first movie, the sequel, *Beneath the Planet of the Apes*, works up to a provocative climax. In the final scenes Taylor is still struggling with the hostility and anger that typified his character throughout the first film. Right at the end, he is effectively the last conversable human being on Earth since all his fellow talkers have been killed in clashes with the gorilla army. Of course there may well be some surviving mutant and telepathic humans inhabiting the subterranean passages that were once the tunnels of the New York underground. Elsewhere on the planet there are plenty of the voiceless people, but we are already aware that Taylor regards these as of lower status because of their lack of language. He and Dr. Zaius—the orangutan who is both minister of science and defender of the faith for the apes—play out the final act in the buried remains of St Patrick's cathedral where a nuclear doomsday device has been stored. This cobalt bomb is not only the object of worship for the telepathic mutant humans who live beneath the planet's surface, but is also fully armed and ready to incinerate the entire planet. Mortally wounded, and aware that the simple-minded military gorillas have no comprehension of the evil destructive power of the doomsday device, Taylor begs for help—a plea rejected by Zaius who asks, piously, why he should help Taylor since man is evil and capable of nothing but destruction. In a final act of outrage, Taylor calls out "You bloody bastard" while lunging toward the trigger for the doomsday device. The film ends with his bloody hand clasping and pushing down the lever that condemns him and all other life on Earth to oblivion.

Not long after the appearance of the movie, the Australian logician Richard Routley (later Richard Sylvan), in a landmark paper titled "Is There a Need for a New, an Environmental, Ethic?" put forward a philosophical version of Taylor's final act. Making no reference to the movie, Routley's version is put forward as a philosophical thought experiment imagining that at some time in the future humans are faced with the "collapse of the world system." We're not told anything about what has caused this situation, but apparently a consequence of the collapse means there is only one human being left—the last man. Routley puts it like this:

> The last man (or person) surviving the collapse of the world system lays about him, eliminating, as far as he can, every living thing, animal or plant (but painlessly if you like, as at the best abattoirs). What he does is quite permissible according to basic chauvinism, but on environmental grounds what he does is wrong.

What "basic chauvinism" means here is the human-centered thinking inscribed in liberal economic and political theory, which states that each of us is free to do as he or she pleases provided that in the process we do not directly harm other people, or cause serious damage to ourselves. This kind of chauvinism is the sort of human-centered thinking that Routley attacks in his paper. He extends the idea to an imagined last surviving group of people on the planet—the last people, and asks if they do any wrong when they turn all bits of the land into farming systems, and generally wreck the planet and eliminate most other forms of life. Plainly, such acts would be wrong, he argues, but "chauvinist ethics" has no way of condemning such acts, since no harm is being done to people.

Just as the last man argument can be generalized to the last people, it can be extended to the industrial society as a whole, which continues to increase output and productivity with benefits to people at a terrible environmental cost. The principles of chauvinist ethics, politics and economics, however, provide no basis for protecting nature or saying that industrial society does wrong in changing the environment for the worse. Routley's last man examples are meant to make us rethink human chauvinism, and see our human-centered ways of thinking as a form of human selfishness, which disregards the lives and welfare of other creatures on the planet.

Rage, Madness, and Evil

The end of *Beneath the Planet of the Apes*, directed by Ted Post as an explicit political parable, is chilling and unsettling. Taylor has scoured the universe in search of something better than humans, and actually shares to some extent the apes' low opinion of humankind. But in his last act he embodies precisely the destructiveness and disregard for consequences that he himself abhors. On the other hand, in the context of the first two movies, Taylor's behavior seems not entirely out of character. He is a prideful, angry, driven person, deeply cynical about his fellows, and very much a misfit in any group he encounters.

It was rare for a movie of the day to finish with the destruction of all the leading characters, a remarkably nihilist ending, reflecting the director's attempt to satirize the Cold War mentality and the madness of mutually assured destruction, a theme well-known to audiences at the time not just because of the heightened sense of threat in the midst of the Vietnam War but also thanks to Stanley Kubrick's 1964 *Dr. Strangelove*.

Writer Paul Dehn originally envisaged an optimistic ending in which a reconciliation between human and ape is suggested by the appearance in the final scene of a human-ape hybrid child. Two problems blocked that ending. First, there was an intractable make-up issue, and second it was thought that, as Dehn explained in a 1972 interview in *Cinéfantastique*, "man-ape miscegenation might lose us our G certificate." Richard Zanuck, who demanded that the human-ape hybrid idea be dropped, was no doubt well aware of the audience—and censor—psychology of the day, in which crossing the species barrier was a much bigger deal than destroying the whole planet. That's the very idea Routley challenged: that once all humans have gone from the scene then nothing else matters.

While Taylor may not emerge from the *Planet of the Apes* movies as a wicked or evil man, the last man of Routley's story does so, with a vengeance. One reason for the difference is that in Routley's examples we're provided with no context at all in which to understand what leads to the last man and the last people acting as they do. The movie, by contrast, not only provides a narrative in terms of which to make sense of Taylor, it also provides a setting in which to debate his behavior. For some viewers, it will be obvious that Taylor is the kind of person who always wants to be on top. He is a leader rather than a follower. Yet, as we see later, narratives also have their ambiguities and in this way they reflect the moral uncertainties of everyday life. The *Planet of the Apes* movies can lead to different people giving different interpretations of Taylor's behavior.

The key idea of "basic chauvinism" or anthropocentrism is that only humans are inherently or intrinsically valuable, since humans have special features that put them apart from the rest of all living things. These may be features like consciousness, rationality, high intelligence—or even, in the traditional Christian view, that humans are made in the image of God. Once it's granted that humans have special value, then the value of everything else is to be measured in terms of its contribution (or failure to contribute) to securing the desires and ambitions of humans. If only human beings have moral value, then no wrong is done by wiping out all the non-humans once there are no more human interests to be served.

Routley's 'last man' examples aim to show something wrong with this view. We're meant to find it absurd to think that no wrong is done by wiping out non-human things, but to see instead that it is monstrous for the last human being to destroy the planet and all the nonhuman beings and things on it. The last man argument immediately became one of the most widely cited arguments in the new environmental philosophy, a defense of a new, non-human-centered conception of value. For the non-anthropocentrist, there is intrinsic value in much else besides human life, certainly in the lives of many things that are not human.

Suppose that Taylor's final act of destruction was mad. One way of thinking about the madness is that in triggering the doomsday device, he commits the ultimate folly of those whose thinking is dominated by anthropocentrism. Being human-centered is a kind of racism towards other species (sometimes called 'speciesism'), and there are plenty of things in the movies that show Taylor is under the influence of just such racist-like thinking. Think of the first words ever spoken by humans to the talking apes: "Take your stinking paws off me, you damned dirty ape!" These are typical of the words a racist might use, and Taylor's outburst would seem to confirm that he is profoundly anthropocentric in his prejudices.

In general, other living things do not get much prominence in the first two movies. Perhaps this is in keeping with the focus on human-simian relationships, so that, with the exception of horses, other animal species do not feature much. The bond between horse and rider is well-known to elicit deep feelings, but the movie makers avoid including any sequences in which the ape riders are shown as having any fondness for their horses. The horses are simply transport mechanisms. Ape City is a bleak place, lacking cats, dogs, or rats, hence neither pest nor companion animals are seen in streets or houses.

Travelers in south-east Asia are familiar with the way primates of various kinds seem to get on well with cats, sometimes grooming street kittens, sometimes even seeming to adopt them as companions. Koko, one of the famous signing gorillas, who is credited with a greater mastery of sign language that either Nim or Washoe, had such a well-documented relationship with a number of cat "pets" that Francine Patterson wrote a book about it: *Koko's Kittens*.

There were no doubt good reasons for not adding to production costs in the *Planet of the Apes* series by introducing the theme of other species and companion animals. Still, the absence of human-animal and ape-animal relationships helps the viewer to perceive Taylor's final deed as less destructive than it would have seemed against a more fully-fleshed depiction of interspecies relations. No one left the theater regretting the loss of a splendid horse, or the ending of a beautiful friendship between a warrior gorilla and a cute kitten.

Intrinsic Value and Psychological Presence

If Routley's argument is accepted, then Taylor's supposed madness is no different from the madness of contemporary industrial societies. In them, massive changes to ecosystems and huge destruction of other species are all carried out in the name of economic growth, the short-term profits of hungry shareholders and a utopian industrial fantasy in which all human beings will—one day—live lives of comfortable satisfaction in healthy and rewarding surroundings. Meanwhile, the very fabric of planetary life-support systems is under attack by those who are the strongest purveyors of the utopian fantasy itself.

At the heart of the utopian industrial project is lip service to the idea that human existence has intrinsic value. Even as populations are displaced through development and pollution, the companies driving environmental and climate change insist that they aim to bring better lives to everyone on Earth, and that—at some indefinite future time—poverty and disease will be conquered so that everyone, and not just the rich and privileged, can live long, happy, healthy, and prosperous lives.

Meanwhile, two features mark contemporary industrial capitalism. First, nearly all the attempts to improve what is valuable in human life and human presence have been carried out in a way that reduces immense amounts of non-human presence over the face of the earth. And, as is made abundantly clear in *Rise of the Planet of the Apes* (2011), the project of improving human health and welfare is carried out at the cost of immense cruelty and suffering to animals used in biomedical research. The expansion of human value, in other words, means loss of other value on a huge scale, the very value that Routley demands we do not overlook.

In an additional twist to the story of utopia, there is a second often-neglected aspect of contemporary capitalism. This is that its impact on human beings themselves is uneven. Those who are rich and well-to-do have relatively little to fear in the immediate future from climate change and the other challenges of a depleted planet. In *Rise of the Planet of the Apes*, Will Rodman raises Caesar, the ape destined to spearhead the revolt against humans that will lead to the future dominance of the talking apes. Caesar himself was born to an experimental animal, his mother having become super intelligent as a result of being inoculated with a modified virus developed to treat Alzheimer's disease in human beings. Rodman's father is an Alzheimer's sufferer, and Will makes sure that his father receives treatment with the new drug long before the question of human trials is raised.

Those who are well-connected, like those who are rich, receive the benefits of new technologies, new medicines and other new opportunities long before they trickle down—if ever—to those who are poor, weak, or vulnerable. As with medicine and technology, so it is more generally with environmental issues. The loss of freshwater resources, scarcity of food, loss of low-lying lands and a whole host of other environmental changes will generally impact on those who are poor long before they affect the wealthy and well-insured.

The first two *Planet of the Apes* movies were produced against a background of Cold War tension, the fear of nuclear annihilation, and increasing cynicism about the United States' involvement in Vietnam. Politically, strategically, and morally the situation of contemporary Western society has not changed so much. Worries about nuclear proliferation are still to the fore, and the fear of global climate change and loss of natural resources to sustain our way of life increases daily as information about accumulating risks becomes ever more available. As humankind pursues the project of human self-realization, it seems that the very fabric of planetary support systems is in danger of collapse (as we argue in our book *Understanding Environmental Philosophy*).

So we face a multitude of problems. On the anthropocentric view, human beings are special and require that every effort be made to enhance their lives, improve medical care, develop their societies so that they can flourish, develop and prosper, even at the cost of increasing damage to other animals and other living things. But what right have we as a species to inflict such damage and ask other valuable living things to pay the price for human development?

Was Taylor Evil?

Good people feel frustration and despair when they think about how the lofty desire to spread value leads inevitably to its loss, how business even when conducted with humane intent, and the desire to make human life better, leads to human displacement and impoverishment, animal suffering, species loss and reduction in the planet's ecological viability.

Rise of the Planet of the Apes encourages us to be skeptical about the humane intentions of drug companies who claim to be seeking ways to improve the lives of the sick and infirm even as they answer to the demands of their shareholders as their first priority. Reflecting on these problems, contemporary thinkers are likely to be not much different in their mindset from that of Taylor the cynical and angry space voyager, wondering with declining conviction whether somewhere there is something better than humankind.

Forty-five years on from the first *Planet of the Apes* movie, the future of humanity is still under threat, not just from nuclear Armageddon but also from environmental catastrophe. There is a difference between the two threats. While nuclear Armageddon threatens many kinds of life on Earth, climate change, declining biodiversity, and ecosystem changes pose a particular threat to the survival of contemporary industrial society and the human race itself. While we cannot survive without the planet's support systems, many other species and systems can survive without us. A contemporary, more ecologically inspired version of Taylor might still wander the galaxy searching for something better than man, and might be a character with whose anger and cynical despair many could sympathize. But such a voyager would not destroy the world in his own dying moments, even if he were the last human being in the universe.

So we return to the puzzling questions: Was Taylor mad? Was he evil? In terms of the moral evaluation of his deeds, not character, it can be argued that Taylor's final actions are wrong in three ways.

Suppose, first of all, that we agree with the intuitions prompted by Routley's last man example. That means we give up the human-centered way of thinking about value, and regard other living things as beings of value in their own right.

The action of incinerating the planet destroys immense numbers of valuable beings. Apes, mutants, Nova's people, the horses, all the other animals and the plants on Earth have value that is wiped out by exploding the doomsday device. From the non-anthropocentric point of view, incinerating the planet shows no respect for life and is clearly an evil deed.

From the human-centered viewpoint, Taylor's last act is evil too. The anthropocentrist thinks that only humans have inherent value. But what is it to be human? If rationality evidenced by the power of speech is the criterion for being human, as Taylor himself seems to assume, then the mutants are clearly human and so are the apes. Some writers make a distinction between being a human being (biological category) and being a person (moral category). John Locke, the seventeenth-century philosopher, introduced the idea that persons are morally special through their self-conscious rationality. A rational parrot, for example, would be a very special being, and Locke accordingly devotes some time in his famous *Essay* to discussing the question of whether a parrot might aspire to rationality and be a parrot person (Book 2, Chapter 27). The anthropocentrist who values rationality, and sees it as the essence of being a person, would regard Taylor as having wiped out morally significant beings, since both mutants and ape-persons are clearly rational. Hence the act is a great wrong.

Many people regard our being members of the biologically human species as the morally important thing. Think of how we protect infants and young children, and treat them with special care, long before they show rationality or linguistic skills. Also think of how many people advocate for the human rights of those who are born mentally impaired. But the species view is anthropocentric in that it takes membership of the biological species as something that confers a special dignity and value on people, and so takes human beings as special in this regard. For this kind of species anthropocentrist, it may be that Taylor does no wrong in wiping out the apes, for they are not biologically human. But Nova's people, and arguably the mutants too, would clearly count as human on biological criteria. So yet again, Taylor is wrong to commit the final destructive act.

In short, Taylor's last action is morally wrong from both the anthropocentric and the non-anthropocentric perspectives. He seems to behave rather like one of the ancient emperors in China who would have his household, concubines and slaves entombed alive with him after he dies, hence condemning all of them to death. Is Taylor taking an imperial attitude to the whole planet, as if once he is dead it matters little if anything else remains alive? This would be an evil stance indeed.

Perhaps a kinder view is to regard him as becoming unhinged with grief at the death of Nova. As he and Brent fight in the cell in which the mutants had confined them, he is reunited suddenly with Nova when she calls his name. That single utterance from the previously mute girl, breaks the telepathic control by a mutant that is locking the two men in conflict, and they are able to break free. Yet within moments of being reunited with Nova, Taylor loses her when a gorilla warrior shoots her. Just seconds before that happens, Taylor learns from Brent that the mutants worship a missile which Taylor recognizes as a doomsday device. He describes it with irony as "a lovely souvenir from the twentieth century."

While Brent is openly horrified at the thought of the cobalt bomb burning the planet to a cinder, the cynical Taylor, with a smirk, comments: "How's that for your ultimate weapon?" Once Nova has been killed, Taylor's irony is replaced by something else, a self-centered anger and grief that overcomes any awareness of the moral significance of others:

TAYLOR: Oh God . . . should let them all die, the gorillas and every damned . . . what it comes to. It's time it was finished.... finished . . .

BRENT: Taylor, come on, come on. The Bomb . . .

TAYLOR: Yeah. . . . Why not?

Here there is a clear failure of communication between the two men. Brent is driven by the horror of the impending catastrophe, doing all he can to avoid it. In fact, he is killed while trying to distract the gorillas from interfering with the bomb. Taylor goes to the final confrontation with quite different intentions. "It's doomsday," he says just as Brent is killed, "end of the world." Despite being severely wounded, he determinedly uses his failing power to reach the trigger ("Yeah. . . . Why not?" as he said to Brent moments earlier), while cursing Dr. Zaius for failing to help him along.

In the first *Planet of the Apes* film, Taylor seems inspired by a vision of dignity and nobility, of "something better" than humankind. By the end of the second film, it's evident that he sees no value or dignity in the other kinds of creatures he has encountered. He is intensely critical and judgmental, even of those who would be his friends, such as Zira and Cornelius. Finding the wrecked world that is now the Planet of the Apes, and losing the one being with whom he had managed to build a close and intimate relationship, his own disappointment, frustration, and despair is given vent in a final utterly destructive act. He who dreamed of something better now carries to its logical conclusion the very politics of mutually assured destruction that was at the heart of military strategy during the Cold War.

Had Taylor been less of an idealist about himself and humanity in general, he might have done less damage. If he had been less self-centered, he might have cared more about the other lives around him. The human-centered theory of value is a parallel, at the species level, to a self-centered worldview. So in our present attempts to tackle the challenges of global warming, ever-increasing species loss, world poverty, the displacement of humans and animals from their homes, the loss of intrinsic value on a tremendous scale—what can we learn from Taylor and the *Apes* movies? Just this: to be too self-interested is not only a personal moral failing but also a danger to ourselves and others. Taylor's fate reminds us of the importance of expanding our moral horizons and extending our care beyond ourselves, our communities and our species. Holmes Rolston, one of the fathers of modern environmental philosophy, puts it like this:

> We worried throughout most of the last century, the first century of great world wars, that humans would destroy themselves in interhuman conflict. . . . The worry for the next century is that humans may destroy their planet and themselves with it. . . . Today and for the century hence, the call is to see Earth as a planet with promise, destined for abundant life.

The *Planet of the Apes* movies, taken overall, show how the promise of the planet is easily lost, squandered through human greed and self-interest. After viewing them, we have to hope that it is not already too late to fulfill the Earth's promise rather than to betray it.

22

Planet of the Degenerate Monkeys

Eugene Halton

I can't get rid of the idea that somewhere in the Universe there must
be a creature superior to man.

—George Taylor, *Planet of the Apes*

Philosophic Prequel: Fable of the Degenerate Monkey

Once upon a time there was a degenerate monkey, degenerate in
the sense of not maturing as quickly as the wild Others, in being
newborn-like much longer, something the biologists call neoteny.

The Others were blessed with robust instincts, which sel-
dom led them into blunders. What they knew instinctively the
degenerate monkey could only get from guessing, with a good
amount of blundering thrown in. But the degenerate monkey
was blessed with good guessing, sensing with awareness, even
if not yet knowing. The very "weakness" of its plastic and flexible brain, proved, under the right conditions, to be its greatest
strength.

The degenerate monkey found that by closely observing the
Others, it could guess the right things to do more often than
not. The living instinctive truths embodied in the diverse creatures and living habitat surrounding it were its great teachers.
It discovered that it was a true child of the Earth, literally, in
its genetic, physiological constitution.

Its beliefs allowed for the fact that the newest portion of its
brain, its prefrontal cortex, through which it learned to make

279

art and speak, was also the most immature part of its brain, precisely because it was the latest to evolve. It may not have even known this consciously, but it lived the fact through beliefs which allowed that the mind of nature, the spirit living in and through all things, was a great teacher, and of a higher order of intelligence. It found that in attuning to and marveling at the instinctive maturity of the Others, it could find its own maturity.

It learned that by hunting like a bear, it could catch the seal. It learned that by acting like a seal, it could attract the bear and hunt it. Immersed in the intelligence of the Others, it learned the sacred game of life, which included the taking of life, the game of predator and game. In revering the sacred game and its rules of sustainable sustenance, it became a harbinger of life. Its attunements to a wide range of habitats and life, not only through observation, but also through ritual, artistic, and practical communicative and cooperative activities among its own kind, allowed it to spread around the globe, creating a planet *of* degenerate monkeys, but not *for* degenerate monkeys. Its relation to the community of life was one of networking with the Earth.

It learned so well that eventually it thought itself mature enough to change the rules of the game: instead of finding its maturity in attuning to and marveling in the instinctive intelligence of the Others, it reversed the process. It began living in settled ape-clusters, which were artificial neoteny environments. It began to turn the Others into degenerate forms like itself, that is, no longer wild, but selectively dematured, domesticated.

The ape reshaped The Others, turning them into mirrors of its newborn-like, dematured self, genetically as well as behaviorally. It domesticated itself with and through them, fixing partial aspects of their full instinctive intelligence. It turned them from wild wolves into domesticated dogs, from aurochs—oxen—into cows, from mouflon into sheep, from wild independent grasses into dematured grasses—wheat, barley, rice—codependent on human cultivation for survival. Even though domesticated, it remained a wild body itself, albeit a degenerate monkey, new-born like, neotenous.

All the while the neotenous or newborn-like ape neotenized its world, living from its domesticated food and walling itself into its cities. It changed its relation to its habitat, physically and spiritually, also walling in its reverence for life, for the game of life it participated in, as predator and prey. It walled that reverence into self-mirroring gods and human-centered (or anthropocentric) consciousness.

It became a spectator at creation, networking with its progressively human-centered reflections of itself, its gods and goddesses of fertility, its domesticates, losing in the process the direct interplay with the wild Earth. It fell prey to the mirror of Narcissus. In moving away from direct participation, it narrowed circumambient creation to the human focus, elevating the dematured human to an object of worship, devaluing the wild other to a slave, devaluing the bulk of its own population into slaves and functionaries of its exalted ego, personified in the form of a divine king.

Degenerate monkey became proud of itself, losing its sense that, as a dematured, newborn-like primate, it required the relationship to the wild others in order to find its maturity. But with its self-mirroring environment as an illusory matrix, effectively walling it off from the instinctive intelligence of the wild others, the shut-up monkey went mad. It went mad within its self-created house of mirrors, its Gods, kings, saviors, prophets, science, machines, its agriculturally created population explosion, its transformation of the "fertile crescent" and other habitats originally teeming with life into desert, and the entire ant-farm it had made of itself. It went mad with itself and called its madness progress.

It went from being a child of the Earth, engaged in communicative attunement, to a civilized infant, wanting ever more. Yet it thought itself the be-all and end-all of evolution and the creation's purpose. And in its civilized infantilism, its unlimited expansionism, it raged against its true mother, the earth, Gaia, the living ecological intelligence on which it depended to find its maturity.

Its homicidal rage was a murderous suicidal call for help, one might say, the rage of a two-year old backpedaling in its mind to the womb. But it found itself murdering that which was its own source, and so it was in reality backpedaling to nothingness, backpedaling, until. . . .

Once upon a time there was a degenerate monkey.

Beware the Beast Man

Near the end of 1968's *Planet of the Apes*, Cornelius, the ape archaeologist and historian, reads from the sacred scrolls: "Beware the beast Man, for he is the Devil's pawn. Alone among God's primates, he kills for sport or lust or greed. Yea, he will murder his brother to possess his brother's land. Let him not breed in great numbers, for he will make a desert of his home and yours. Shun him; drive him back into his jungle lair, for he is the harbinger of death."

Well, this does not present a very pretty picture of humanity. But it does speak truths civilized people either don't know or do not want to hear, not of uncivilized peoples so much as the costs of agriculturally based civilization itself, and its inventions such as mass-killing war, property and poverty, over-population, and devastated ecosystems.

Philosopher Charles Peirce, the founder of American pragmatism and a leading mathematician of his time, drew an unflattering portrait of man similar to that of the sacred scrolls, depicting him, with some humor, as "a degenerate monkey." As he put it in 1901, "man is but a degenerate monkey, with a paranoiac talent for self-satisfaction, no matter what scrapes he may get himself into, calling them 'civilization,' and who, in place of the unerring instincts of other races, has an unhappy faculty for occupying himself with words and abstractions, and for going wrong in a hundred ways before he is driven, willy-nilly, into the right one."

Homo sapiens, man the knower, is the way we humans like to distinguish ourselves from the rest of nature. But if we consider ourselves as degenerate monkeys, *Homo errans*, or *man the blunderer* would have been a better term, calling attention to our softened instinctive intelligence, our greater "plasticity," as the biologists call it, in contrast to the "unerring instincts of other races," as Peirce put it elsewhere.

Peirce's concept of *degenerate monkey* is not mere monkey business, but contains a serious philosophical outlook. It attempts to draw attention to our prolonged newborn-like nature, which biologists call neoteny. He means "degenerate" both in the mathematical sense of a genetic falling away from a pure form, in this case from more quickly matured genomes of other primates, and he also means it in the more everyday sense in which the newer portion of the human brain, the prefrontal cortex, which allows the capacities for symbolic and rational communication, for language, can also contribute to monkeying-around hubris. The degenerate monkey in this sense can get into some bad scrapes, falsely idealizing them as "civilized."

I take Peirce's term "degenerate monkey" as not limited to moderns, but applicable to *Homo sapiens sapiens*, the technical term for anatomically modern humans, generally. Considering humans as degenerate monkeys is a key to understanding human development, precisely because we need to attune ourselves to the intelligence of the wild environment, drawing its intelligence into our dematured, blundering selves through intuitive inference, or what Peirce termed abductive inference, our gift for guessing, as well as other ways of thinking, and therein finding our maturity.

Alien Nation

Which is it: is man one of God's blunders, or is God one of man's blunders?

—FRIEDRICH WILHELM NIETZSCHE, *Twilight of the Idols* (1889)

The alien is typically a symptom of human alienation, projected out into fantastic form. Those visitors from outer space? They usually represent fears of how our science and technology are running away with us, ruinously. In *Planet of the Apes* humans become the visitors in space ships, but the aliens are both the intelligent apes they discover, and the humans who are "ape-like" savages. *Planet of the Apes* presents us with specters of ourselves, alienated not only from our humanity, but alienated *in* our humanity.

That's precisely why my friends and I had to see *Escape from the Planet of the Apes* when it came out in 1971. Some fans identify with movies by acquiring costumes similar to those in the movie. But we thought we'd be clever by escaping *into* the movie at the nearby drive-in theater, sneaking in by foot through a hole in the fence with a couple of six packs of beer, moving a bench from the snack bar area to a spot where an auto should be, and creating a stereo sound for ourselves with a speaker at either end of the bench.

From the opening scenes, where the three astronauts returning to contemporary Earth turn out to be the chimps Zira, Cornelius, and another colleague from the future, through Cornelius's account of a future dramatic rise of the apes when a certain Aldo would be the first to utter No! to his human masters (which actually dropped out of the plots of sequels and never occurred in them), to the tragic killing of Zira and Cornelius and surprise ending survival of their offspring Caesar, we were riveted.

We couldn't really articulate why we liked it so much, but the revolt against authority was in the air, even if our prank was simply apolitical fun. *Escape from the Planet of the Apes* was the counter-culture in pop form, complete with expressions of racism, militarism, and scientific hubris which called for resistance. But all of that serious stuff of resisting authority also spoke directly to our youthful exuberance in sneaking in, playing, "like an angry ape . . . such fantastic tricks before high heaven as makes the angels weep," as Shakespeare put it in *Measure for Measure*. Only in this case I hope the angels would laugh. Given the fantastic tricks that accompanied the establishment of agriculture and civilization, of history, they could use a break.

Monkeying to Mayhem

Agriculture and civilization, which propelled man from "his jungle lair," expelled us from the living wild habitat through which we attuned ourselves to the mature communities of life in which we found ourselves, and which provided the means for our immature brains to reach relatively sustainable maturity. In citified ape-compounds civilized man learned to kill "for sport or lust or greed," as the sacred scrolls of the apes put it. Cain the agriculturalist learned to "murder his brother to possess his brother's land." Humans began to "breed in great numbers," turning "the fertile crescent" in Mesopotamia into "a desert of his home" (remember "Operation Desert Storm" of 1991?).

Humans continue to breed in great numbers, now at seven billion. Refinements in the mechanization of agriculture made it possible to feed more people, and that has led to those people breeding more people, which has led to more agriculture to feed more people: the endless cycle which began with agriculture ten thousand years ago, now amped up radically through modern technology. This is the scenario of civilization since its origins, forcibly driving out surrounding foragers who are believed to "waste" the habitat because they do not cultivate the land in endless expansion of population and food needs, a scenario duplicated in *Beneath the Planet of the Apes*. There the gorilla military commander Ursus calls for an invasion of the Forbidden Zone:

> We must replenish the land that was ravished by the Humans with new, productive feeding grounds. And these we can obtain in the once Forbidden Zone. So now it is our holy duty to enter it.

Agriculture and its offspring, civilization, have been called progress. The progress that they made can also be seen as one step forward and two, three, or more steps backward. The evidence, from nutritional, ecological, societal, archaeological, and anthropological studies is unmistakable. Agriculture, settlement, and civilization brought about a transformation of humankind, a transformation involving whole new forms of society, ways of living in huge power clusters called cities, a whole new centralization of power and power complexes, with far greater hierarchy and social inequality, time required for work, and a devastation of the human body from reduced nutrition and increased work demands, literally resulting in people becoming four to six inches shorter on average, wherever it developed.

The increase in height of people in industrial societies in the past hundred years or so is merely a return to average heights of people from before agriculture, as numerous anthropological and archaeological studies show. Human socialization practices changed, including the spacing of births from an average of every four years to every two, as well as the relation of humans to the Earth, and the human mind itself.

The degenerate monkey evolved into being through a long evolutionary narrative of foraging, but departed from that narrative through the advent of agriculture, settlement, and civilization. This change is called history and progress, but from another perspective might be called regression. Degenerate monkey needs the mindset of foraging, or its moral equivalent, to find its maturity. It just might be that without it, without that attunement to the Others, monkey goes mad, monkeying in its mirror of itself, fatally fixated, like Narcissus, and with similar results: planet of the civilized degenerate monkeys, monkeying to mayhem. That is precisely what happened both to the humans in their original nuclear war described in *Beneath the Planet of the Apes*, and to the apes driven to invade the Forbidden Zone in the same movie, a decision which resulted in the ultimate destruction of the living Earth.

The *Planet of the Apes* series pictured an atomic war and its aftermath, which remains a real possibility for our own foreseeable future, despite the end of the Cold War. But numerous other scenarios of the consequences of unsustainable living now compete with it: global warming and mass famine; viral pandemics such as swine or avian flu, induced by mutation-breeding manure lagoons of huge slaughtering operations—the "primordial soup of the Apocalypse," such as emerged in La Gloria, Mexico in 2009; or genetic recombination gone wrong, whether resulting in resistant bacteria, dangerous "Frankenfoods," or in a scenario similar to that pictured in the recent 2011 reboot, *Rise of the Planet of the Apes*, a global pandemic of the ALZ-113 virus: medical monkeying gone awry. Therein lies the tragedy of the degenerate monkey who is us. Yes, we "learn." But learning unhinged from our special evolutionary requirements becomes a way of spelling suicide. And that is what we infantilized apes are spelling globally today.

Charlton Heston may not arrive back from the future in time to change things. It will take more than a Hollywood sequel to change the likely ending: Once upon a time there was a degenerate monkey.

Doomsday Machine

In the end, the monkey mirror held up by these movies tends to downplay another real ingredient in the dehumanization of humanity. It too is a portion of ourselves, just as the ape in us is a portion of ourselves. But it is a far more deadly portion when falsely elevated into a ruling principle, truly the "harbinger of death" written about in the sacred scripture of the apes. It is the idealization of the machine, the schizoid machine, the overweening projection of degenerate monkey's highly elaborated prefrontal cortex severed from the community of passions which had grounded it in its evolution into being. This is the alien of the *Terminator* and *Matrix* movies, but it also haunts the *Planet of the Apes* series as well, though playing second fiddle to the ape as other.

The human mutants who worship the doomsday Alpha Omega bomb in *Beneath the Planet of the Apes* have developed extraordinary powers of communication through telepathy and telepathic hypnosis, unlike their mute above ground fellow humans. A note in the script for the movie states of the mutant named Verger that: "he shares facial characteristics common to all the city's denizens: great beauty; an unwrinkled skin; deep-set eyes in shadowed sockets; and that slightly accentuated definition of the lip-line which, in men and women of our own day, is often accounted sexy. We are about to learn one other remarkable attribute which he shares with his fellows." We learn that attribute during the height of their sacred ceremonies, when the mutants face the golden bomb rocket, and lift their hoods to reveal that they have lost their skin and wear rubber face masks.

They use actual speech in facing the bomb, saying, "I reveal my Inmost Self unto my God!" That self, sadly, is one incapable of true face-to-face interaction, despite its abilities to communicate at distances. It can get into other minds through telepathy, but it has utterly lost the living Earth, literally entombed in the subterranean post-nuclear New York. All it can really honestly "face" is the bomb machine, that symbol of the destruction which ravaged their DNA, yet which gives them ultimate hope of invulnerability. But a strange invulnerability it is, for in using it to defend themselves, they would also destroy themselves and all life.

They worship the cold-war strategy of "mutually assured destruction," but also something more. They worship *deus ex machina*, literally, the god out of the machine, the technical device which promises to save and redeem us. These mutants, possibly the weirdest group of characters to appear in the entire series, might actually represent the most accurate prophecy of the entire *Planet of the Apes* series, not as found in the Sacred Scrolls, but as found in our own time today.

Those mutants prefigure the loss of face-to-face communication that is occurring today in the name of the Holy Facebook. They engage in faceless "telecommunication," like the Facebookies of today, who excessively outsource face time to faceless virtual interaction, frequently "masked" in pseudonyms, through telecommunication. Consider: a recent Kaiser Foundation study in 2010 found that American children 8–18 years of age reported spending a whopping 7 hours and 38 minutes of media screen time per day, actually 10 hours and 45 minutes including multitasking squeezed into those 7 hours, 38 minutes, which also does not count schoolwork. For 'tweens between 11 and 14 years old it is actually 8 hours and 40 minutes per day. If someone sleeps for 8 hours and is involved with school for 8 hours, then virtually all remaining available time is totally enscreened time.

This represents a significant loss of face-to-face contact and tactile connection to a virtual world that is supposed to be there as a convenience, a means to self-direction, toward what I call self-originated experience, where you are engaged in the moment, emotionally available to the moment, and capable of self-determination. Social media can be all of that, yet for many kids and even adults, it seems instead to be a refuge where, "I reveal my Inmost Self unto my God!"

Yet our faces are subtle sources of gestural and empathic communication. Mind reading, it turns out, is a neurological reality, not only through mirror neurons, but also through micro-muscular mimicry below the level of awareness, through which one attunes to another in a face-to-face interaction, feeling inferentially another's emotions and potentially also intentions. Recent studies have shown that not only do "unwrinkled" Botox recipients, like the rubber-masked mutants, lose the ability to express their emotional states facially because of their facial muscle paralysis, but that they also suffer impaired ability to "read" the emotional states of their partners through subtle, subconscious micro-mimicry. This shows how one's own micro-muscular mimicry of others is a communicative practice which can atrophy from disuse, resulting in impaired empathy.

The mutants, despite their advanced telecommunicative prowess, were also notably deficient in empathy, for example, hypnotically inducing their human visitors to try to kill each other. But the possible empathy-deficient mutants we might be brewing today don't need to worship the bomb and practice torture. That is so old-school, so Orwell. We have transitioned to the conditioning of slavish unempathic conformism through pleasure techniques, as first envisioned by Aldous Huxley in his 1932 novel, *Brave New World*, with its soma, promiscuity without relationships, and systematic methods of desensitization to emotions.

In his 1949 letter to his former student George Orwell, congratulating him on his new book *Nineteen Eighty-Four*, Huxley predicted that within the next generation pleasure conditioning would replace pain conditioning as a more efficient means of control:

> Within the next generation I believe that the world's leaders will discover that infant conditioning and narco-hypnosis are more efficient, as instruments of government, than clubs and prisons, and that the lust for power can be just as completely satisfied by suggesting people into loving their servitude as by flogging them and kicking them into obedience.

That next generation of the nuclear age saw the introduction of the screen, in the form of television, into virtually all American households, conditioning infants and adults to gaze in narco-hypnotic distraction. The cold war ended, yet the screen may prove in the end more powerful than the bomb.

Our god out of the machine is the device we always have at hand or nearby, which makes us feel good to use, and which, as we depend on it more and more, pressing its buttons thousands of times every day, pushes our buttons unwittingly "unto our god."

The cult of the machine, inclusive of the human elements that are part of it, first hatched in the bureaucratic organizations of ancient civilization, which included explicit religious worship of the apparatus of the state, especially through divine kingship, and then came to dominance in the modern, secular era, though as an implicit, religious-like belief, symbolized through the clock. This watershed development has proved to be not simply an extension of our tool-using capabilities, but more a Frankenstein that has taken on a life of its own.

Humans, being so adaptively flexible, have been able to climb way out on the limb we have been sawing off, but once we started believing in the metaphor that the universe is a giant clock, we began ticking toward nullity. Neuroscientists need to realize that the machine-model of the brain is hyperbole, exaggerating the automatic aspects of our being and radically undervaluing and even negating the spontaneous and creative aspects, as well as the deep tempered capacities of the passions. These are not merely "subjective," but are real capacities produced by millions of years of engagement with wildness.

Mind, as Peirce and fellow pragmatist George Herbert Mead said, is a relational, communicative process of conduct between the individual and the habitat, not something enclosed in a brain. When that relation becomes contracted from the attunement to the wild intelligible habitat of the surrounding community of life to other dematured humans and their likenesses, and then even further contracted to projections and idealizations of the automatic portions of the human psyche, as though the living world is but a schizoid machine, then perhaps we can understand why Emerson said: "The end of the human race will be that it will eventually die of civilization."

Planet of the Regenerate Monkeys

We have been undergoing revolutionary new findings in the past few years that reveal that the planet of anatomically modern humans of the past 100,000 years or so was one shared with a variety of other humans. As anthropologist Chris Stringer put it recently, "there might have been as many as six different kinds of humans on the Earth," including both Neanderthals and Denisovans, whose DNA are found in contemporary human DNA. They all disappeared, despite some interbreeding, for reasons that are not yet clear.

There are threats that the other great ape species living today could become extinct too, as many other animal species have, not because of natural conditions, but because human expansion has literally been a harbinger of death. It's time to consider how to remake human civilization into a harbinger of life, a question that animates a number of the movies in the series, but is especially highlighted in the conclusion of the last of the original series, *Battle for the Planet of the Apes*. There the Lawgiver, speaking to the integrated class of young human and ape children, says, "But as I look at Apes and Humans living together in friendship, harmony and at peace, at least we wait with hope for the future." Yet the camera turns to the statue of Caesar, "Our Founder," which sheds a tear as the movie closes, perhaps suggesting what we know will be a degeneration into race hatred and hostility between apes and humans, the "same old, same old" of civilizational hubris, culminating in the destruction of the Earth from the Alpha Omega bomb.

Despite the ubiquitous cruelty between apes and humans in the series, there are numerous moments when the primate touch empathically bridges the interspecies gulf: Zira putting her hand on Taylor's in her office after she discovers he can write, or Taylor's kissing her on the lips near the end of *Planet of the Apes*, and her return kiss to fellow scientist, the human Dr. Lewis Dixon, in *Escape from the Planet of the Apes*. But perhaps the best example is found in circus owner Armando's warm sympathy for Cornelius and Zira and his subsequent raising, as we discover in *Conquest of the Planet of the Apes*, of their son Milo, later named Caesar, who will later lead the rebellion of the apes. Armando was devoted to Saint Francis, "who loved all animals," and practices that devotion by risking his life, and ultimately losing it, on behalf of his adopted Caesar and the promise of life he holds.

The empathic bonding between ape and man found in the relations of these characters in *Planet of the Apes* may seem overly "sentimental" to some. In many ways it is, though I think "idealized" is a better term. But it also does strangely break through the human-centered portrayal of apes in the series to show unexpected possibilities to overcome dehumanization. Certain deep sentiments, such as the capacities for empathy, for mothering, for dreaming and playing, that we share with other primates and even with non-primate mammals, may turn out to be the mightiest weapon against the destructive tendencies of the unrestrained mechanization of life today, whose imagined catastrophic consequences are pictured in the *Planet of the Apes* movies. They are among our oldest primate and mammal capacities, yet crucial for our most newly acquired, characteristically human capacities, such as the self, speech, and rational reasoning, to function optimally and not pathologically.

Though we may think ourselves modern, we retain Pleistocene bodies, as ecological philosopher Paul Shepard put it, and Pleistocene needs, bodied into being over our longer two million year evolution. What Shepard termed "the sacred game," the dramatic interplay of predator and prey, reminds us of that older evolutionary story, wherein degenerate monkey emerges into being wide-eyed in wonder at circumambient life, a child of the earth foraging for edible, sensible, thinkable, and sustainable wisdom.

Consider what happened to that ape that became human in the past two million years, thanks to the community of mature, instinctive life to which it attuned itself. What is two million years in the long term view of evolution? What if we could redirect our science, technology, and civilization today away from its idealization and worship of the machine and inflated projections of the human, and toward an idea that the further creation and pursuit of truth, goodness, and beauty involves a re-attunement to all-surrounding life, not isolation from it?

A creature aware that its destiny is tied to its origins, and that it must, perhaps for the first time, come to terms with itself as a degenerate monkey requiring self-controlling, sustainable limits to its civilization at all levels of institutions and beliefs, toward the purpose of a sustainable, proliferating planet of life? A new civilization capable of relating to the earth not as something put here for humans, but as something marvelous out of which humans were bodied forth to serve?

We might just find a creature in two million years quite different from the futures envisioned in *Planet of the Apes*, which remain trapped in the constrictive frame of "history." We might find a planet where biodiversity is itself regarded as a great teacher, a planet teeming with immense varieties of life, revered and enhanced by a somewhat recognizable, but transformed life form. We might find the planet of the regenerate monkeys.

References

Andrews, Kristin Alexandra. 2012. *Do Apes Read Minds? Toward a New Folk Psychology*. Cambridge: MIT Press.

Aristotle. 2009 [350 B.C.E.]. *Nicomachean Ethics*. Translated by W.D. Ross. World Library Classics.

Ashby. Arved. 2004 *The Pleasure of Modernist Music*. Rochester: University of Rochester Press.

Atwood, Margaret. 2011. *In Other Worlds: SF and the Human Imagination*. New York: Doubleday.

Ayer, A.J. 1936. *Language, Truth, and Logic*. London: Gollancz.

Barrow, J.D., and F.J. Tipler. 1986. *The Anthropic Cosmological Principle*. Oxford: Clarendon.

Baylis, François, and Jason S. Robert. 2004. The Inevitability of Genetic Enhancement Technologies. *Bioethics* 18:1.

Bekoff, Marc. 2007. *The Emotional Lives of Animals*. Novato: New World Library.

Benn, Stanley. 1967. Egalitarianism and the Equal Consideration of Interests. In Pennock and Chapman 1967.

Bentham, Jeremy. 2007 [1789]. *An Introduction to the Principles of Morals and Legislation*. New York: Dover.

Bonds, Mark Evan. 2006. *Music as Thought: Listening to the Symphony in the Age of Beethoven*. Princeton: Princeton University Press.

Booker, M. Keith. 2007. *Alternate Americas: Science Fiction Film and American Culture*. Westport: Praeger.

Boulle, Pierre. 1963. *Planet of the Apes*. Translated by Xan Fielding. New York: Vanguard.

Brennan, Andrew. and Y.S. Lo. 2010. *Understanding Environmental Philosophy*. London: Acumen.

Brown, Royal S. 1994. *Overtones and Undertones: Reading Film Music*. Berkeley: University of California Press.

Butler, Judith, Ernesto Laclau, and Slavoj Žižek. 2000. *Contingency, Hegemony, Universality: Contemporary Dialogues on the Left*. New York: Verso.

Call, Josep, and Michael Tomasello. 2008. Does the Chimpanzee Have a Theory of Mind? 30 Years Later. *Trends in Cognitive Sciences* 12:5.

Cage, John. 1962. Interview with Roger Reynolds. *Generation* (Ann Arbor, Michigan).

Carroll, Noël. 1988. Mystifying Movies: Fads, Fallacies in Contemporary Film Theory. New York: Columbia University Press.

Cavalieri, Paola, and Peter Singer, eds. 1994. *The Great Ape Project: Equality Beyond Humanity*. New York: St. Martin's.

Morris, Simon Conway. 2003. *Life's Solution: Inevitable Humans in a Lonely Universe*. Cambridge: Cambridge University Press.

Cook, David. 2000. *Lost Illusions: American Cinema in the Shadow of Watergate and Vietnam, 1970–1979*. Volume 9 of Charles Harpole, ed. *History of the American Cinema*. New York: Scribner's.

Daniels, Norman. 1985. *Just Health Care*. New York: Cambridge University Press.

Davies, B. 1986. *Storm over Biology: Essays on Science, Sentiment, and Public Policy*. Buffalo: Prometheus.

Dawkins, Richard. 1976. *The Selfish Gene*. Oxford: Oxford University Press.

Dennett, Daniel. 1981. *Brainstorms*. Cambridge: MIT Press.

Ekman, Paul. 2001. *Telling Lies*. New York: Norton.

Fallis, Don. 2011. Lies, Incorporated. In Wittkower 2011.

Feldman, Leslie Dale. 2010. *Spaceships and Politics: The Political Thought of Rod Serling*. Lanham: Lexington.

Fodor, Jerry. 1984. Observation Reconsidered. *Philosophy of Science* 51.

Foer, Jonathan Safran. 2009. *Eating Animals*. New York: Little, Brown.

Fouts, Roger. 1997. *Next of Kin: What Chimpanzees Have Taught Me about Who We Are*. New York: Morrow.

Francione, Gary L. 2006. Animals: Property or Persons? In Sunstein and Nussbaum 2006.

Gorbman, Claudia. 1987. *Unheard Melodies: Narrative Film Music*. Bloomington: Indiana University Press.

Gould, Stephen Jay. 1989. *Wonderful Life: The Burgess Shale and the Nature of History*. New York: Norton.

Guilbaut, Sergei. 1983. *How New York Stole the Idea of Modern Art: Abstract Expressionism, Freedom, and the Cold War*. Chicago: University of Chicago Press.

Greene, Eric. 1998. *Planet of the Apes as American Myth: Race, Politics, and Popular Culture*. Middletown: Wesleyan University Press.

Gross, Charles. 2012. Disgrace: On Marc Hauser. *The Nation.* <www.thenation.com/article/165313/disgrace-marc-hauser>.

Earle Hagen. 1971. *Scoring for Films: A Complete Text.* New York: Criterion.

Hare, Brian, Josep Call, B. Agnetta, and Michael Tomasello. 2000. Chimpanzees Know What Conspecifics Do and Do Not See. *Animal Behaviour* 59:4.

Hare, Brian, Josep Call, and Michael Tomasello. 2001. Do Chimpanzees Know What Conspecifics Know? *Animal Behaviour* 61:1.

Heinlein, Robert. 1947. Jerry Is a Man. *Thrilling Wonder Stories* 31:1.

Hess, Elizabeth. 2008. *Nim Chimpsky: The Chimp Who Would Be Human.* New York: Bantam.

Hobbes, Thomas. 1651. *Leviathan.* London: Andrew Crooke.

Juengst, Eric. 1997. Can Enhancement Be Distinguished from Prevention in Genetic Medicine? *Journal of Medicine and Philosophy* 22.

Kant, Immanuel. 1993 [1785]. *Grounding for the Metaphysics of Morals.* Indianapolis: Hackett.

Keeton, William T., James L. Gould, and Carol Gould. 1986. *Biological Science.* New York: Norton.

Kittay, Eva. 2009. The Ethics of Philosophizing. In Tessman 2009.

Lacan, Jacques. 2006. *Écrits.* New York: Norton.

Locke, John. 1979 [1689]. *An Essay Concerning Human Understanding.* Oxford: Clarendon.

Mader, Sylvia S. 1987. *Biology.* Dubuque: Brown.

Mannison, D., M.A. McRobbie, and R. Routley, eds. 1980. *Environmental Philosophy.* Canberra: Australian National University, Research School of Social Sciences.

McMahan, Jeff. 2005. Our Fellow Creatures. *Journal of Ethics* 9.

McNeil, D.G. 2012. Bird Flu Paper Is Published after Debate. *New York Times* (June 22nd).

Mill, John Stuart. 2002 [1861]. *Utilitarianism.* Indianapolis: Hackett.

Mills, Charles W. 1998. *Blackness Visible: Essays on Philosophy and Race.* Ithaca: Cornell University Press.

Monk, Ray. 1990. *Ludwig Wittgenstein: The Duty of Genius.* New York: Free Press.

Mukhopadhyay, Carol C., Rosemary Henze, and Yolanda T. Moses. 2007. *How Real Is Race?* Lanham: Rowman and Littlefield.

Nattiez, Jean-Jacques. 1990. *Music and Discourse: Toward a Semiology of Music.* Princeton: Princeton University Press.

Nussbaum, Martha. 2007. *Frontiers of Justice.* Cambridge: Belknap.

Patterson, Francine. 1987. *Koko's Kitten.* New York: Scholastic.

Peirce, Charles Sanders. 1979. *Charles Sanders Peirce: Contributions to The Nation, Part Three: 1901–1908.* Lubbock: Texas Tech University.

Pennock, J. Roland, and John W. Chapman, eds. *Equality*. New York: Atherton.

Pinker, Steven. 2011. *The Better Angels of Our Nature: Why Violence Has Declined*. New York: Penguin.

Plato. 2000 [350 B.C.E.] *Republic*. Mineola: Dover.

Plato. 2011 [380 B.C.E.]. *The Trial and Death of Socrates*. Indianapolis: Hackett.

Quine, Willard V. 1960. *Word and Object*. Cambridge: MIT Press.

Regan, Tom. 1983. *The Case for Animal Rights*. Berkeley: University of California Press.

Rolston, Holmes, III. 2012. *A New Environmental Ethics: The Next Millennium for Life on Earth*. New York: Routledge.

Rousseau, Jean-Jacques. 1978 [1762]. *On the Social Contract*. New York: St. Martin's Press.

Routley, Richard. 1973. Is There a Need for a New, an Environmental Ethic? *Proceedings of the 15th World Congress of Philosophy* 1. Sophia: Sophia Press.

Routley, Richard, and Valerie Routley. 1980. Human Chauvinism and Environmental Ethics. In Mannison, McRobbie, and Routley 1980.

Ruse, Michael. 1988. *Homosexuality: A Philosophical Inquiry*. Oxford: Blackwell.

———. 1996. *Monad to Man: The Concept of Progress in Evolutionary Biology*. Cambridge: Harvard University Press.

———. 2012a. *The Philosophy of Human Evolution*. Cambridge: Cambridge University Press.

———. 2012b. "A Man's Gotta Do What a Man's Gotta Do" and Other Memorable Lines from "Philosophy and Film." *Soundings: An Interdisciplinary Journal* 95.

Sandel, Michael. 2012. *What Money Can't Buy: The Moral Limits of Markets*. New York: Farrar, Straus, and Giroux.

Saunders, Francis Stonor. 2000. *The Cultural Cold War: The CIA and the World of Arts and Letters*. New York: Norton.

Schaler, Jeffrey A., ed. 2009. *Peter Singer Under Fire: The Moral Iconoclast Faces His Critics*. Chicago: Open Court.

Scherziger, Martin. 2004. In Memory of a Receding Dialectic: The Political Relevance of Autonomy and Formalism in Modernist Musical Aesthetics. In Ashby 2004.

Schoenberg, Arnold. 1975. Composition with Twelve Tones I (1941). In Stein 1975.

Segerstrale, Ullica. 2000. *Defenders of the Truth: The Battle for Science in the Sociobiology Debate and Beyond*. New York: Oxford University Press.

Shepard, Paul. 1973. *The Tender Carnivore and the Sacred Game*. New York: Scribner's.

Shettleworth, Sara. 2013. *Fundamentals of Comparative Cognition*. New York: Oxford University Press.

Singer, Peter. 2009 [1975]. *Animal Liberation*. New York: Harper Perennial.

———. 2011. The Troubled Life of Nim Chimpsky. *New York Review of Books*. <www.nybooks.com/articles/archives/2011/oct/13/troubled-life-nim-chimpsky>.

Singer, Peter, and Jim Mason. 2006. *The Way We Eat: Why Our Food Choices Matter*. Emmaus: Rodale.

Smith, David Livingstone. 2005. Natural-Born Liars. *Scientific American Mind* 16:2.

Stein, Leonard, ed. 1975. *Style and Idea: Selected Writings of Arnold Schoenberg*. Berkeley: University of California Press.

Stich, Stephen. 1978. The Recombinant DNA Debate. *Philosophy and Public Affairs* 7.

Stravinsky, Igor. 1962. *An Autobiography*. New York: Norton.

Sunstein, Cass, and Martha Nussbaum, eds. 2006. *Animal Rights: Current Debates and New Directions*. New York: Oxford University Press.

Tessman, L., ed. 2009. *Feminist Ethics and Social and Political Philosophy*. New York: Springer.

Turner, Frederick Jackson. 2010 [1893]. *The Significance of the Frontier in American History*. Mineola: Dover.

Frans de Waal. 2011. *Moral Behavior in Animals* [video file]. <www.ted.com/talks/frans_de_waal_do_animals_have_morals.html>.

Warren, Karen. 2000. *Ecofeminist Philosophy: A Western Perspective on What It Is and Why It Matters*. Lanham: Rowman and Littlefield.

Whiten, Andrew, and Richard W. Byrne. 1997. *Machiavellian Intelligence II*. Cambridge: Cambridge University Press.

Williams, Bernard. 2009 [2006]. The Human Prejudice. In Schaler 2009.

Wittgenstein, Ludwig. 1953. *Philosophical Investigations*. New York: Macmillan.

———. 1969. *On Certainty*. New York: Harper.

Wittkower, D.E., ed. 2011. *Philip K. Dick and Philosophy: Do Androids Have Kindred Spirits?* Chicago: Open Court.

Žižek, Slavoj. 2009. *The Sublime Object of Ideology*, Second edition. New York: Verso.

———. 2010. A Permanent Economic Emergency. *New Left Review* 64.

Žižek, Slavoj, and Christopher Hanlon. 2001. Psychoanalysis and the Post-Political: An Interview with Slavoj Žižek. *New Literary History* 32:1.

About the Authors

KRISTIN ANDREWS is an Associate Professor in the Department of Philosophy and Cognitive Science Program at York University, in Toronto. She is the author of *Do Apes Read Minds? Toward a New Folk Psychology* (2012) and has done extensive research into the minds of dolphins, human children, and orangutans, including investigations of the pantomime behavior of orangutans and Charlton Heston.

JONAS-SÉBASTIEN BEAUDRY is a DPhil candidate at the University of Oxford, where he served as a treasurer for the Oxford Animal Ethics Society. His work and research focus on the rights of women, poor and indigenous people, and the mentally disabled. He has worked at the Supreme Court of Canada, the Canadian Human Rights Commission, the Inter-American Court of Human Rights, the International Court of Justice and the Ape City Tribunal.

ANDREW BRENNAN is chair of philosophy and pro vice-chancellor for graduate research at La Trobe University in Melbourne. He and Norva Lo have collaborated on a range of books and papers on environmental philosophy, forgiveness, and the puzzle of whether humans can aspire to any kind of simian dignity.

JASON DAVIS works at Macquarie University in Sydney. He has written chapters for several books in Open Court's Popular Culture and Philosophy Series, including *Dexter and Philosophy: Mind over Spatter*, *Anime and Philosophy: Wide Eyed Wonder*, and *Manga and Philosophy: Fullmetal Metaphysician*. When he fails to complete tests, it's because he loathes bananas.

DON FALLIS is Professor of Information Resources and Adjunct Professor of Philosophy at the University of Arizona. He has written articles on lying and deception, including "What is Lying?" in the *Journal of Philosophy* and "The Most Terrific Liar You Ever Saw in Your Life" in *The Catcher in the Rye and Philosophy: A Book for Bastards, Morons, and Madmen*. In 1991, he was a PhD student in philosophy at the University of California, Irvine, where the *Conquest of the Planet of the Apes* occurred. But for the life of him, he can't remember a mob of angry apes trying to burn down the campus.

LESLIE DALE FELDMAN is Professor of Political Science at Hofstra University and author of *Spaceships and Politics: The Political Theory of Rod Serling* (2010). Her parents are great science fiction fans, and her former babysitter always said, when *Planet of the Apes* was on TV, "Les, the Apes are on!"

LORI GRUEN teaches at Wesleyan University and writes about animals and ethics. She has documented the history of the first one hundred chimpanzees in the US <http://first100chimps.wesleyan.edu> and is currently working on a book that draws lessons from the lives of the chimpanzees she has come to know, respect, and love.

EUGENE HALTON is a harmonica player and guerilla philosopher who teaches in the sociology department of the University of Notre Dame. His books include *The Meaning of Things* (co-authored, 1981), *Meaning and Modernity* (1986), *Bereft of Reason* (1995), and *The Great Brain Suck* (2008). He has just completed a book on pragmatism in the twentieth-first century. Hopefully it will still provide useful guidance after the Great Ape Revolution.

JOHN HUSS is a songwriter and philosopher who teaches at The University of Akron. His other works include *Lipchitz* (co-authored with the John Huss Moderate Combo), *Johnny Cash and Philosophy: The Burning Ring of Truth* (co-edited with David Werther), and *Use Your Head* (co-authored with Loch Phillipps and Lee Skaife). He still can feel the shock of seeing the Statue of Liberty waist deep in sand on the TV in Ricky Lesser's basement. See? The revolution did happen on television.

GREG LITTMANN has written on evolutionary epistemology, philosophy of logic, *The Big Bang Theory*, *Breaking Bad*, *Doctor Who*, *Dune*, *Ender's Game*, *A Game of Thrones*, Ridley Scott, *Terminator*, and *The Walking Dead*. He's a member of the community of tall, shaved chimpanzees with big noses, also known as *Homo sapiens*, and teaches philosophy at Southern Illinois University Edwardsville.

NORVA Y.S. LO is a senior lecturer in Philosophy at La Trobe University, Melbourne, who has written on ethics, environmental philosophy, and the philosophy of David Hume. She is particularly interested in movies that explore the dark side of human nature but equally those that inspire cross-species friendships (see this book's front cover).

SHAUN MAY lives in London where he's currently finishing a PhD applying Heidegger's philosophy to humor. He's also a theater director and producer who specializes in doing odd shows in weird spaces—his most critically acclaimed show being an opera in an Ikea store. Like Caesar, he's much better at solving the Lucas Tower than you would expect from looking at him.

TOM MCBRIDE has taught at Beloit College for nearly forty percent of a century. He is Professor of English and Keefer Professor of Humanities. Along with Ron Nief he's the co-creator of *The Annual Beloit College Mindset List* and co-author of *The Mindset Lists of American History* (2011). He's written on Shakespeare, Conan Doyle, Raymond Carver, and Saul Bellow. When asked, he denies that Dr. Zaius reminds him of college deans he has known.

WILLIAM L. MCGINNEY teaches Music History at the University of North Texas. He has written on the film music of Aaron Copland, the music of Emerson, Lake, and Palmer, and science-fiction movie scores. Although he has never met a talking ape, as a child he dreamed of growing up to be a scholar and scientist like Dr. Cornelius.

DAVID L. MORGAN received his PhD in theoretical particle physics from William and Mary, and his research has appeared in *Physical Review* and the *Astrophysical Journal*. He is the recipient of a Sloane/EST commission for the play "The Osiander Preface." When not devoting time to thinking about space he devotes space to thinking about time.

MASSIMO PIGLIUCCI is an evolutionary biologist and a philosopher of science at the Graduate Center of the City University of New York. His latest cogitations can be found in *Answers for Aristotle: How Science and Philosophy Can Lead Us to A More Meaningful Life* (2012). As a biologist he has worked on plants, not apes, but as a member of the Order Primates, he feels qualified to pontificate about them anyway.

BERNARD E. ROLLIN is the author of eighteen books including *The Frankenstein Syndrome* (1995) and *Animal Rights and Human*

Morality (1992), and co-editor of *Harley Davidson and Philosophy: Full Throttle Aristotle* (2006). He is University Distinguished Professor of Philosophy at Colorado State University, where he is also University Bioethicist. His areas of research include animal ethics, animal pain, and animal consciousness. Having testified before Congress on animal research, he knows what it's like to be Taylor on trial.

MICHAEL RUSE teaches philosophy and film at Florida State University, and is founding editor of the journal *Biology and Philosophy*. Although he has written a number of books on philosophy and evolution, including *Homosexuality: A Philosophical Inquiry* (1988), *Darwinism and Its Discontents* (2008), and *Science and Spirituality: Making Room for Faith in the Age of Science* (2010), deep down he would rather like to be a bonobo.

RALPH SHAIN teaches philosophy at Missouri State University and wrote his dissertation on the philosophy of time. He specializes in Continental philosophy and contributed a chapter to *Led Zeppelin and Philosophy: All Will Be Revealed* (2009) on the struggle for recognition called "Your Time Is Gonna Come." When not devoting space to thinking about time he devotes time to thinking about space.

CHAD WILLIAM TIMM is an assistant professor of education at Grand View University in Des Moines, Iowa. He has written on radical education, Axis POWs in Iowa, and popular culture and philosophy, including *The Hunger Games*. While attempting to solve the Lucas Tower puzzle in less than thirty seconds he experienced an identity crisis, realizing he was destined to lead junior faculty in a global ape revolution of their own.

TRAVIS MICHAEL TIMMERMAN is finishing his PhD in philosophy at Syracuse University. He specializes in ethics and death, but only because studying the *Planet of the Apes* series is not properly recognized as a philosophical discipline. When not reading or writing philosophy, he eagerly awaits *Dawn of the Planet of the Apes*.

SARA WALLER is an Associate Professor of Philosophy at Montana State University, where she studies animal minds and analyzes the vocalizations of dolphins, coyotes, wolves, and feral cats. She thinks that speech, language, and making noise in general have a lot to do with ensuring fair and just treatment on Planet of the Humans and Other Critters as well as on the Planet of the Apes.

JOHN S. WILKINS has a PhD in history and philosophy of science from the University of Melbourne, where he is an honorary (and jolly good) fellow, and teaches at the University of Sydney. He has published a book on the history of species concepts, and has another on classification coming out this year. He is currently at work on yet another book exploring submission behaviors, threat stares, and dominance hierarchies in philosophy departments.

Index

abortion, selective, 160
Abrahams, Mort, 245
Academy Awards (Oscars), 193, 194, 198, 200, 201
acting, 193, 194, 197–99, 201
Adam and Eve, 148, 149
Adorno, Theodor W., 216
alpha males, 174
Alpha Omega Bomb, 287–291
Andreasen, Robin, 249
animal liberation, 85; see also Singer, Peter
animals: behavior, 8; communication, 8–11, 42–43, 167, 174–75; Heidegger on, 257; human relations with, 271; intelligence, 21; moral status of, 67–82; pain, 49–50; research, 43, 47–48; thought, 5–7
Anscombe, Elizabeth, ix–x
anthropic cosmological principle, 160
anthropocentrism, 270–71
anti-hero, 224
anti-miscegenation laws, 250
anti-Semitism, 160
Ape City, 125, 131, 137, 266, 271
Appiah, Kwame Anthony, 253
Arab Spring, x
Aranha, Caroline, 55, 237, 239

Aristotle, 85, 293; ethics, 59–60; logic, 117–18, 120
Armando, 29, 87, 103, 291
Atwood, Margaret, 212

Bambi, 143
Barrow, J.D., 160
Battle for the Planet of the Apes (movie), ix, 95; and race, 251, 252; anti-speciesist message, 81, 248, 290
Baylis, François, 57, 61–63
belligerence, 146, 151
Beneath the Planet of the Apes (movie), 86, 250; annihilation in, 253, 267, 269; deceit in, 30; Malthusian aspects, 285–86; mutants in, 29, 95, 287; muteness in, 25; Nova in, 32; telepathy in, 88, 287; time travel in, 99; post-apocalyptic aspects, 151
Bentham, Jeremy, 81
Beverly Hillbillies, 150
biological essentialism, 247
biological realism, 247
Boulle, Pierre, ix, 27, 30, 32, 69, 111
Brave New World, 212, 289
Brent, 25, 29, 99, 151, 276

Bright Eyes, 17, 20, 150, 233

Caesar, 53–60, 177–189,
    231–243; Andy Serkis as,
    193–201; autonomy of, 172;
    confinement of, 168, 169, 171;
    deceptive ability, 30; escape of,
    175; genetic enhancement of,
    53–60; identity crisis of,
    231–243; intelligence, 16, 17,
    20, 87; leadership, 81, 85, 103,
    106; moral aspects, 94,
    177–189; privilege of, 273;
    signing of, 3, 8, 10, 23; rise of,
    255–262; speaking ability, 19
Cage, John, 218–19
Cain, 284
Carroll, Noël, 220
cave, 147, 148, 149, 151, 155
censorship, 129–130, 134, 270
Chambers, John, 200–01,
chimpanzees, 30, 177–78, 195,
    297; captive, 167–176; circus,
    103; digital, 193–201;
    research on, 19–20, 36–38, 92;
    folk psychology of, 9; genetic
    enhancement of, 53–59;
    genome, 249; human friend-
    ship with, 84; language, 258,
    266; mirror test, 234; moral
    psychology, 177–189;
    retirement, 300; sex, 155;
    speech, 23, 106; status in Ape
    society, 125, 128, 133–35,
    139
Chimpsky, Nim, 92, 258
Civil Rights Movement, 214
civilization, 31, 135, 142, 147,
    149, 163, 190, 292; collapse of,
    281–86
class, warrior, 132, 137–138
Cold War, 155, 216, 225, 269,
    273
compassion, 60, 94, 132
competition, 146, 188–89

*Conquest of the Planet of the
    Apes*, x, 68, 87, 81, 106, 246,
    254, 291
consciousness, 47, 52, 88; self-,
    266, 267, 270, 281
Copernicus, ix, 196
Cornelius, Dr., 73–74, 116, 134,
    147; in *Conquest of the Planet
    of the Apes* (movie), 249; in
    *Escape from the Planet of the
    Apes* (movie), 74, 101, 106,
    116; in *Planet of the Apes*
    (book), 112; in *Planet of the
    Apes* (movie), 131–35, 140,
    147, 155, 205, 260; and Sacred
    Scrolls, 265, 282; and reverse
    evolution, 131, 134, 147, 155,
    26

Darwin, Charles, 11, 50,,
    180–82, 184
Davidson, Donald, 5
Davis, Sammy, Jr., 245, 252
Dawkins, Richard, 156
Dawn of the Planet of the Apes,
    57
democracy, 141–42, 147, 224, 225
Dennett, Daniel, 28, 35
deontology, 59
Descartes, René, 5, 33, 34, 50,
    51, 232, 238, 259
deus ex machina, 287–89
devil, 143, 265, 282
de Waal, Frans, 19, 179
Dixon, Dr. Lewis, 30, 36, 38, 83,
    291
DNA, 156–57, 249, 287, 290
Dodge, 44
Douglas, Donna, 150
Drysdale, Sonny, 150

Earth, ix, 100, 111, 265–67,
    272–77, 280–81, 285, 290–92
egoism, rational, 178

education, 16, 128–29, 136
Einstein, Albert, 44, 99–102, 112
Emerson, Ralph Waldo, 290
endangered species, 175
epistemology, 246; of ignorance, 246
Eubulides, 55
Escape from the Planet of the Apes (movie), 101–03, 121, 137, 175, 260, 266; backward time travel in, 111, 113, 116, 118, 119; parallel timelines in, 106, 107; plot, 113
Evans, Maurice, 200, 214, 254
ethics, 58; chauvinist, 269; consequentialist, 58; deontological, 59; emotivist, 46–47; environmental, 267, 268; Kantian, 178; virtue, 58, 59–60
evolution, convergent, 182; cultural, 260; heresy of, 131; human, 162, 189; question of progress in, 154, 161; reverse, 135, 146–47, 261; theory of, 131, 135
evolutionary tree, 182

Facebook, xi, 287–89
family, 29, 91–92, 138, 238–39
Fellowship of the Holy Fallout, 151
fertile crescent, 281, 284
Flintstones, 146
Fodor, Jerry, 6, 197
Forbidden Zone, 69, 80, 151, 155, 214, 266, 285, 286
Fouts, Roger, 266
Francione, Gary, 80
Franciscus, James, 151
Franco, James, 77, 193, 198–99
Freud, Sigmund, 237
frontier thesis, 150

Galen, Dr., 139
Galileo Galilei, ix, 49, 196
Garden of Eden, 149
genes, 29, 157, 160, 185, 186; therapy, 157
genetics, 160, 186; and race, 249; counseling, 160; determinism, 185; diversity, 57; engineering, 53, 54, 55, 57; enhancement, 53, 56–57, 61–63, 157, 173, 177
Goldsmith, Jerry, 220–24, 226
Goodman, Nelson, 11–12
gorillas, 33, 125, 127–28, 137, 147, 167; in Ape City, 127, 131–33, 137, 251; silverback, 188
Gould, Dana, 254
Gould, Stephen Jay, 154
Great Ape Project, 267
Green Belt, 145
Greene, Eric, 27, 223, 246
Griffin, Donald, 8

Hasslein, Otto, 89, 95, 102, 103, 116; on the nature of time, 119–120; Curve Theory of time travel, 44–45, 99, 106
Hauser, Marc, 34
Heinlein, Robert, 28
Hess, Elizabeth, 266
Heston, Charlton, 144, 150, 153, 214, 286; balls of, 140;
Hobbes, Thomas, 143, 144, 145, 146, 189; *Leviathan*, 143, 179
Holbrook, Hal, 254
Hollywood, Classical, 219–220; traditional, 216, 223
Homo errans, 282
homosexuality, 160, 185
Honorius, Dr., 129, 131, 135, 140, 196
human nature, 62, 143, 181, 182, 185; John Locke on, 88; pre-Darwinian view of, 180;

Rod Serling on, 144, 146, 152; Thomas Hobbes on, 145, 179; Jean-Jacques Rousseau on, 148

humans, 131, 135–36, 141–42, 156, 261; as pinnacle of creation, 182; captive, 168; empathy of, 179; evolution of, 161, 162; future, 268; genetic diversity of, 249; in *Rise of the Planet of the Apes*, 178, 186; lack of soul in, 140; mutant, 151, 267, 268; similarities to other primates of, 183–84; sociobiology of, 158

Hume, C.W., 48

Hume, David, 52, 160; *Dialogues Concerning Natural Religion*, 160

Huxley, Aldous, 289; *Brave New World*, 212

Icarus, 44

ideological fantasy, 241–43

ideology, 42–43, 241–42; Nazi, 41–42; religious, 43; scientific, 41–52

intelligence, 26; and language, 15, 23; dangerous, 22; instinctive, 280–82; measurement of, 21, 22, 24; octopus, 20; of nature, 280, 283; quotient (IQ), 17, 85, 185

interests, 68, 80; ape, 84, 80; chimpanzee, 171; equal consideration of, 81, 84, 87, 89; group, 83; human, 82, 83, 89, 81; moral weight of, 84; of other species, 95

self-, 178

Jacobs, Arthur P., 200, 245, 252

Jacobs, Steven, 55, 56, 63

Juengst, Eric, 54

Julius, 145

justice, 60, 93, 139, 140; City of, 126–28; social, 253

Kant, Immanuel, 59, 178; *Critique of Judgment*, 215

Kass, Leon, 61–62

Keepers of the Divine Bomb, 32, 34, 289

Kennedy, John F., 150, 151

Koko, 27, 33, 271

Kubrick, Stanley, 200, 226, 269; *2001: A Space Odyssey*, 200, 226, 254

La Gloria, Mexico, 286

Lacan, Jacques, 232–38, 240

Landon, Dodge, 16, 188–89, 257

Landon, John, 44, 87, 136, 146, 148, 152

language, 15–16, 23, 175, 209; and intelligence, 15, 17, 23–24; and mind, 8; and silence, 25; and thought, 5–6; barrier, 18; shared, 3, 4; tyranny of, 16–18

Laurel and Hardy, 151

Lawgiver, The, 143, 290

linguistics, 236

Lloyd Morgan's Canon, 35

Locke, John, 88, 275

logic, 44–45, 118, 210

logical positivism, 44–46, 52

Long Island, 146, 148

Lovejoy, E.A., 180

Lull, Raimond 180

makeup, 198, 200, 201, 247; digital, 195, 200

manifest destiny, 150

March of the Wooden Soldiers (movie), 151

Matrix, The (movie franchise), 287

MacDonald, x, 26, 30, 94

McDowall, Roddy, 144, 149, 200

Mead, George Herbert, 290

meaning, 45, 213–220; in music, 213–14, 215, 218–220; and syntax, 258; logical positivist view of, 45; of symbols, 20; semiotic view of, 236–39

Meredith, Burgess, 148

Mérou, Ulysse, 31, 32, 33, 112, 114

Mesopotamia, 284

meta-ethics, 60

metaphysics, speculative, 44

Mill, John Stuart, 8, 58

Mills, Charles W., 251, 252, 253

Milo, Dr., 25, 31, 38, 101

Milo, Baby, 87, 103, 106, 116, 121, 291

minds, 6; and environment, 12; animal, 48, 259; as habitat relation, 290; of nature, 280; problem of other, 6–8; rational, 139

mindreading, 4–5, 8–11, 32–38, 288

Minnesota Multiphasic Personality Inventory, 18

missing link, 135

modernism, 215–17

Mooney, Paul, 252

Moore, G.E., 207–211

moral considerability, 71–80

moral status, 19, 74–82; of apes, 265–66; of humans, 265

Morsi, Mohamed, x

music, instrumental, 213, 215; modernist, 215–18, 220, 221, 224–27; twelve–tone, 221, 222, 224, 226

mutually assured destruction, 287

Narcissus, 281, 286

Nattiez, Jean-Jacques, 219

neoteny, 279–283, 291–92

New Frontier, 150, 151

New Hollywood, 216

New York, 146, 148, 151, 267, 287

Newton, Sir Isaac, ix, 44; laws of motion of, 107

Nietzsche, Friedrich Wilhelm, 283

Nova, 4, 150, 152, 223; as feral child, 187; communicative capacities of, 4, 10, 18; intelligence of, 24–25, 80; as love interest, 32, 91; death of, 89, 276

nuclear war, 95, 148, 149, 151, 158, 286

nuclear weapons, 62, 156, 273

Nussbaum, Martha, 83

Operation Desert Storm, 284

orangutans, 125, 127, 129–131, 133–35, 137, 139, 147

Oroonoko Indians, 148

Orwell, George, 288–89; *Nineteen Eighty-Four* (novel), 289

Oscars; *see* Academy Awards

overhypothesis, 11–12

Paine, Thomas, 152

Pallas, Peter Simon 180

Peirce, Charles, 219, 282–83, 290

physics, 99–109; equations of, 113–14; laws of, 101–02; time-symmetry of, 101, 115

Pinto, Freida, 199

Planet of the Apes (1968 movie), 3, 41, 67, 125–142; as controlled hallucination, 211–12; evolutionary issues in, 154; message of, 163;

music for, 213–227; scariness
of, 167; Serling devices in,
148–150, 151
Planet of the Apes (2001 movie),
82, 87
Planet of the Apes (novel); see
Boulle, Pierre
Planet of the Apes (franchise),
ix–xi, 3; anti-speciesist
message of, 86–77; as
cautionary tale, 95, 142, 277;
as story of moral progress
84–85; inconsistencies in,
105–06; lessons of, 26;
prejudice in, 16; political
themes in, 201; racial issues
in, 245–254
Planet of the Apes (TV series),
"Escape from Ape City,"
87
Planet of the Apes (planet), 127,
208
Planet of the Apes (musical),
254
Plato, 88, 145, 146; criticism of
divine basis for ethics, 88–79;
on the soul, 139–140, 142;
Republic, 126–142, 145, 149,
184, 210
Popper, Sir Karl, 194
power, ability to corrupt,
139–142
prejudice, 68, 146, 150, 266;
arbitrary, 92; human, 90;
liberal, 61–62; linguistic, 16,
17, 26
primitive, 214, 218, 222, 223
Project Nim (movie), 92, 258;
Singer's review of, xii, 27
propositions, logical versus
empirical, 206
psychologist's dilemma, 48–49

Quine, Willard Van Orman,
23–24

race, 245–254; ontology of, 247,
251, 252
Regan, Tom, 69, 267
Relativity: special, 99–100;
general, 102, 112
religion: and science, 43–44;
ape, 265–66; as tool for
political control, 125–26,
129–131, 134–35, 140–41;
David Hume on, 52, 160
revolution: ape, 231; American,
ix; scientific ix, 196; sexual,
ix
Ring of Gyges, 145
Rise of the Planet of the Apes
(movie), x, xii, 3, 68, 81, 87,
231–243, 255–262; portrayal
of drug companies in, 274;
sound editing in, 170;
morality in, 178; visual effects
in, 195, 201
Robert, Jason Scott, 57, 61–63
Rodman, Charles, 53, 57, 58, 177
Rodman, Will, 53, 56–58, 63, 77,
187, 273
Rousseau, Jean-Jacques, 148,
179
Routley, Richard, 268–270, 272,
274
Ryder, Richard, 68

sacred scrolls, 85, 131, 140, 146,
265, 282
San Bruno Primate Shelter, 3,
13, 30, 87
Saussure, Ferdinand de, 219,
236–37
Schaffner, Franklin, 265
Schoenberg, Arnold, 221
science, 131–34; ideology of,
41–52; limitations of, 5; of
race, 248; philosophy of, 8–8,
44–47, 196; and ethics, 46, 48,
52; social, 157–58
Sepkoski, Jack, 162

Serling, Rod, ix, 144–152, 204; optimism of, 149; pessimism of, 149

sex, ix, 137–38; interracial, 250; interspecies, 250

sexual orientation, 160, 185

Shakespeare, William, 210, 234, 284

Shepard, Paul, 291

signified, 236–38

signifier, 236–241

Singer, Peter, xii, 68, 69, 83; *Animal Liberation*, 68, 81, 297; anti-speciesist views of 84, 86, 87, 90; views on personhood, 27

social contract, 145

Socrates, 194, 198

speciesism, 68–82, 84–94, 266, 271

Star Wars (movie), 227

state of nature, 143

state of war, 145

Statue of Liberty, 148, 152

Sterling, Bruce, 211

Stewart, 149

Stravinsky, Igor, 215, 222, 223; *The Rite of Spring*, 222, 223

Stringer, Chris, 290

Swift, Jonathan, 89–90

Tahrir Square, x

Taylor, George, 67, 83, 222–25, 276–77; anger of, 276; as anti-hero, 224; as "Bright Eyes," 17; captivity of, 147, 167–68; destiny of, 121; linguistic capacity, 3, 16, 27, 42, 132, 257; misanthropy of, 223, 266; relationship with Nova, 10, 32, 187; relationship with Zira, 7, 67, 94, 163, 291; speciesism of, 83; trial of, 48–50, 86–87, 196

Terminator, 287

time: arrow of, 102; scale, 163; travel, 99–109, 111–121

Tocqueville, Alexis de, 147, 148

Tower of Hanoi, 20

translation, indeterminacy of, 23–24

Turner, Frederick Jackson, 150

turtles, orangutan fear of, 11

Twain, Mark, 254

Twilight Zone (TV show), 144, 148, 149, 150, 151, 204; "Time Enough at Last," 148, 149, 151; "Third from the Sun," 148; "Two," 149; "Probe, 8—Over and Out," 149; "The Rip van Winkle Caper," 149; "On Thursday We Leave for Home," 149; "The Old Man in the Cave," 149; "Eye of the Beholder," 150; "One More Pallbearer," 151; "The Shelter," 148; "People Are Alike All Over," 144

tyranny of the majority, 147

United States, 57, 84, 141, 216; factory farming in, 80; race in, 251; involvement in Vietnam, 273

Ursus, 285

US Supreme Court, 250

Verger, 287

Verne, Jules, 212

war, 95; in Vietnam, 214, 225, 269, 273; nuclear, 148–49, 151; of all against all, 145–47

Warhol, Andy, 199

Washington, George, 152

Washington, Martha, 152

Washoe, 266, 271

wealth, 127, 132, 142
Wittgenstein, Ludwig, 45, 194;
  On Certainty, 204–211;
  Philosophical Investigations, 35
women, social role of, 136–37
World War I, 215
World War II, 155, 184

Zack, Naomi, 253
Zaius, Dr., 69–71, 86–89, 121,
  131, 147; and the cave,
149–150, 155, 210; and the
Sacred Scrolls, 146; as
ideologue, 43; at Taylor's trial,
205; clothing of, 69, 147;
destruction of evidence, 131,
147, 155, 211; elitism of, 139;
in *Beneath the Planet of the
Apes*, 267, 268, 276;
misanthropy of, 69–70, 89
Zanuck, Darryl, ix
Zira, Dr., 131, 134–35, 137, 140,
  147, 150, 224, 284, 291
Žižek, Slavoj, 240, 241, 242–43